THE NUDE
IN BLACK AND WHITE

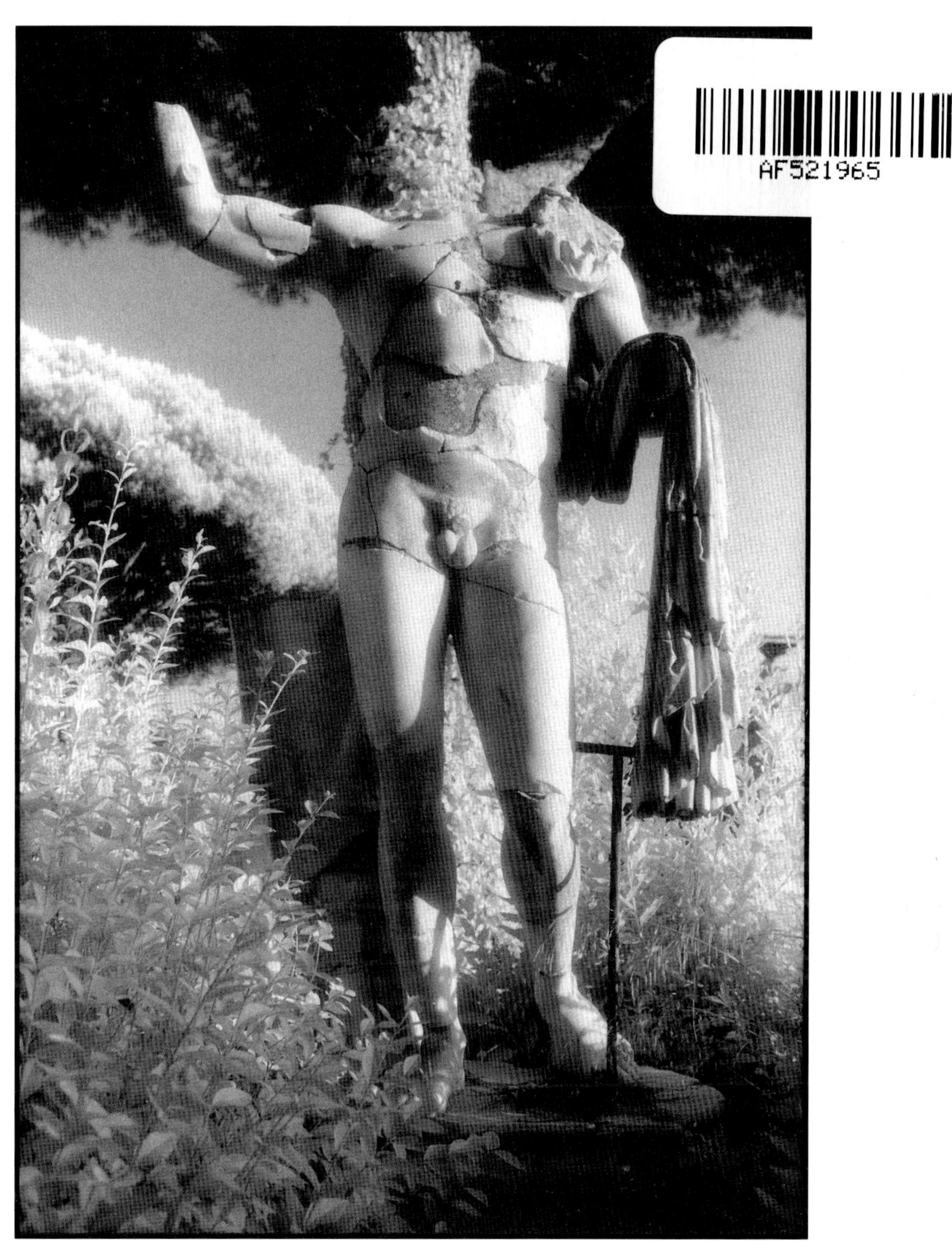

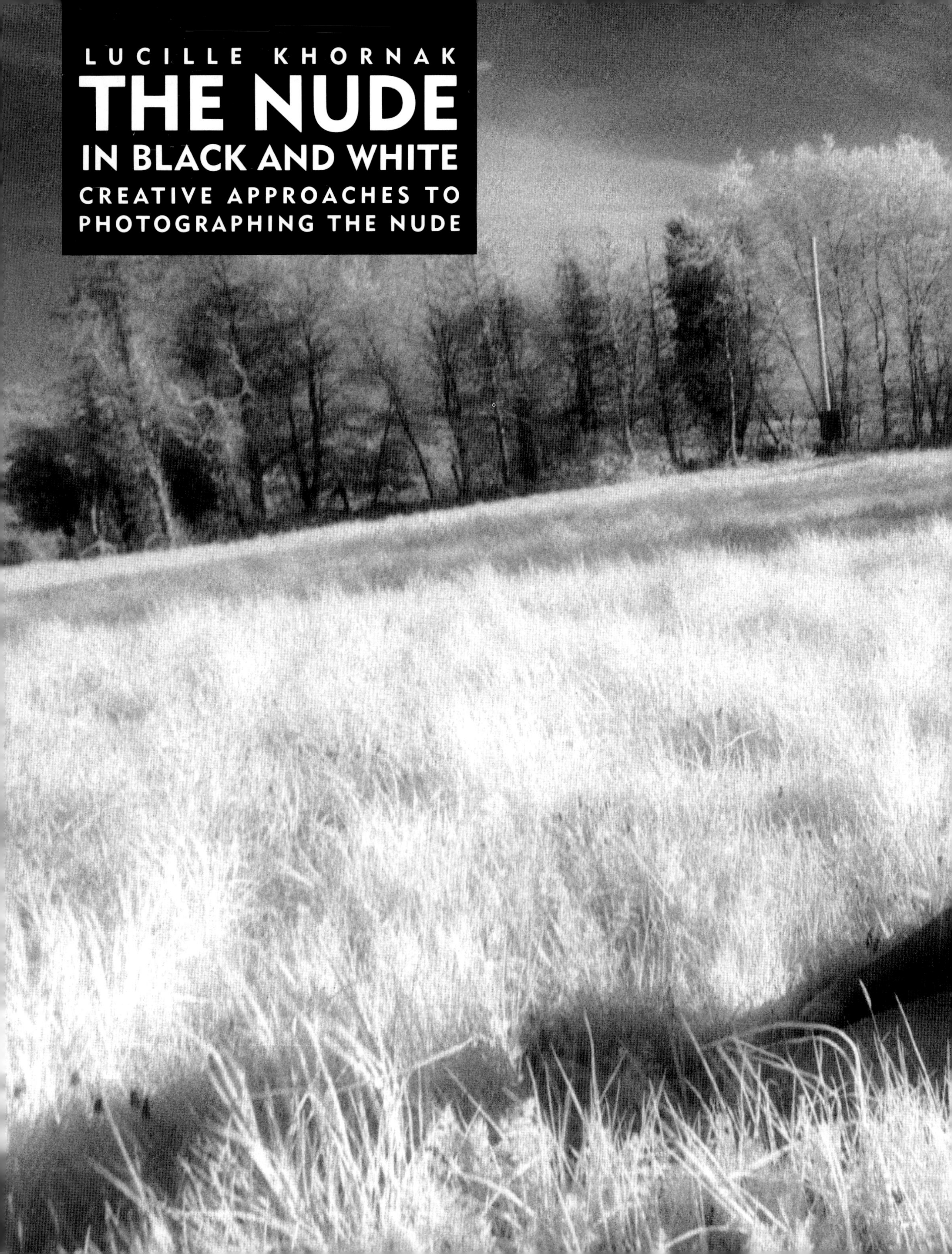
LUCILLE KHORNAK
THE NUDE
IN BLACK AND WHITE
CREATIVE APPROACHES TO
PHOTOGRAPHING THE NUDE

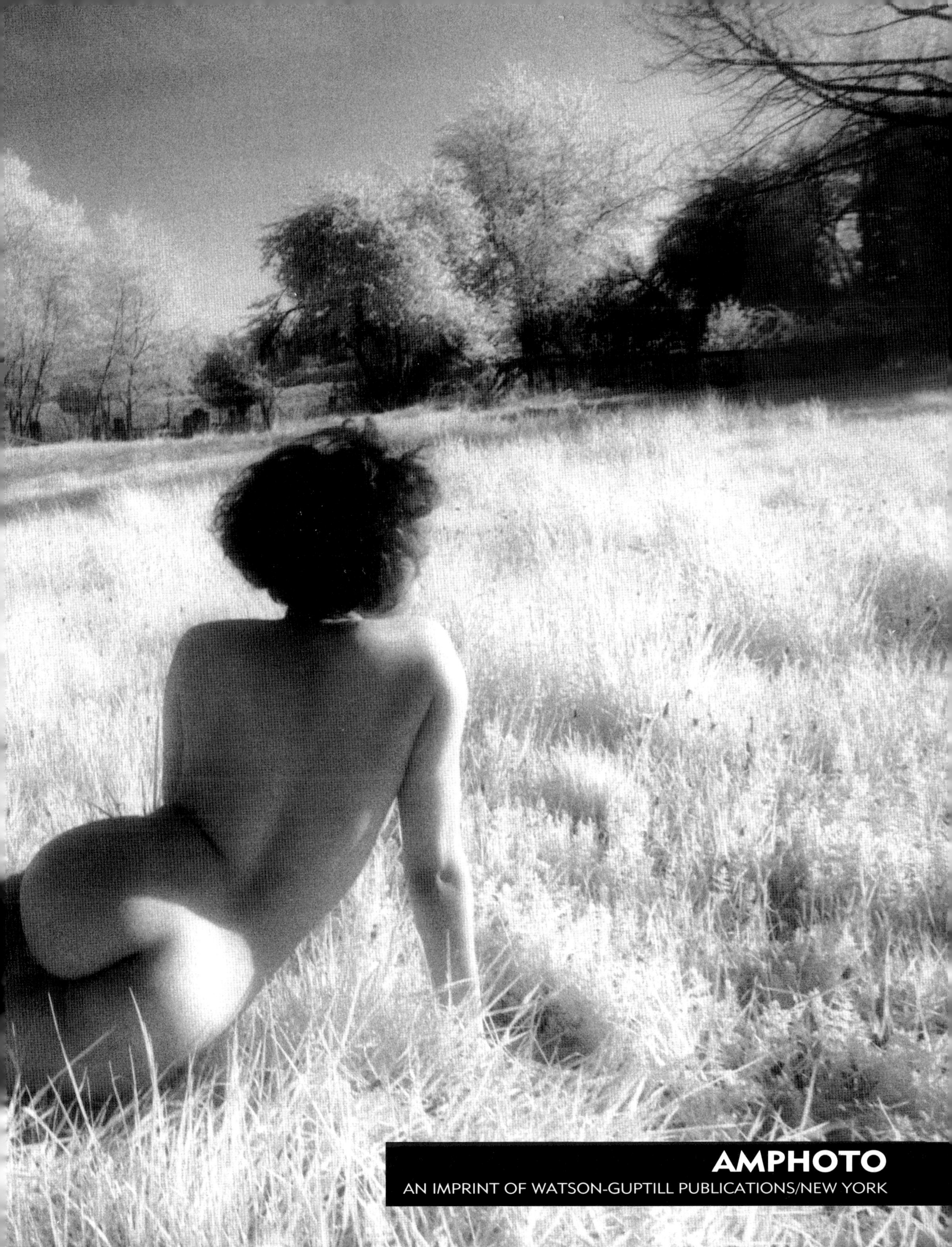
AMPHOTO
AN IMPRINT OF WATSON-GUPTILL PUBLICATIONS/NEW YORK

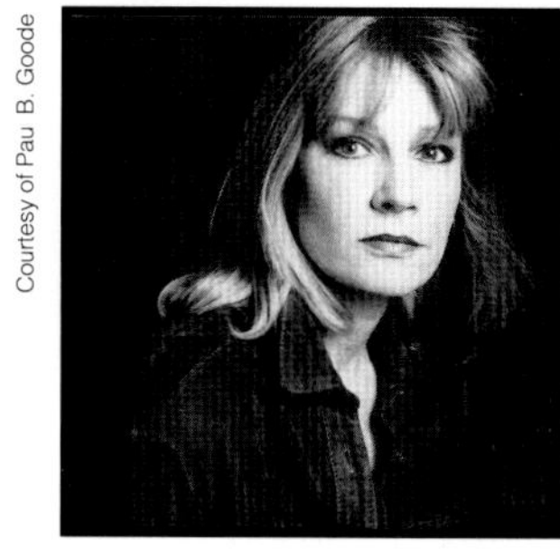

Courtesy of Pau B. Goode

Lucille Khornak, a commercial and fine-art photographer, lives and works in New York City but travels extensively to photograph and lecture, as well as to exhibit her work. She has had a number of gallery and museum shows in New York, California, and Lisbon. Khornak has taught workshops on fashion and beauty photography at the Palm Beach Workshops in Florida. She is the author of several books, including *Fashion Photography* (Amphoto, 1989). Khornak's pictures have appeared in such major publications as *New York* magazine, *Vogue*, *Harper's Bazaar*, *Newsweek*, and *The New York Times Sunday Magazine.*

Acknowledgements

I would like to express a special thank-you to two close friends, Olga Victoria Karras and Gerald Kornblau, who extended themselves beyond the call of duty. I don't know what I would have done without them . . . I cherish our friendship.

I would also like to thank the following:
Arista Photo Labs, Peter Brown, Ted Carrasco, Stephanie Kornblau, and Frank Murphy for their input; Arista Photo Labs and Schneider Erdman for their photographic-printing expertise; all the models who exhibited faith and confidence in my artistic integrity; all the creative artists who contributed their time and energy; Amphoto Senior Editor Robin Simmen, who believed in my work; Amphoto Editor Liz Harvey, for her expert editing; Dyna-Lite and Polaroid, for their support; and my husband, Robert, for always being there.

First published in 1993 in New York by Amphoto,
an imprint of Watson-Guptill Publications,
a division of BPI Communications, L.P.,
1515 Broadway, New York, NY 10036

Printed in the United States of America

Library of Congress Cataloging-in-Publication Data

Khornak, Lucille.
The nude in black and white / by Lucille Khornak.
Includes index.
ISBN 0-8174-5088-2
1. Photography of the nude. 2. Photography of the nude—Handbooks, manuals, etc. 3. Khornak, Lucille. I. Title.
TR647.K47 1993 93-28353
778.9'21—dc20 CIP

1 2 3 4 5 6 7 8 9/01 00 99 98 97 96 95 94 93

Editorial concept by Robin Simmen
Edited by Liz Harvey
Designed by Jay Anning
Graphic production by Ellen Greene

To Mom and Dad

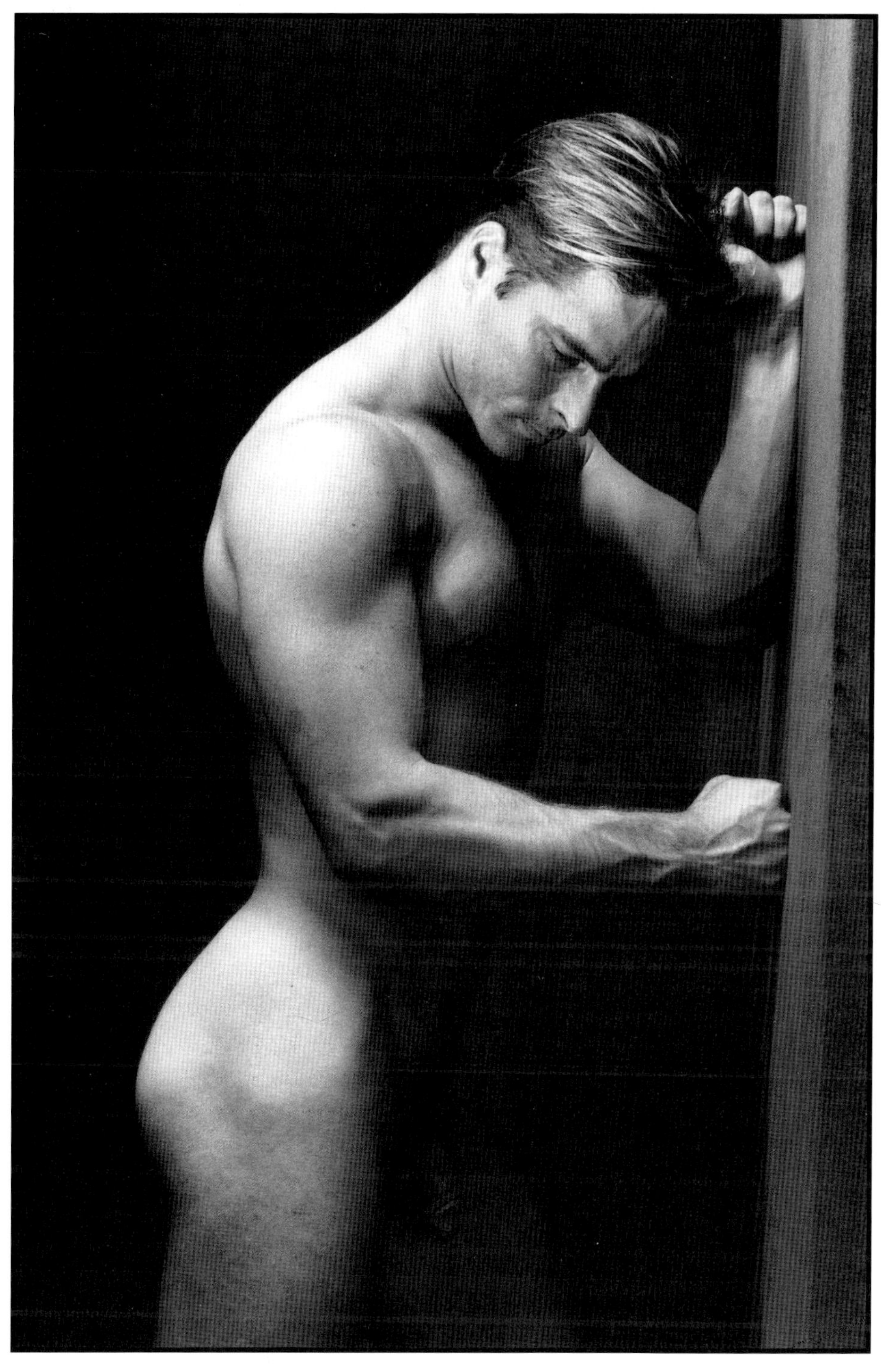

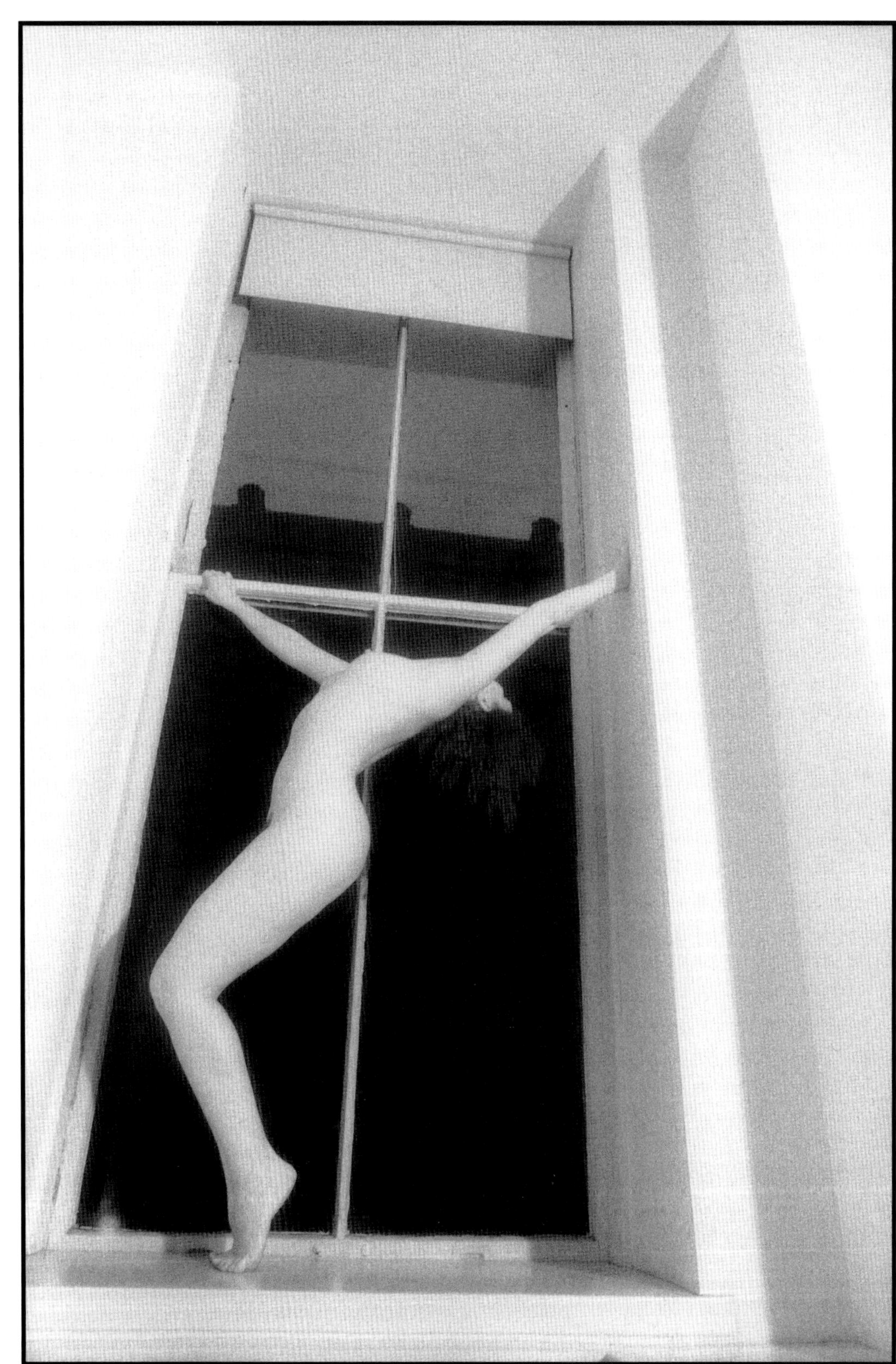

CONTENTS

INTRODUCTION

I remember vividly that while I was growing up, my mother was fascinated with the nude figure. She was attracted to and collected figurines. These images are embedded in my memory, and I can see how I was influenced by my early environment. Although I was unaware of it at the time, the nude was gradually becoming part of my own visual vocabulary.

Nevertheless, when I first started photographing nudes, I was uncomfortable asking models and "everyday" people to take off their clothes. So I decided to tell only a few people about my interest in doing nudes. I did, however, advertise my black-and-white work in a magazine in Europe because Europeans are always so advanced in their styles. One day, a male model called me, said that he'd seen my work in Europe, and asked to come by and show me his portfolio. When he arrived, I looked through it and asked him if he wanted to pose nude in exchange for pictures; he agreed.

I could sense immediately by the model's pictures that he was interested in the bizarre and that he had a creative side. Up to this point, I'd photographed only a few nudes, but I'd decided to pursue this type of photography more vigorously. I believe that when you make a decision to go after something and really focus on your objective, it will start to happen.

I was fortunate that my interests led me along this path. Today, nude models are now used quite commonly in advertising. In fact, more and more companies whose products have nothing to do with the body opt to use partial nudity in their advertisements. For example, Calvin Klein, one of the advertising field's biggest clients, uses nude models in clothing and fragrance campaigns. In addition to hair salons and health clubs, companies that require partially nude models manufacture perfume, lingerie and underwear, and pantyhose, as well as such bath products as soap, towels, and body lotions. These companies often utilize the human figure in their marketing strategies to suggest romance and illusion, two compelling forces. Beautiful bodies can sell almost anything.

After all, the human body is the art form most universally admired. The body, in a myriad of shapes and sizes, is the basis of figural art, which has evolved significantly from one civilization to the next. Ancient Egyptians sculpted nudes that appeared completely lifeless because they believed that the human spirit couldn't be captured. The Greeks, on the other hand, depicted the ideal human form. In addition, they celebrated if not worshipped the male form, and beautifully draped the female figure. The Romans created portrait-like statuary true to life. Clearly, the nude figure is an integral part of the art and art history of every one of the world's great cultures. The nude has been variously represented in sculpture, drawing, painting, collage, and photography. And the tradition continues.

My own entree into the nude-photography field took me somewhat by surprise. I never thought about being a photographer when I was very young; my dream was to become an actress. After a few years of studying and being part of the Hollywood scene, however, I moved to New York to model, and three years later, I decided to move behind the camera. I wanted to make people more beautiful than they were. Involved in the glamorous business of photographing attractive female and male models, I continually found myself surrounded by "beautiful people." As time passed, I realized that the world isn't all beauty and perfection. I started to see beauty in imperfection. Gradually, I became more and more interested in photographing the human figure and went from images depicting the bizarre and the extreme to images portraying fantasy, reality, and the shapeliness of the form.

Although I shoot many variations of the nude, I don't approach the human body in a sexually explicit manner. I also feel strongly that since the world isn't made up of perfect bodies, I don't have to limit myself by photographing only "10s." As an artist, I'm challenged by the human figure and its unparaleled beauty and endless forms of expression. My biggest problem is finding people with imperfect bodies who will permit me to photograph them. When I ask if I might photograph them in the nude, time after time I hear something like, "Well, maybe when I lose 15 pounds and I'm in better shape, I'll think about it." I can often visualize a picture of a particular person in the nude, but I'm not always able to convince that person to disrobe.

How an individual expresses movement, form, shyness, or boldness is all part of the identity process. Many people are content and feel at ease in their overweight bodies, while others feel that they shouldn't be photographed unless their bodies are in great shape. If, however, your subjects are comfortable in front of the camera, they feel free to expose who they really are. If your subjects are uncomfortable, you can capture their shyness or, perhaps, some wild part of their personality that they somehow suppress. I portray the human figure with my own sensibility and perspective, working with the subject and using the highest degree of artistry that I am capable of.

As a photographer, I liberate and expose some of my subjects' innermost thoughts. Fantasies are an essential product of the human brain. As a photographer and a creative individual, I attempt to illuminate many of these fantasies. An intimate situation, sexual or otherwise, between nude models can parlay itself into an interesting moment on film.

When I'm photographing nude subjects, I usually don't go into the session with a preconceived idea. I assess the situation at hand and "go with the flow." The subject might need some time in order to feel comfortable or might never feel relaxed during the shoot. Whatever happens, it is my responsibility as the photographer to capture the moment—and my vision—on film.

Photography is a process. It is about self-discovery and how you relate to the world. It is about boundaries and how you continue to explore within these confines and beyond them. In some ways, photographers are like painters. It takes years for their style to develop. At one point, however, everything seems to come together, and the strength of their body of work becomes evident.

Black-and-white photography is a particularly powerful means of expression that involves many intriguing variables. A wide range of film types, developing techniques, and printing processes provides rich, creative opportunities. For example, you can use texture and composition to increase an image's power. And when you photograph a subject with two different types of film, you end up with two completely different images. Black and white enables you to maintain complete control of your work. One image can inspire many interpretations, and you can create many moods from the same setup via the film, paper, filters, and exposure you choose. Ultimately, the way you decide to interpret negatives and your subject matter becomes your style.

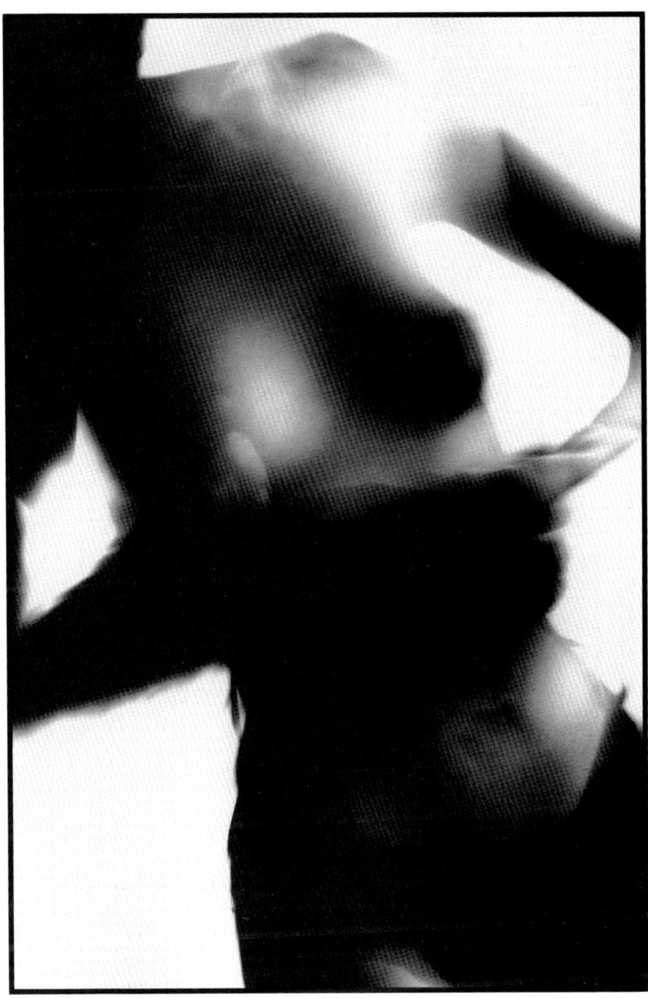

Seeing in black and white is different from seeing in color, which is how you view the world. In black and white, you must first start to translate colors into shades of gray; you must learn how to deal with the absence of color and with chiaroscuro, the interplay of light and dark. A photograph that is successful in color might not translate well in black and white. Of course, the opposite is also true. Try this revealing exercise: shoot the same image in color as well as black and white, and compare the results.

At the very beginning of my photographic career, I learned the process of shooting in black and white by taking many courses at the New School in New York City, as well as in various other classes. I rented a darkroom by the hour and would spend 8 to 10 hours at a time printing. My black-and-white photographs had a fine-art quality and were personal

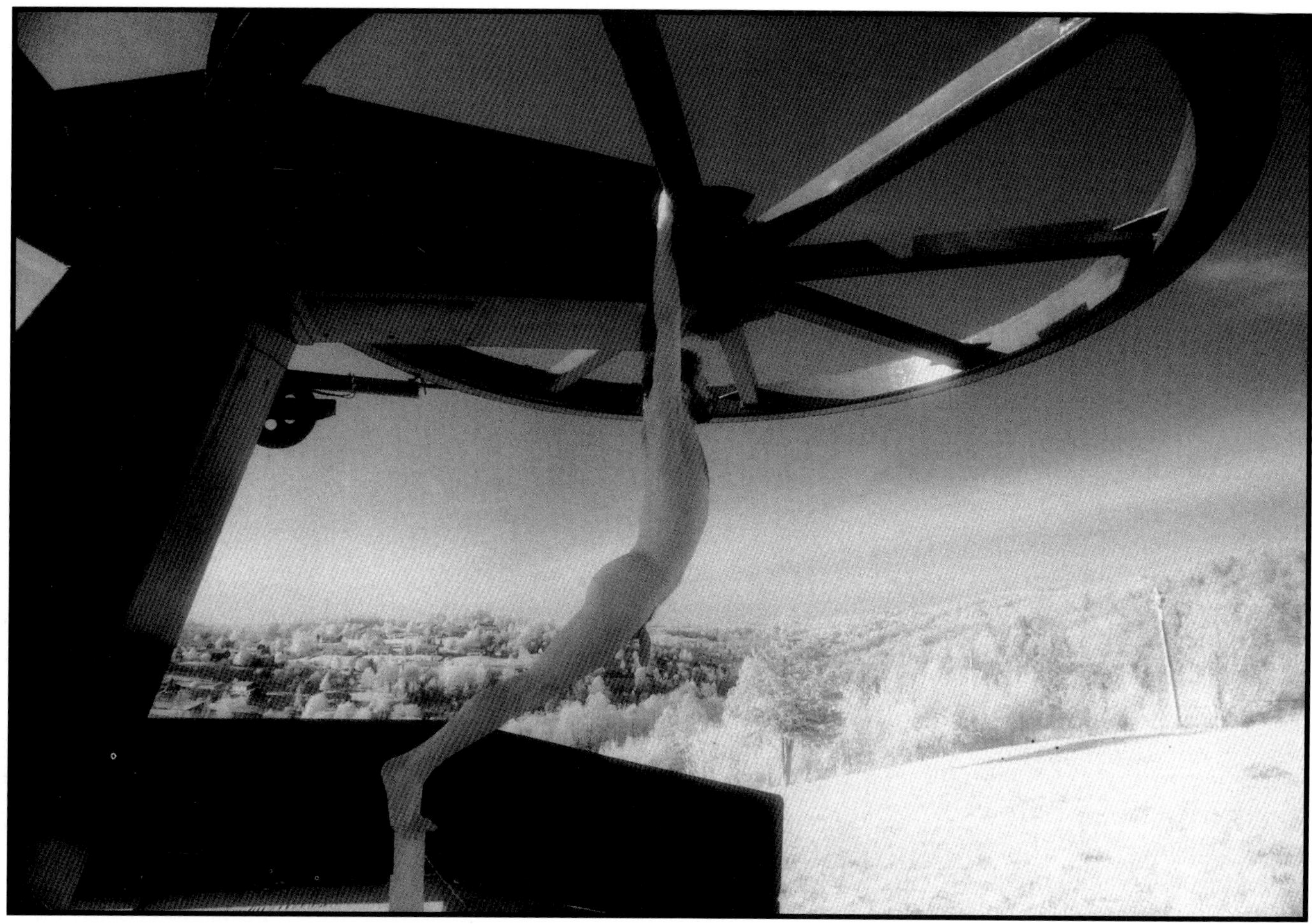

interpretations of images and situations that, at the time, didn't lend themselves to commercial applications. The advertising field sought color images that were clear, direct, and to the point. In my photographs, I always try to tell a story or attempt to make viewers think about what is going to happen next. I like capturing a single dynamic moment within the context of a story.

After mastering the basics of black and-white printing, I studied platinum printing, which adds another dimension to the print. I continued to shoot in black and white as my career progressed and some of this work was exhibited in small gallery shows; however, my real focus came to be color. I was concerned about maintaining a career with an income, and color images were the means to that end.

But my career path veered off in a dramatic direction when I was shooting an assignment in Portugal. During my stay, I was able to arrange a museum exhibition of my black-and-white photographs. This show led me to pursue my own point of view. I started to advertise my black-and-white work, and the response was incredible. Until this point, I regarded black and white as a medium suitable for the fine-art world only and never really thought about using my black-and-white images commercially. But the advertising world had changed: It now embraced black-and-white photography. My timing was perfect.

Throughout my commercial career, my black-and-white work has featured fashion models, portraits, and nudes. Since I do a great deal of fashion shoots, models are readily available to me. I enjoy photographing the nude in black and white because it is a total departure from fashion photography. The body, which in my fashion shots is beautifully attired, is now completely exposed, and each body is unique. Furthermore, each model reveals himself or herself in an incomparable way and has a personal rhythm. Choreographing movements and then capturing them on film are fascinating processes.

For me, photographing the nude is about sculpture and beauty. Beauty lies in the eye of the beholder, of course, so something beautiful to one person might be disturbing to someone else. Depending on how the body performs, I can see sculptural qualities in the model's movement, at which time I press the shutter. I believe that this split second is the high point of my vision. I'm continually searching for and experimenting with new avenues of expression, as well as challenging my visual insight by searching deeper and deeper into the form, the lines, and the motion of the body.

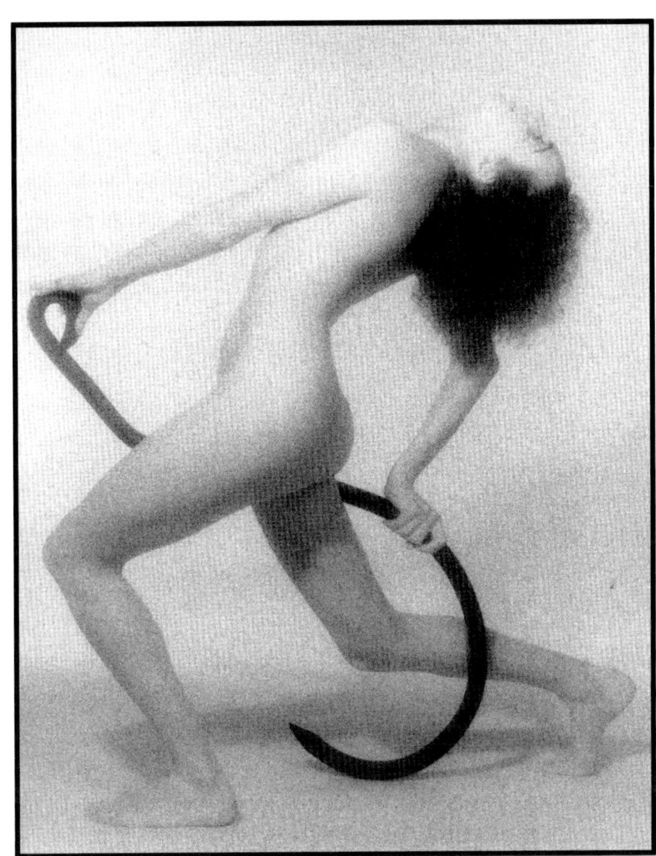

Another reason I prefer photographing the nude in black and white is the timeless quality of the resulting images. Working with the nude gives me the opportunity to deal with the body as sculpture, as a graphic element, and as a form that I can define and redefine with light. How you use light can transform an ordinary picture into something special, a work of art. The intensity of the illumination, or the lack of illumination, establishes a mood by bringing out the tonal qualities of black and white. Light can also tell a story, flatter or enhance the human form, and emphasize the roundness of or flatten anatomical features. Although I like to shoot in available light, I also enjoy working with strobe light in the controlled environment of the studio.

Nude photography will undoubtedly continue to challenge the imagination, just as black-and-white photography continues to inspire photographers because it offers unlimited opportunities for creative expression. New technological advances in film processes will also continue, and the photographers of tomorrow will be encouraged to work with these new mediums. Photography had its beginnings in black and white, and the future of black and white promises classic, seemingly endless approaches to photographing the nude.

Shooting in black and white will guide you through a process of self-discovery. Your likes and dislikes will surface in a way that might astonish even you. In this book, I document the human form within the framework of a variety of scenarios and supply technical notes for each picture. You can apply the approaches, techniques, and information to your own work; however, you must ultimately determine the direction and style of your finished photographs. I wish you luck in your explorations and your inevitable discoveries!

GALLERY

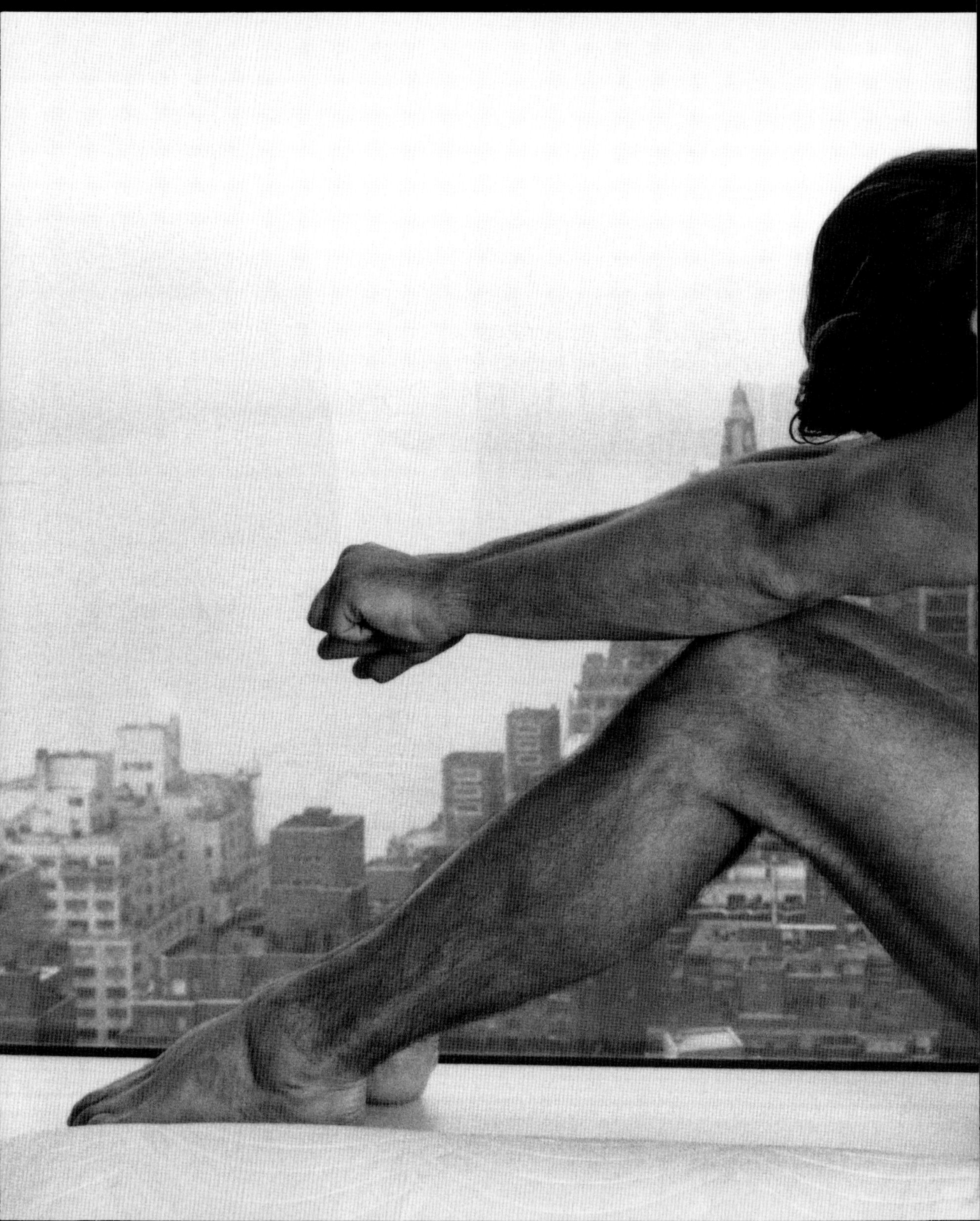

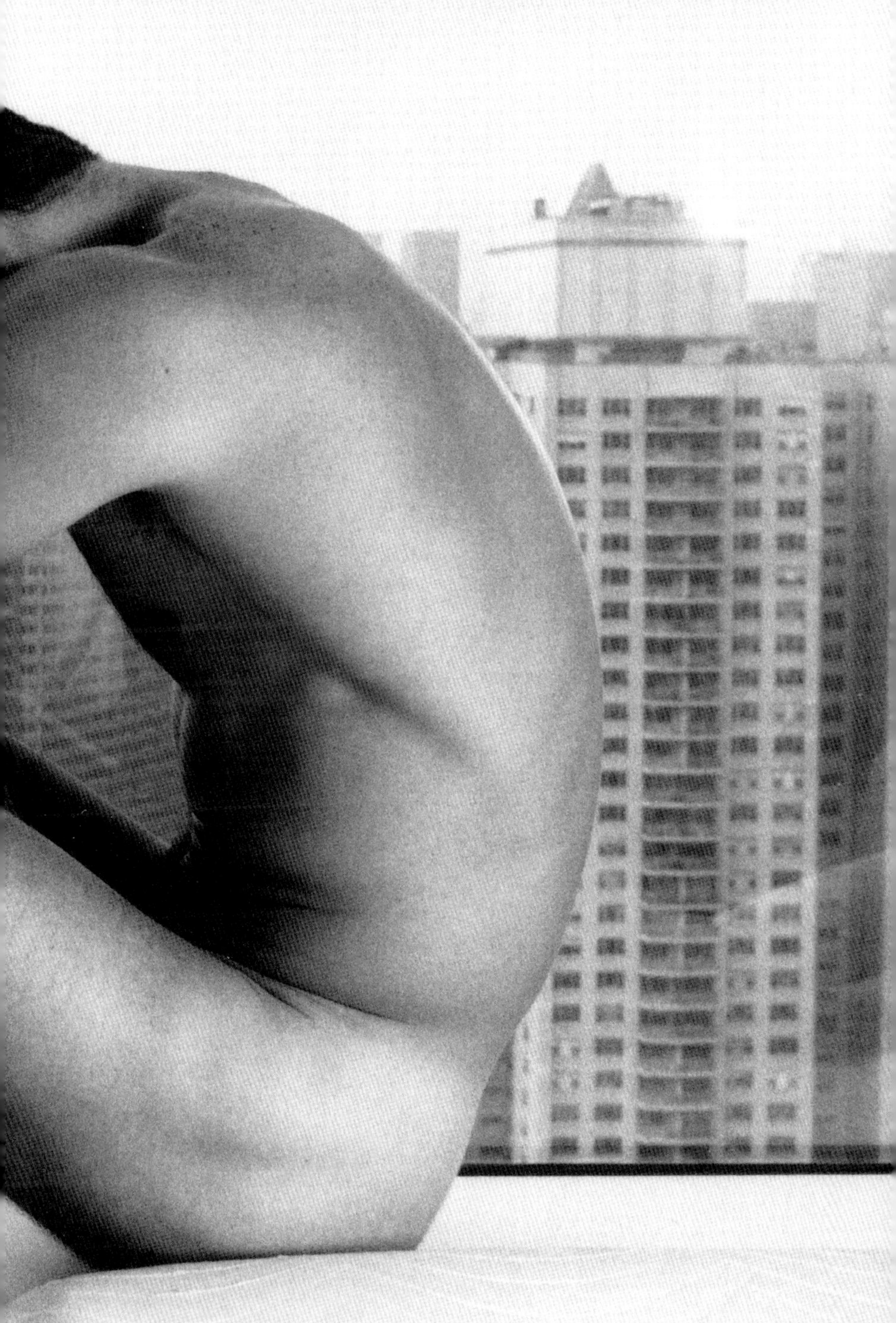

THE BODY IN MOTION

Human anatomy has always intrigued me. These photographs of models in motion represent some of the results of my unending efforts to capture the sculptural form of the human body as it stretches, bends, jumps, leaps, and contorts, as well as interprets music, within and without. When you look at these pictures of the body in motion, imagine what happened just before I froze that particular moment and what occurred right afterward. Each body in motion offers either a fragment of a complete story or, as you can see from this series of shots, a beautiful range of expressions.

When model Kenn Wells initially came to meet with me, we discussed my desire to capture movement (see pages 24–29). He pleasantly surprised me by disclosing that he'd been one of the dancers in the original Broadway production of the musical *Cats*. The choreography in this play is simply incredible, so I immediately knew that I had a very good subject to work with. When Kenn and I continued our conversation, we decided to go one step further and use body paints. After I mentioned that I wanted an animal motif, we agreed to attempt to reproduce zebra stripes. Of course, Kenn would be able to move around freely as he posed; his movements didn't have to mimic those of a zebra! When Kenn and I first met to go over this shoot, I had no idea that editing the photographs from his session would be such an enormously difficult task: There were so many wonderful pictures to choose from.

The high-spirited and/or graceful movements of some people beg to be recorded on film. While working with some models, I simply can't stop photographing them, and, perhaps just as important, they can't stop feeding my camera. I always play music on the set to create a mood that the model invariably responds to. When you are on a roll, keep shooting until the session comes to its natural end.

Carmela proved to be a wonderful model. When she and I first spoke about her session, I told her that I wanted to shoot some great body movement (see pages 20–23, 55). I also urged her to practice in front of a mirror before the shoot so that she wouldn't be stiff on the set. Having taken ballet lessons, Carmela assured me that she knew what I was looking for. On the day of the shoot, she didn't disappoint me.

As my model moves for me, I am flexible and creative. I consider almost every shoot as an opportunity to experiment and to push beyond my limits by using various lenses and films. Just because a model is moving as you work doesn't mean that every shot you finally choose has to portray him or her in motion. For example, if I find a specific form exciting while a model is moving, I'll ask the model to hold that pose while I compose the scene in my camera. The resulting picture might not express movement—in fact, it might clearly depict a complete absence of movement—but it came about at a session during which I directed the model to move around freely.

While the series of pictures I made during Kenn's session reveals his fluid, continuous movements, Carmela's series is more varied. Her natural, elegant motions inspired me to do closeups and long shots, and to photograph her body contorted as well as relaxed.

A professional nude model who poses for art-study classes, Regina Hawkins is another subject who knows how to move in front of the camera (see pages 16–17). She is particularly skilled at effecting subtle changes in position. Even though many of her movements were similar to those of Carmela, Regina expressed them her own way because, in part, she has a different body type. The lines of each individual body register differently in your vision, too. All models coordinate their facial expressions with their various body movements. Some models are stiffer, some are freer, but no two models are exactly alike as they move to the music.

I enjoy observing the way people walk, talk, and gesture. Studying movements and stances can tell a whole story about an individual. In addition, it provides me with the opportunity to recognize and analyze the grace, the fluidity, and the range of motions that can ultimately result in a good photograph. People can hide behind their clothing, whether they're wearing elegant gowns, three-piece suits, or jeans. But when stripped of their clothing, they are naked, or exposed, in every sense of the word.

I want to capture sensitive, sensual, and erotic qualities in a subtle way. I want to capture the dance in every single one of my subjects. Each individual has a unique rhythm, and when photographing someone nude, it is up to the photographer to encourage the subject to set it free.

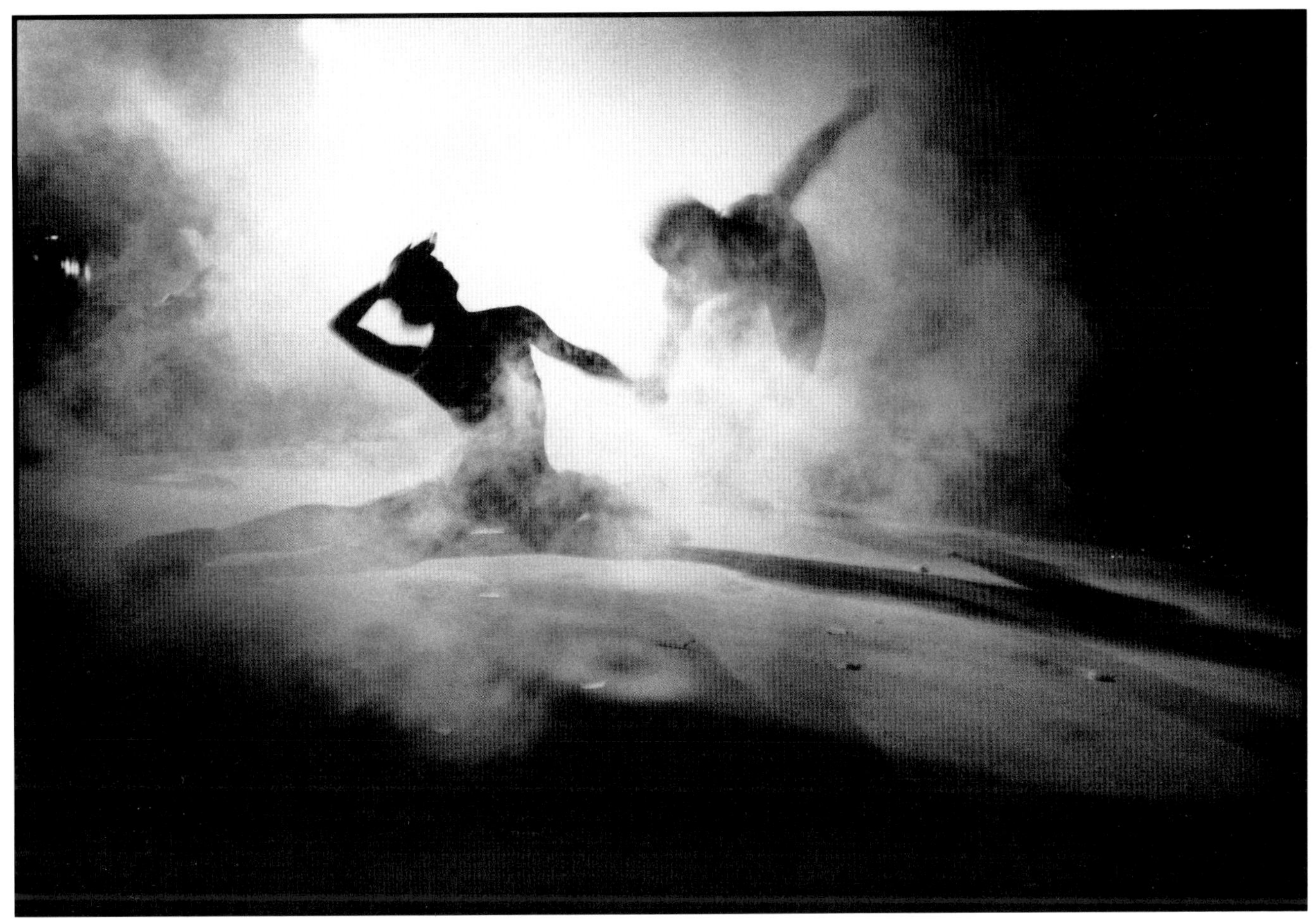

Plate 9

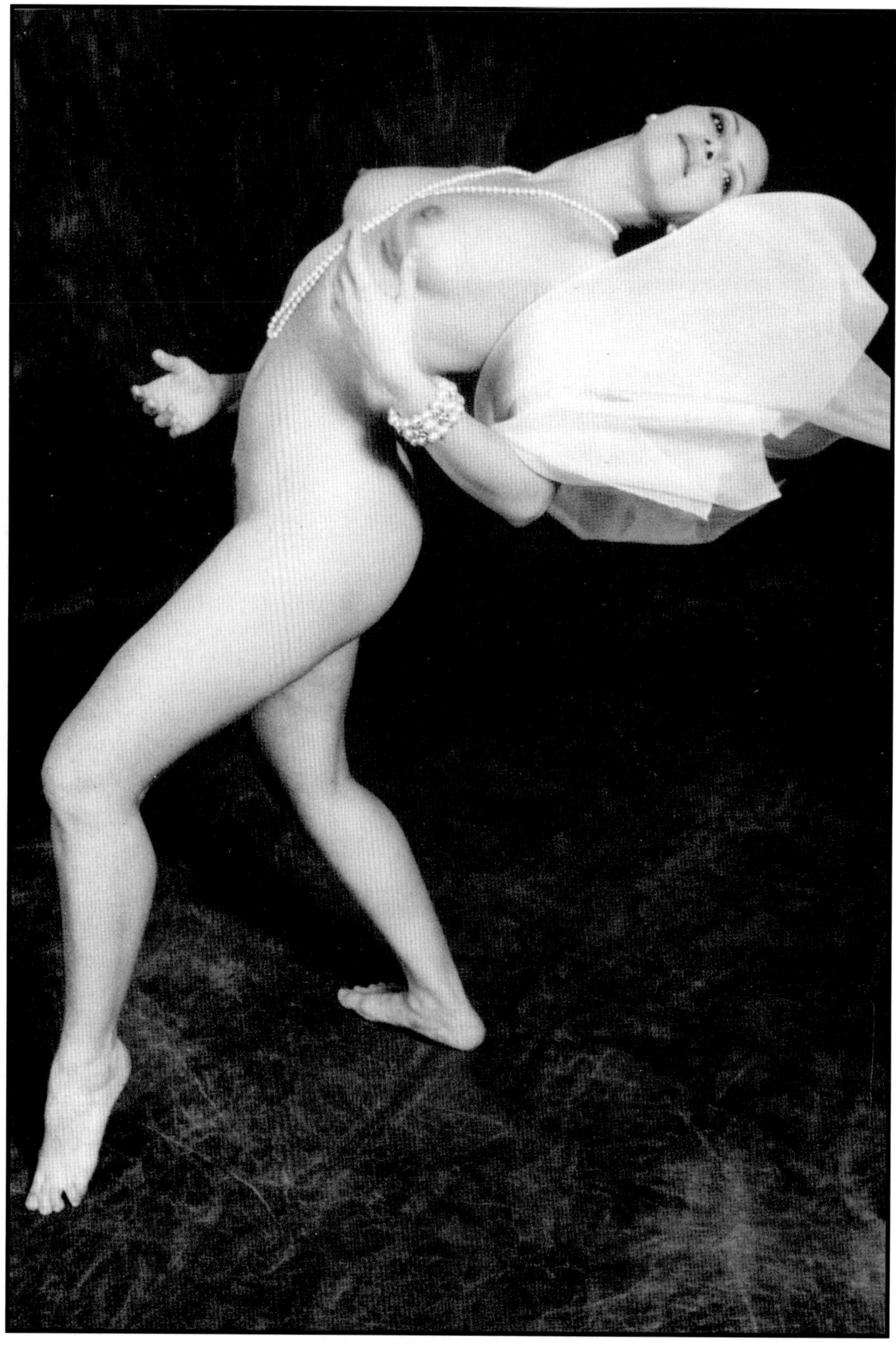

Plate 10

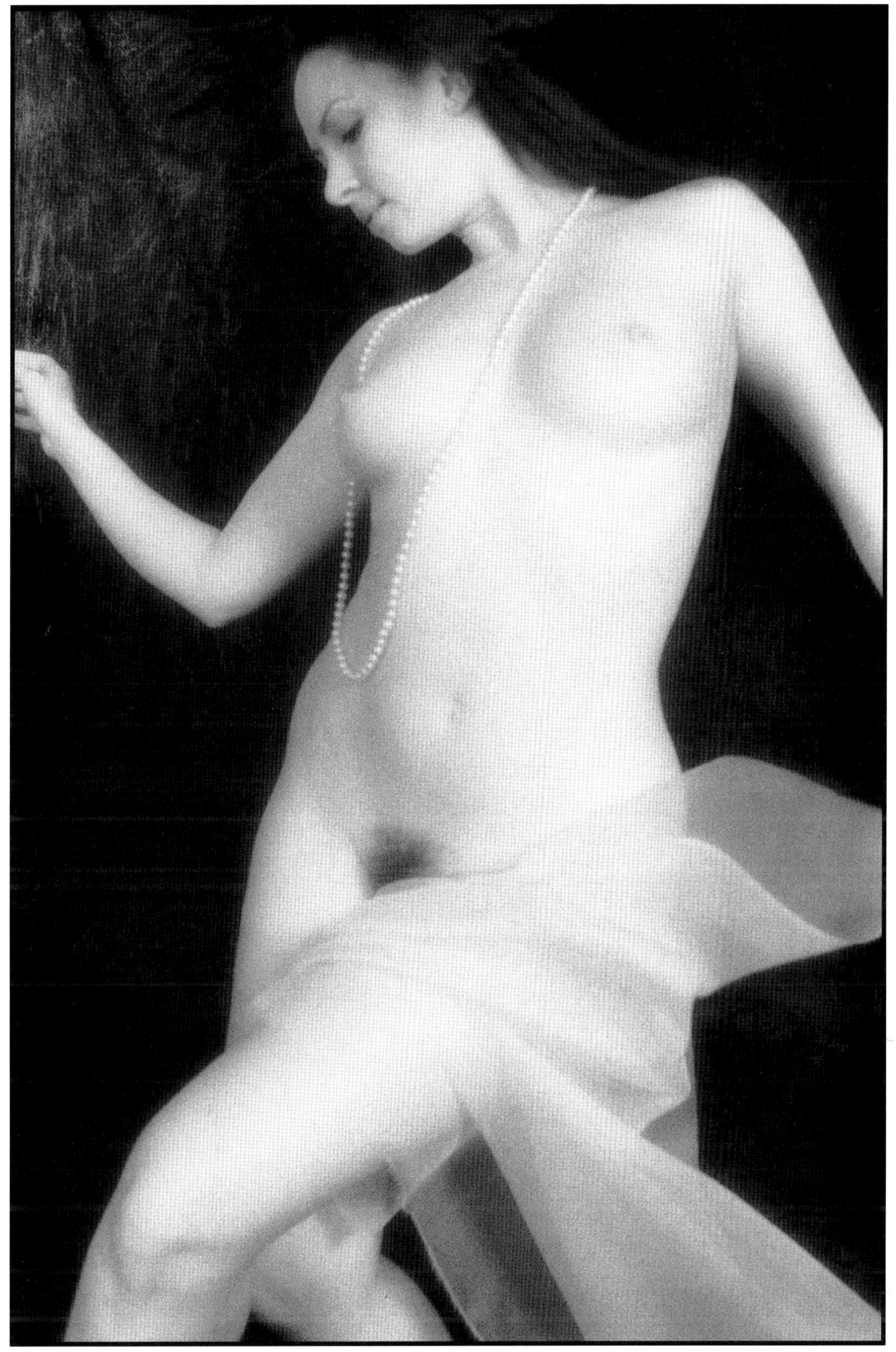

Plate 11

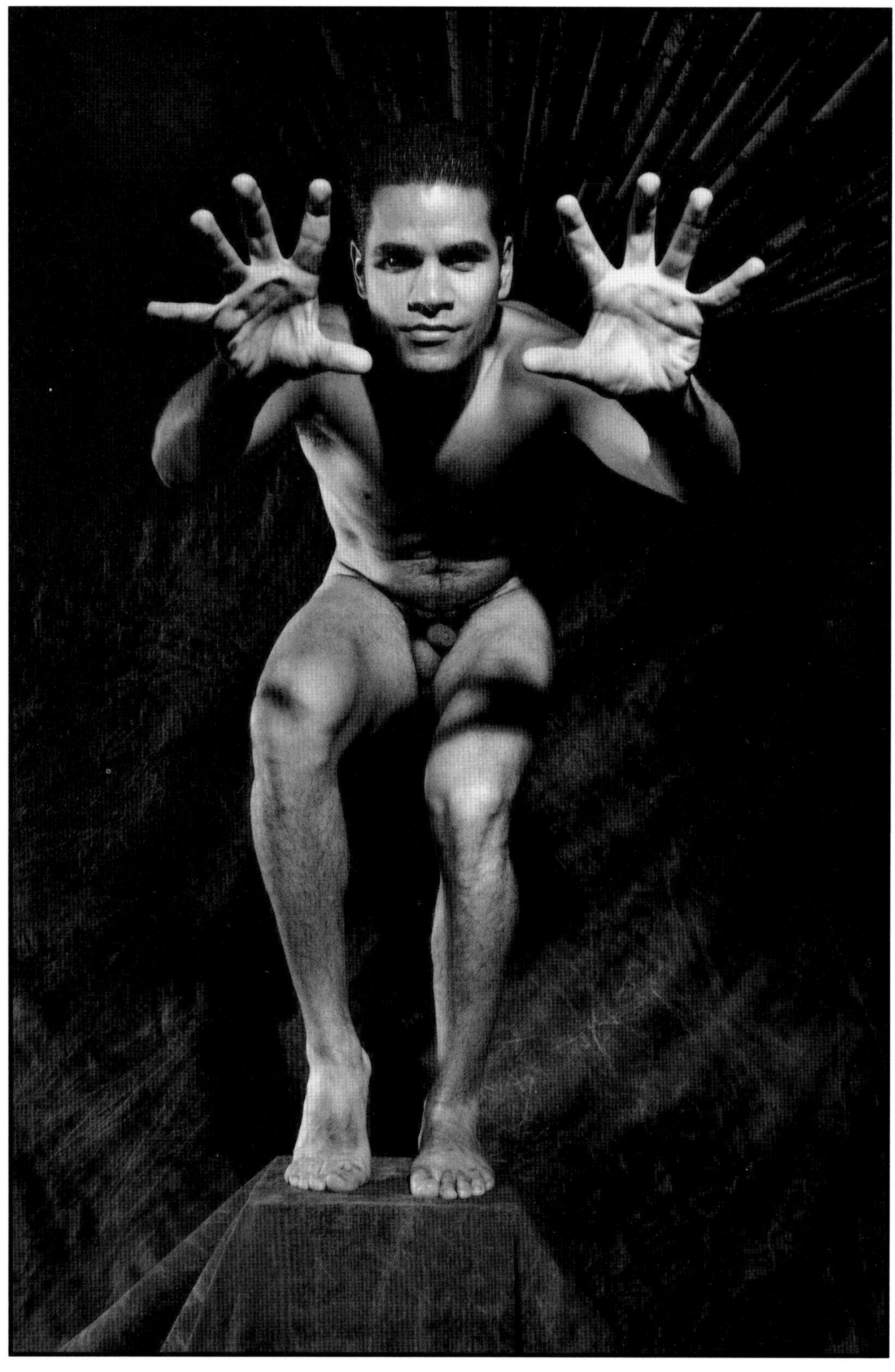

Plate 12

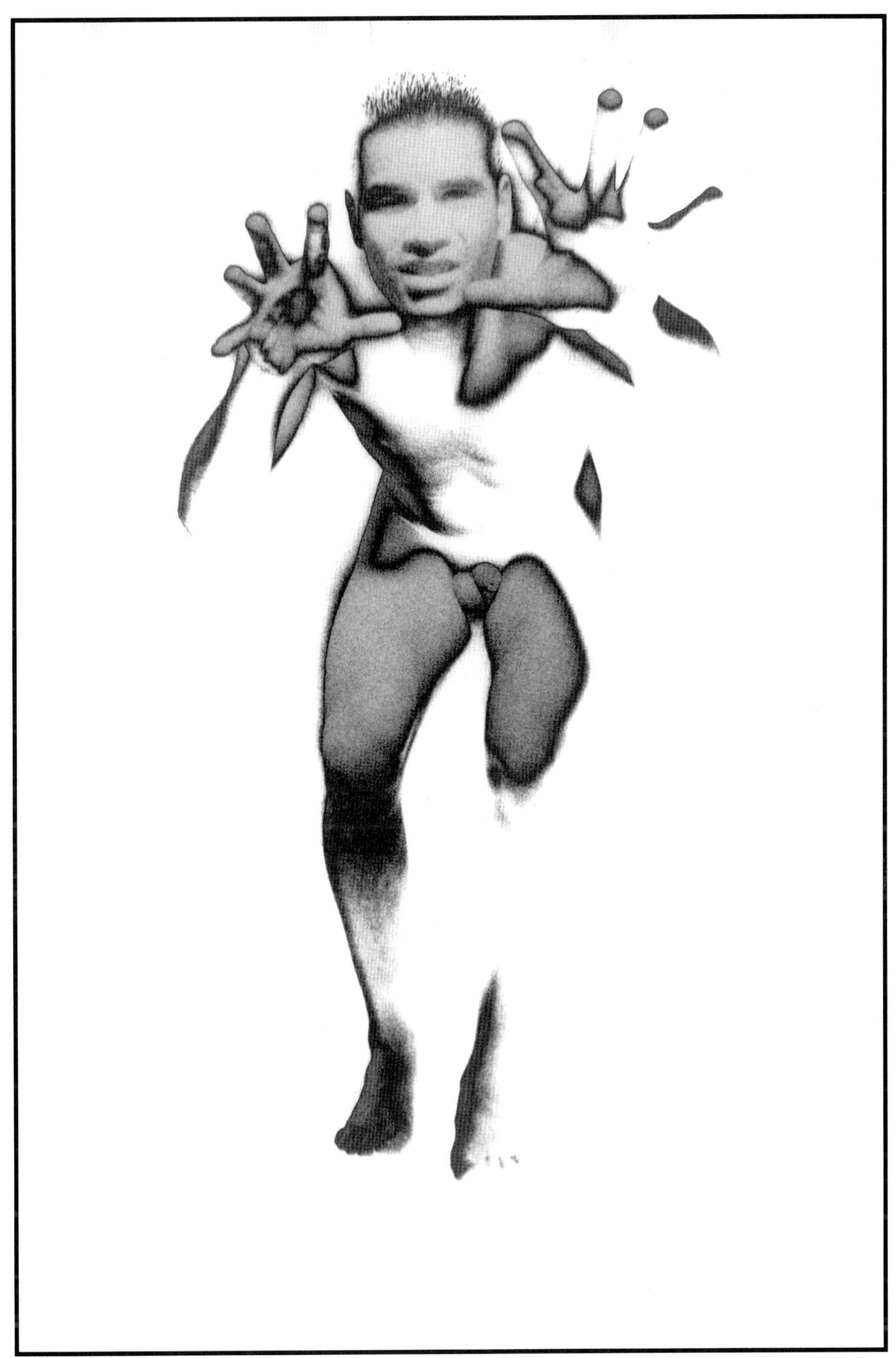

Plate 13

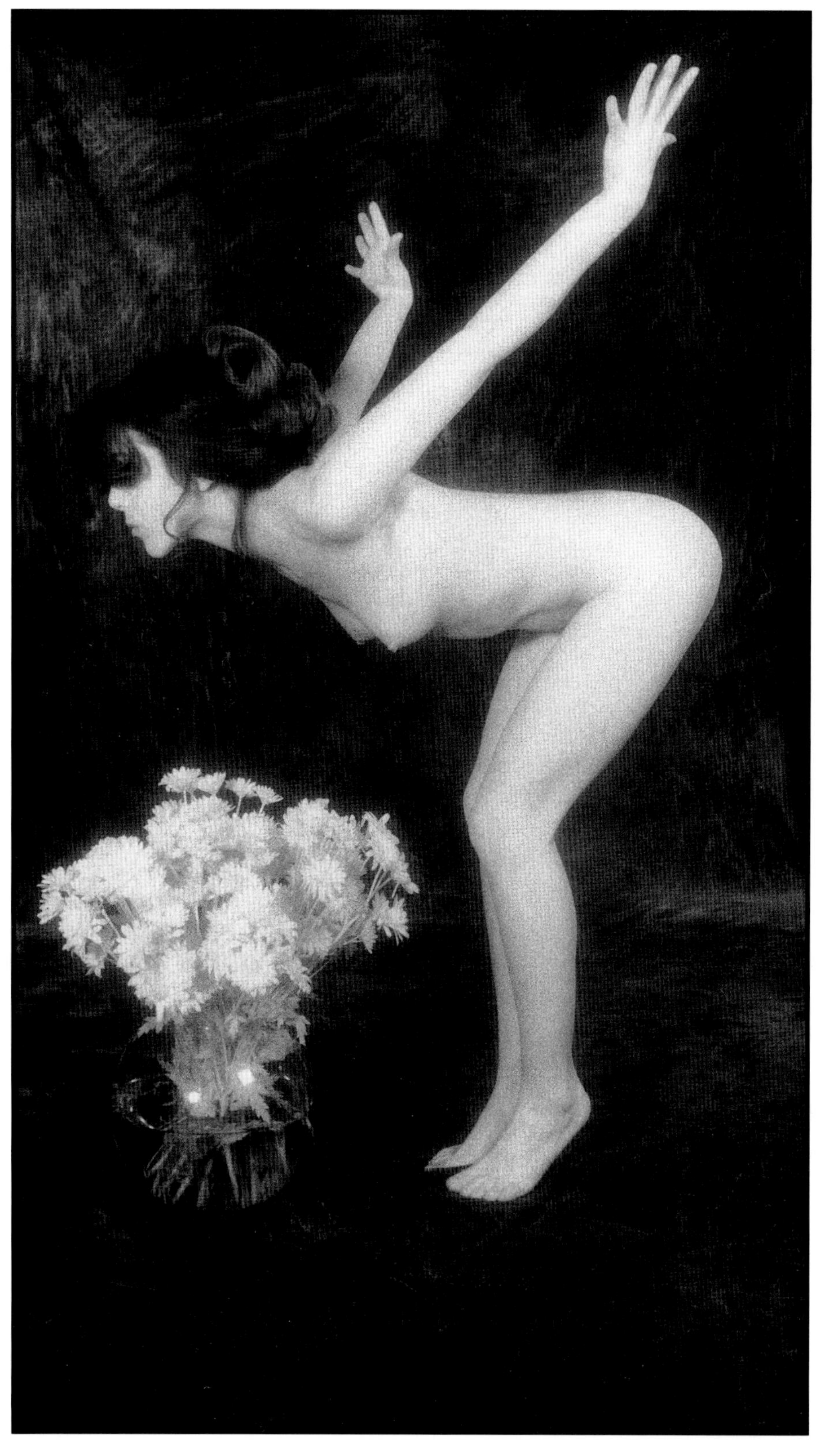

Plate 14

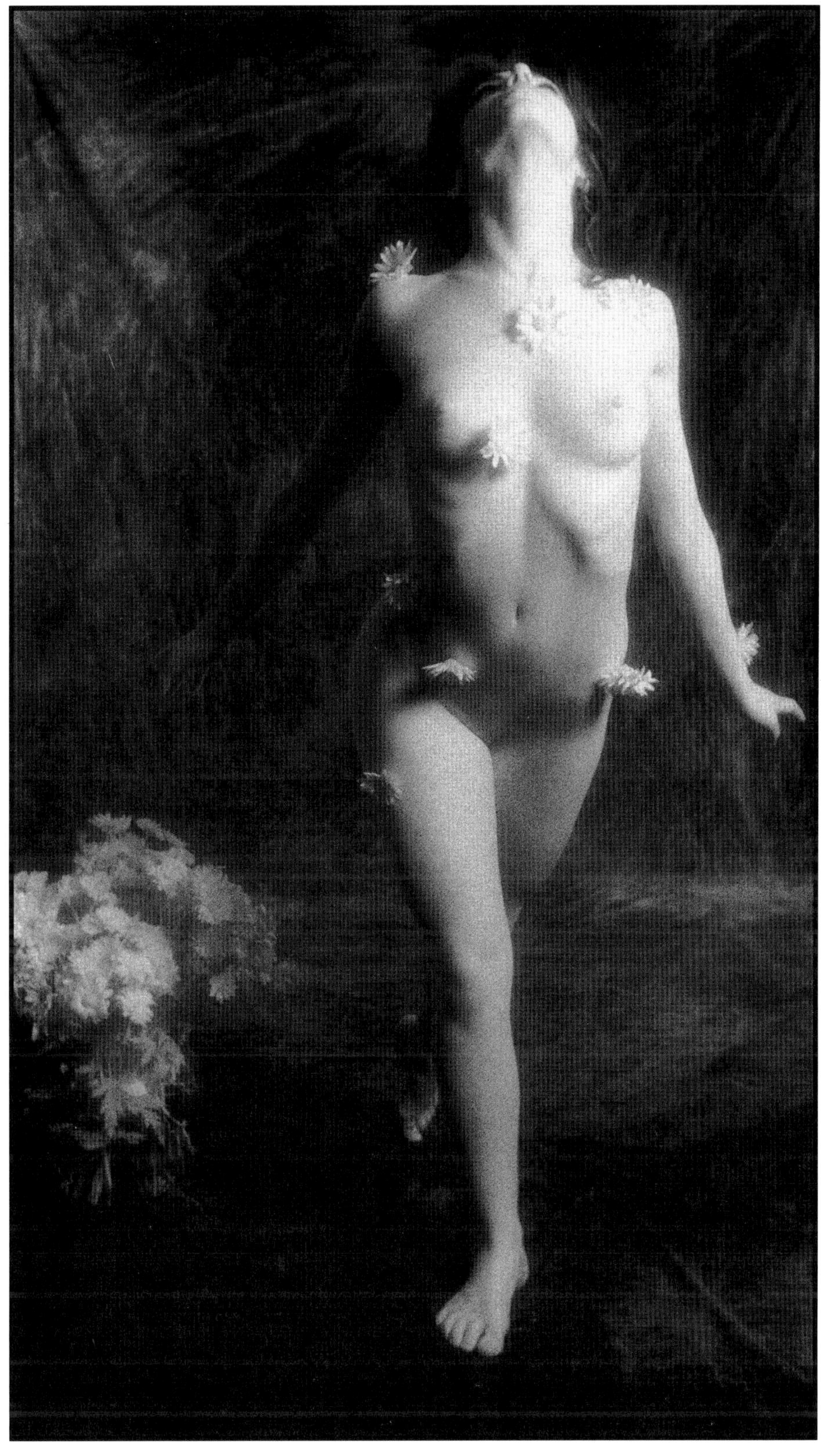

Plate 15

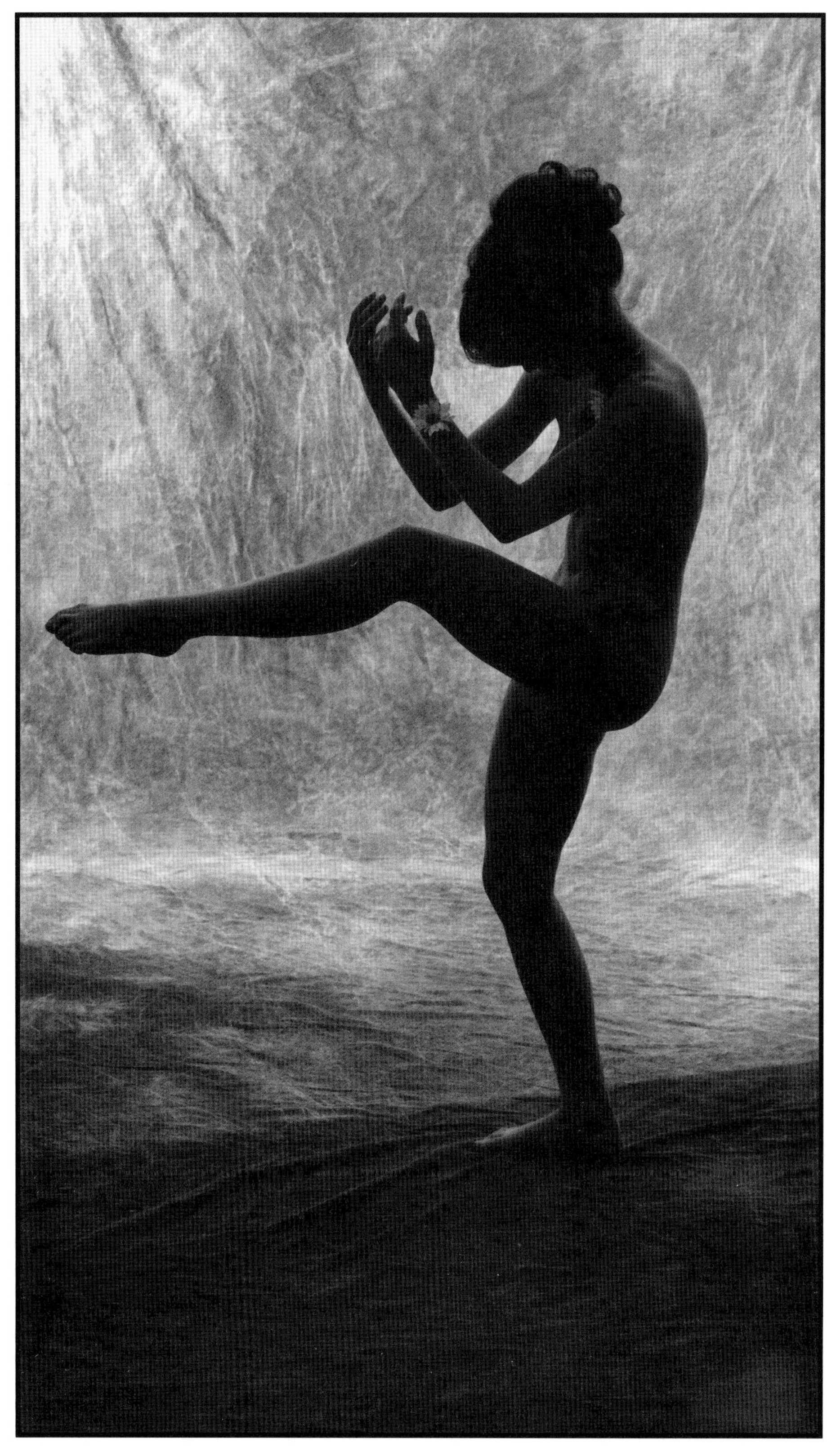

Plate 16

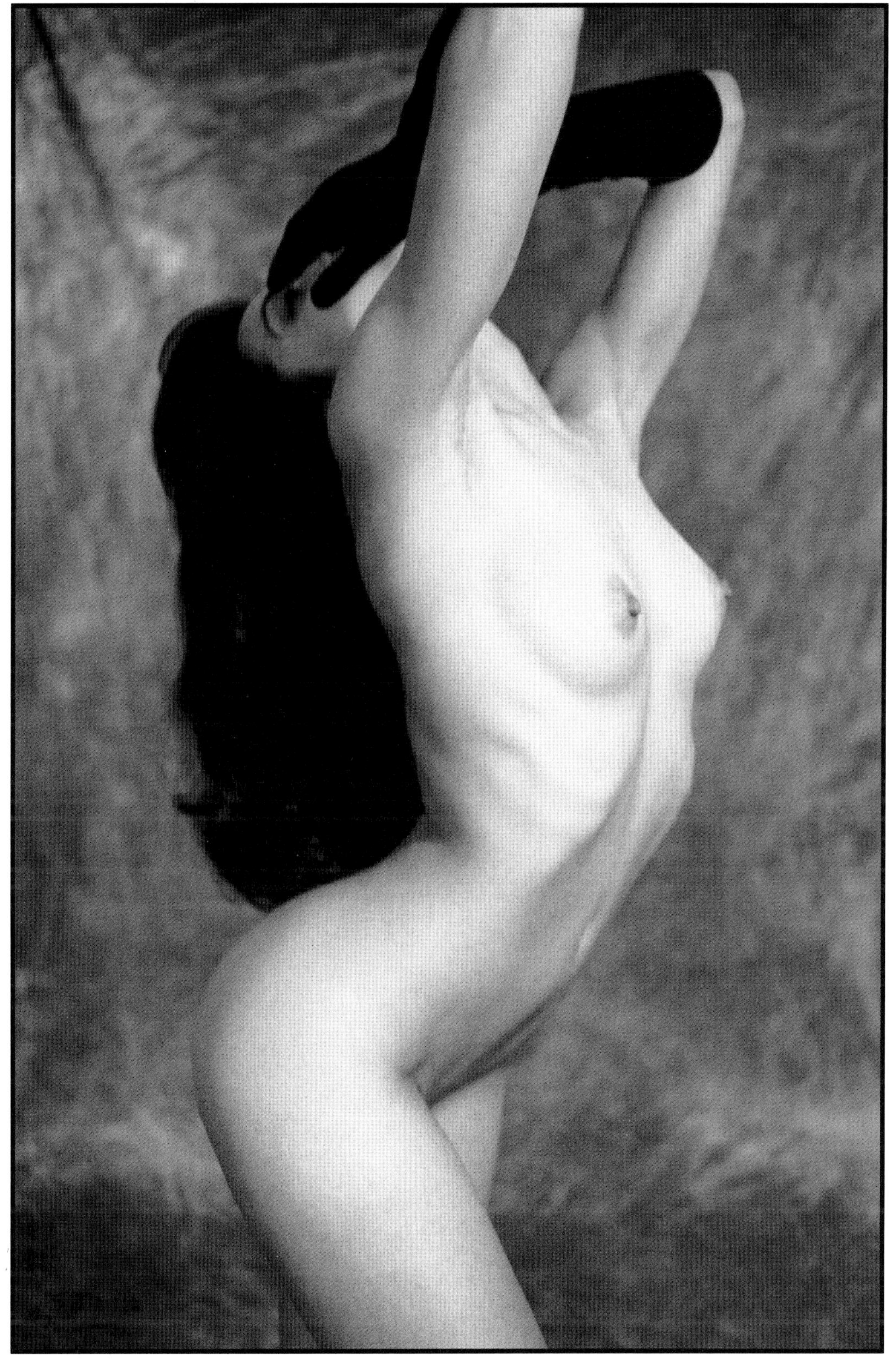

PLATE 17

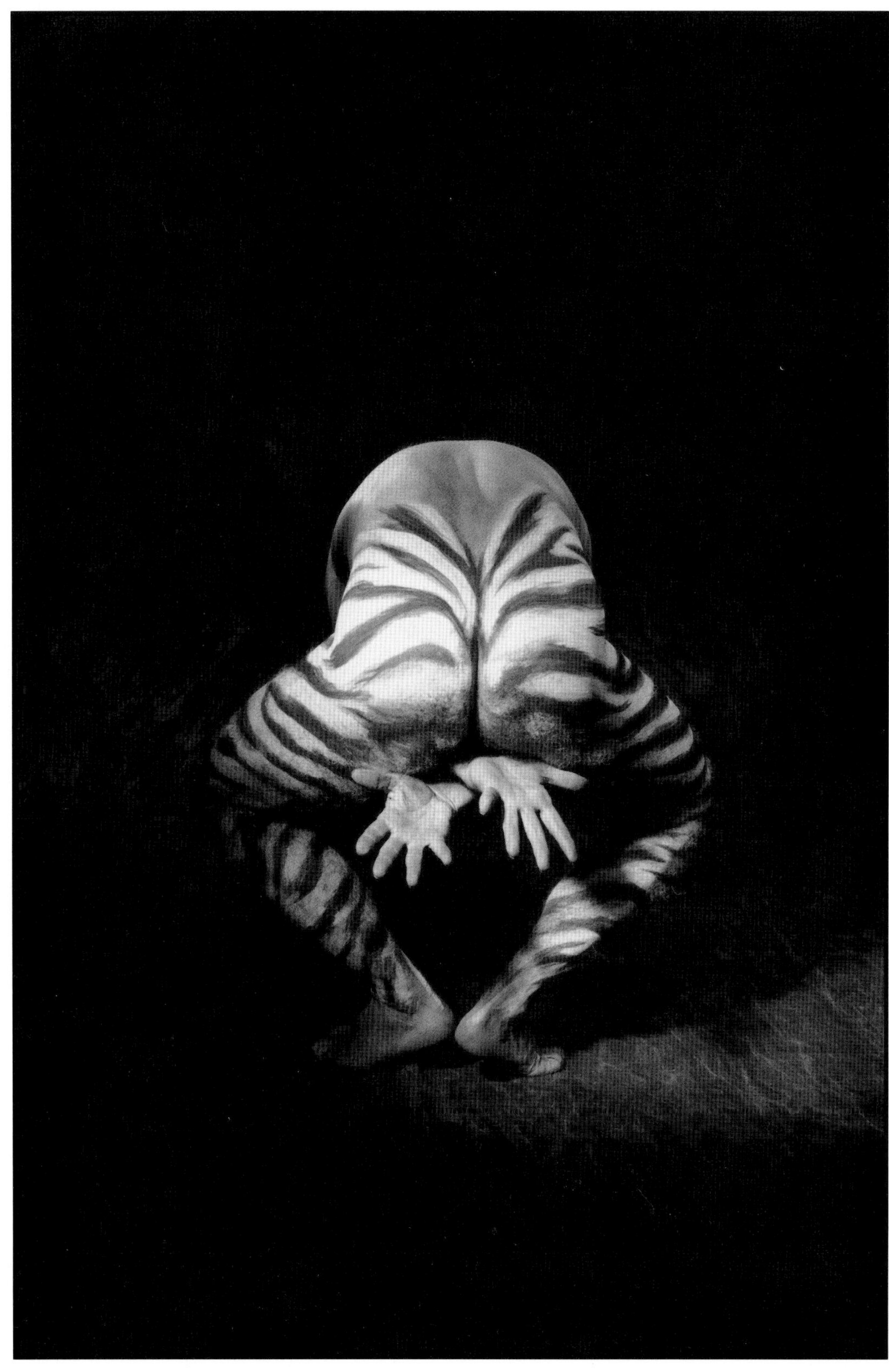

Plate 18

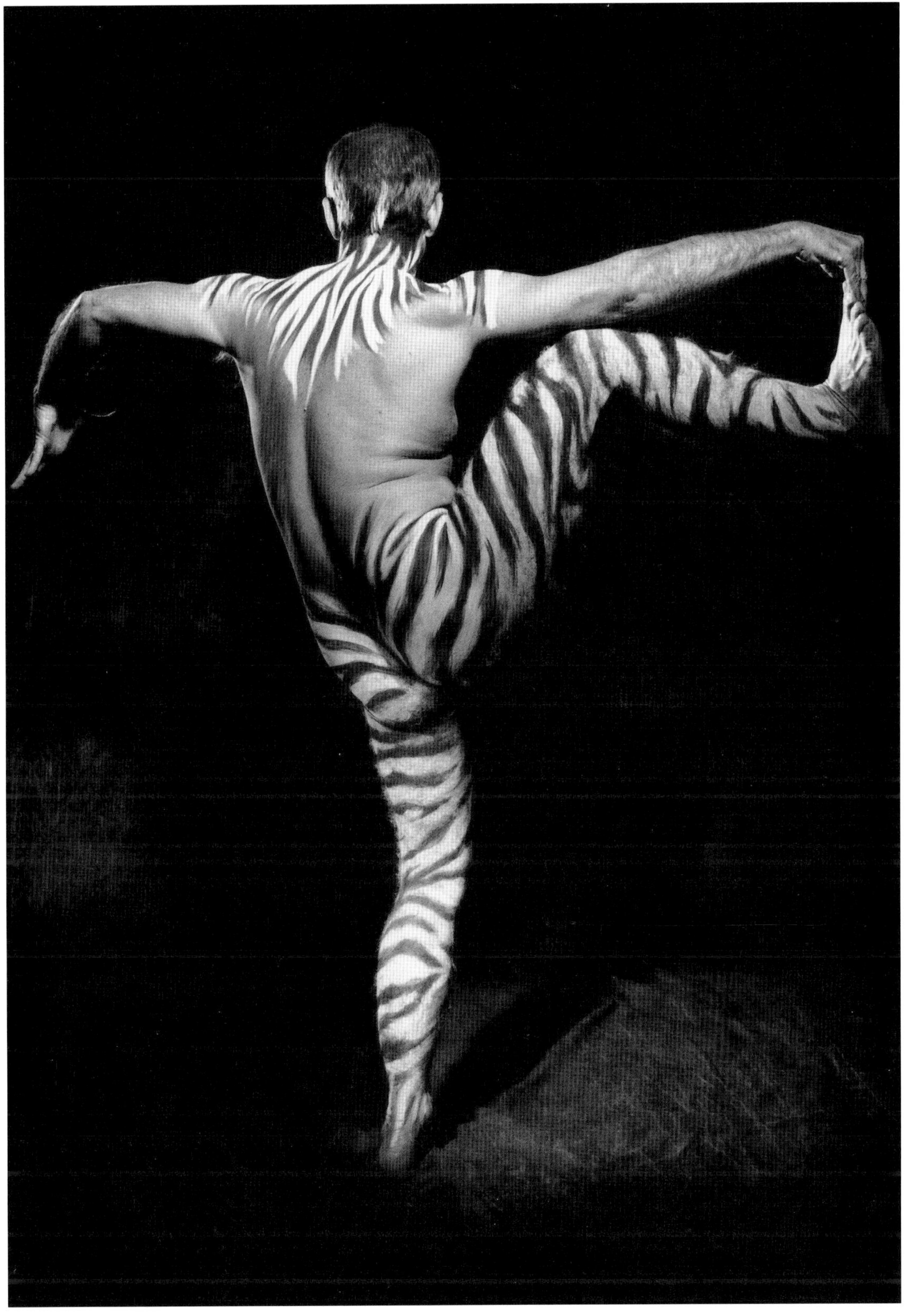

Plate 19

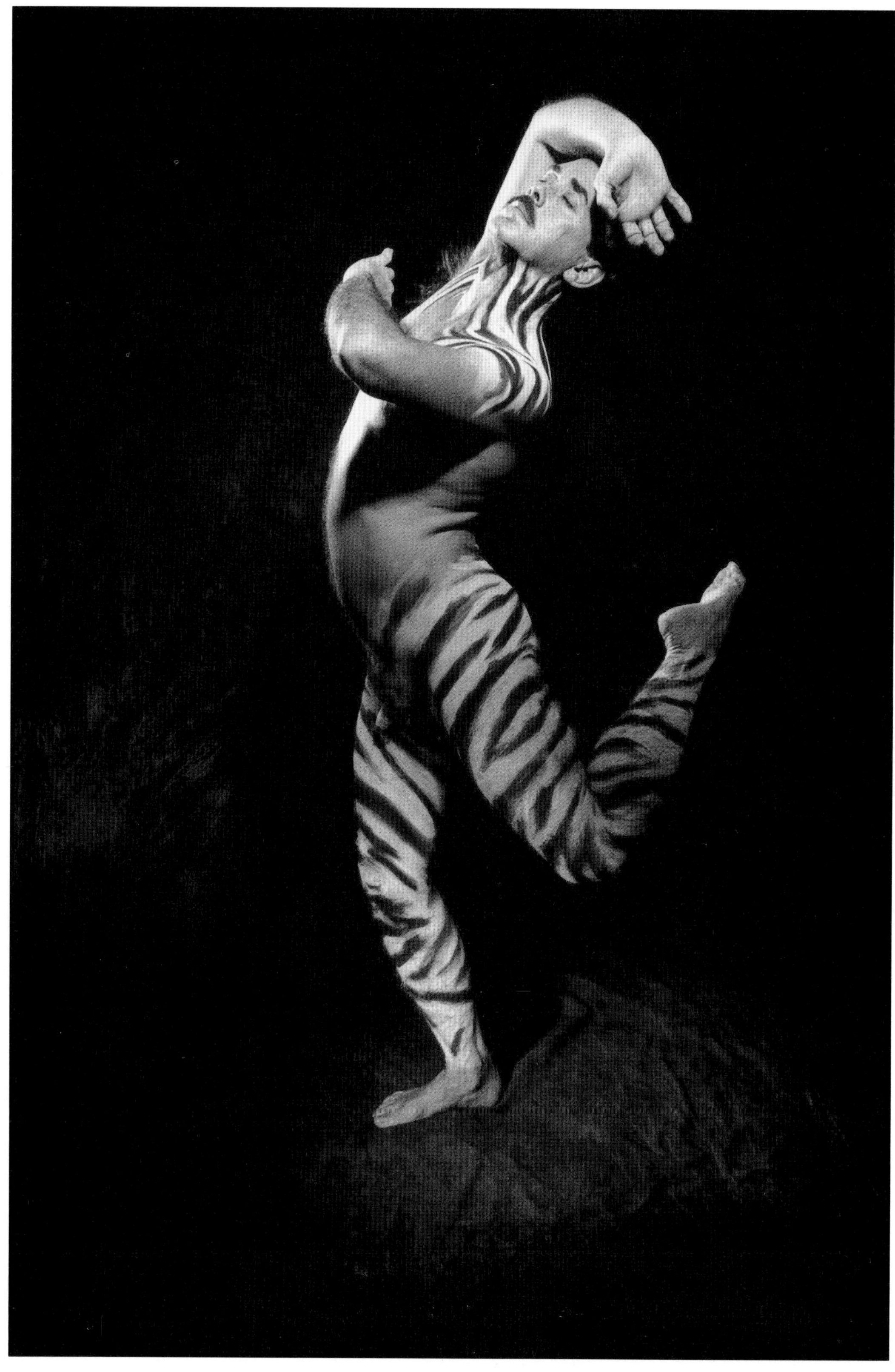

Plate 20

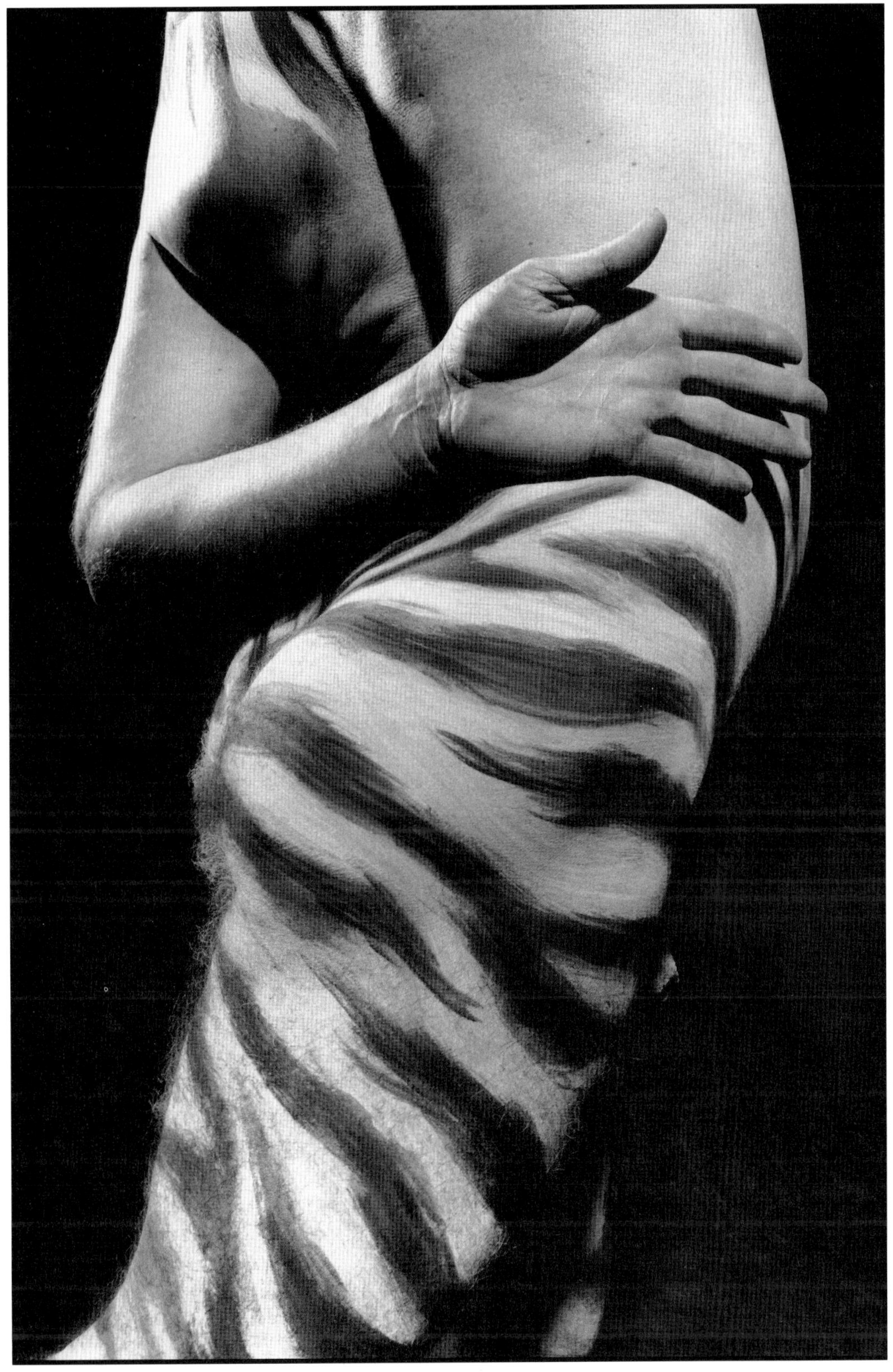

Plate 21

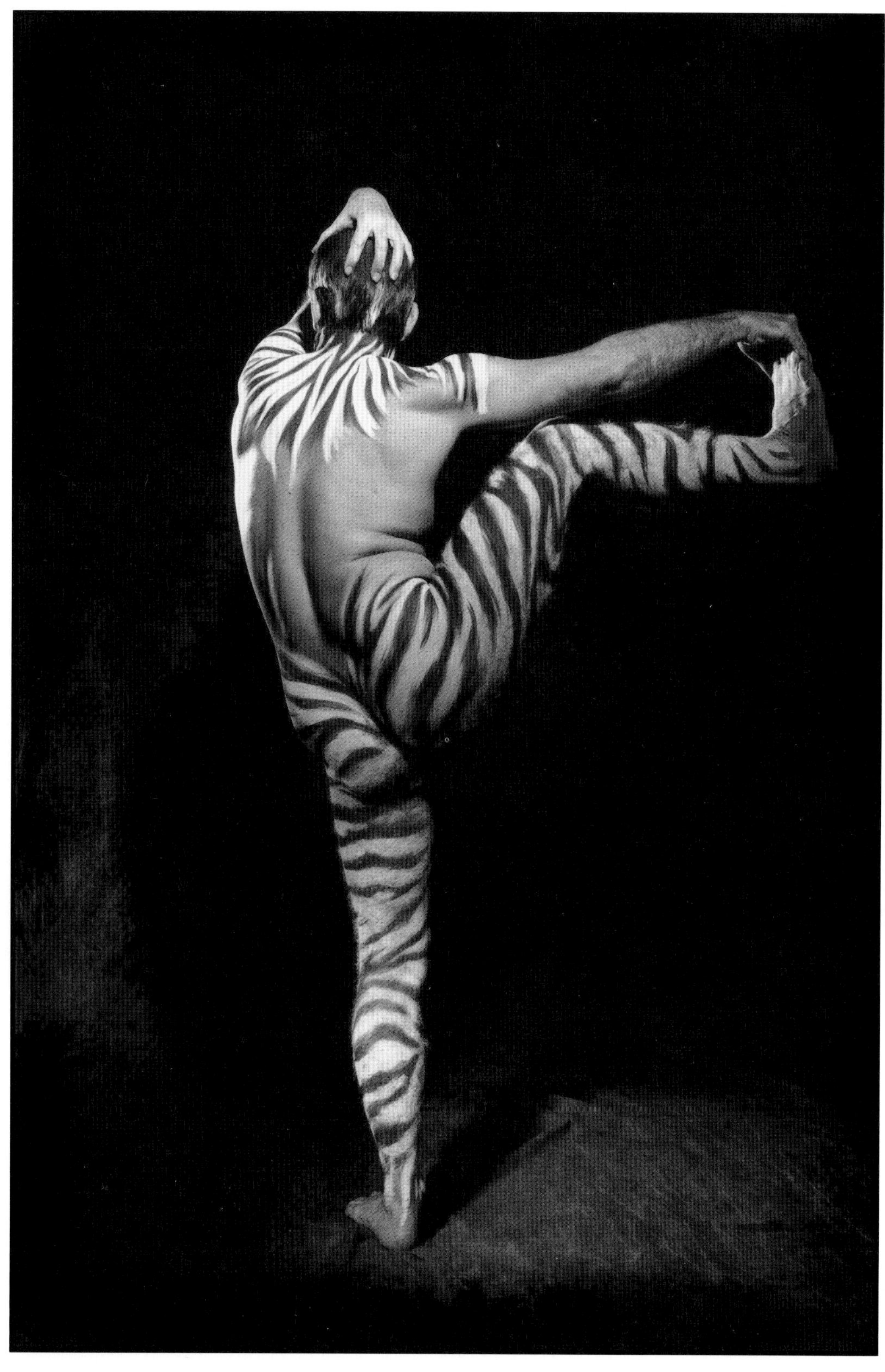

Plate 22

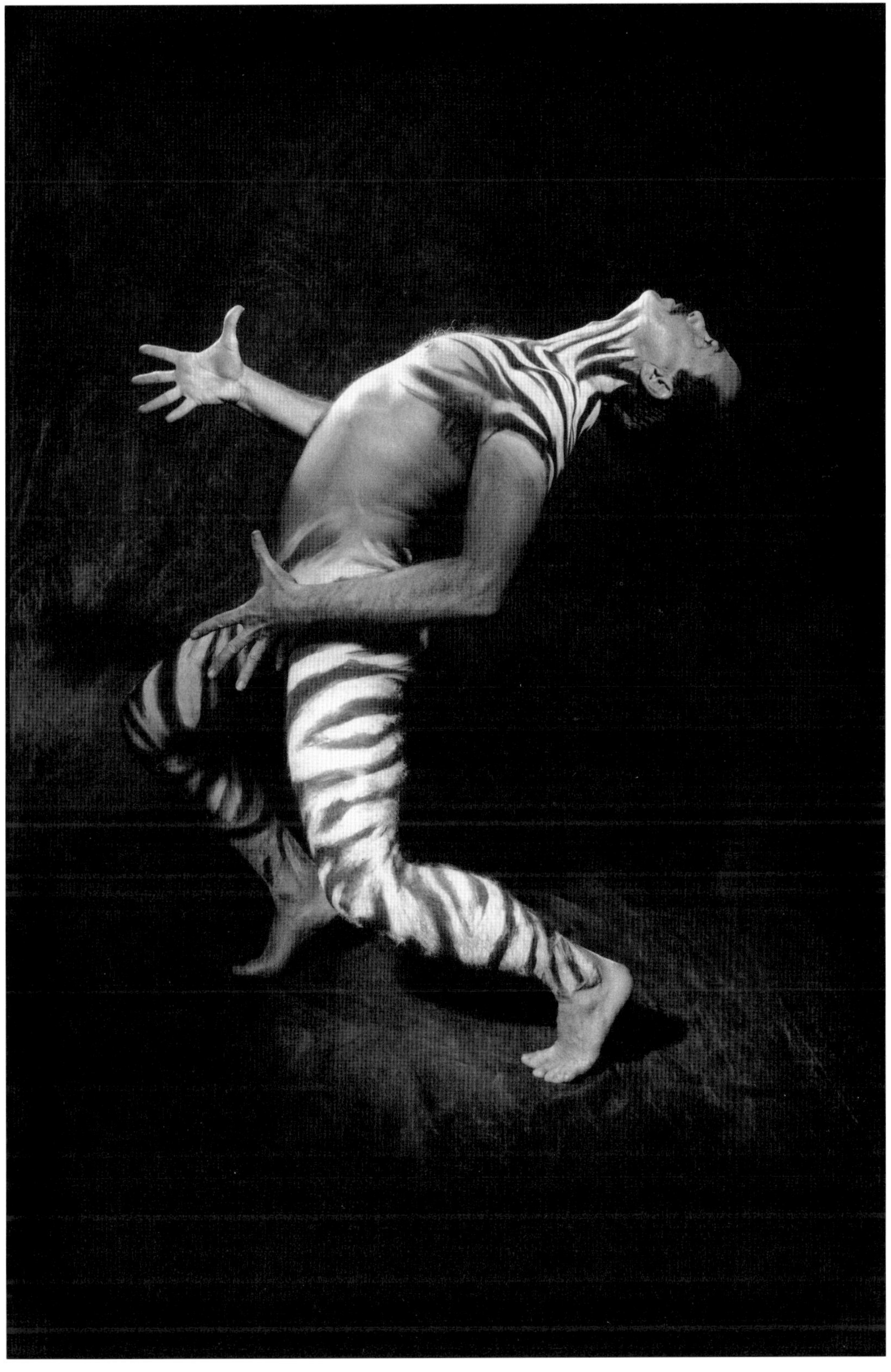

Plate 23

BODIES PLURAL

When bodies interact, there is instant drama. The chemistry that exists between human beings is always a fascinating subject for photographers. For example, when I photograph a nude, I feel as if I'm peering through a keyhole into the privacy of a subject's life. Nude subjects can be lovers, a parent and a child, or two children at play. The moment can be light and tender or highly charged. Something special takes place for an instant; it might be the way the subjects look at each other, or it might be the way they move or their bodies relate to one another. When two people feel comfortable together, they embrace without embarrassment, and their bodies intertwine in an endless number of arrangements, creating wonderful shapes, forms, and expressions.

As a photographer working with several nude subjects, you have the opportunity to capture many aesthetically appealing moments. You can photograph your subjects straight on, or you can go to an extreme and use a wide-angle lens to produce distortion. Sometimes distortion can be unattractive, but at other times it can emphasize a beautiful quality in a photographic image.

I choose to shoot a high degree of intimacy, where sexuality comes to the surface but isn't the primary point of focus. Whatever someone exudes, sensuality or shyness, it is there for you to capture on film. Remember, no two individuals are the same. And when two people are physically attracted to each other, the passion that develops between them ignites the moment. Couples interact as a unit: They give and take and express themselves as one. Of course, the relationship between two people who form a couple will come across differently in your photographs than that of two people who are "just friends."

Often, the interaction between two nude subjects results in a very graphic image. For example, if you position two male models side by side and come in close with a telephoto lens, you can isolate a single body part of each of the men, such as an arm, a leg muscle, or the roundness of a shoulder. Here, you're no longer taking a picture of two individuals. The resulting image shows separate body parts that work well together to create a whole new entity. The interpretation is then left, as always, to the viewers.

Sometimes, however, you'll engage the modeling services of two or more people who simply can't relate to each other. The chemistry just isn't there. Instead of being disappointed, use the disharmony to your advantage and immediately revise your plans for the session. When I see that a shoot isn't working because of the lack of rapport between the models, I challenge myself to come up with solutions. I might do something as simple as change lenses, or I might decide to focus on my subjects' inability to communicate with each other. Introducing a prop can shift the subjects' attention away from themselves. This also enables me to focus on their reactions to the prop. The more intriguing the prop is, the more interesting the models' responses usually are.

You might also run into some difficulty when you use more than two subjects for a shoot. Photographing a number of models together can be confusing unless you are very organized; you should be prepared to make order out of chaos. In addition, if two or more of the models you are about to photograph have never met before, you must give them time to get comfortable with each other. The situation can be awkward initially because, obviously, nude strangers feel even more vulnerable than clothed ones.

It is essential that you understand the relationships that you're attempting to photograph, as well as the importance of directing your subjects well. There is another relationship at work: the exchange that takes place between you, the photographer, and your subject. Depending on your instructions and approach, the moment you record on film can be quite erotic or playful. Once you give your subjects a general scenario, allow them the freedom to write their own scripts.

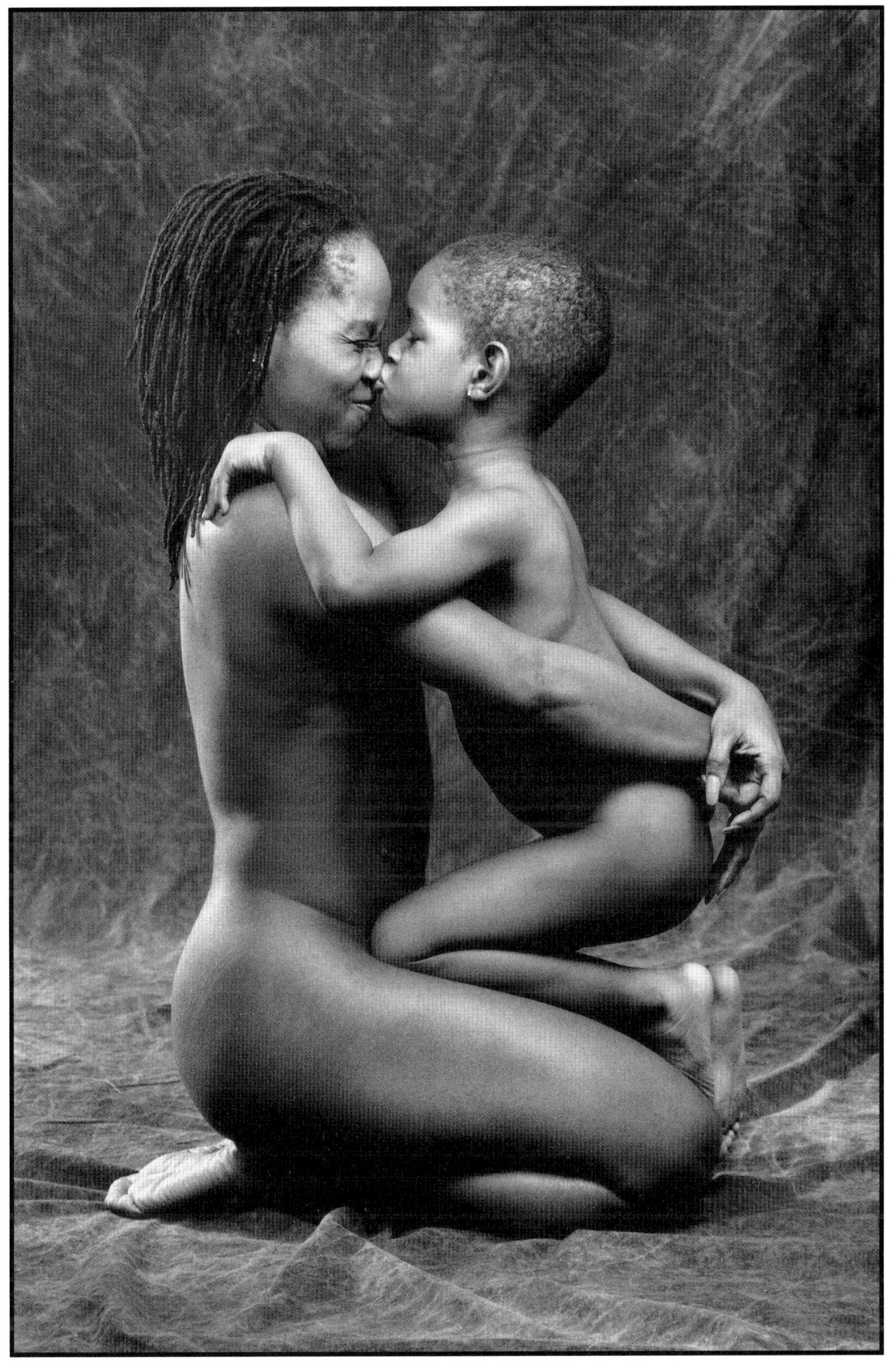

Plate 24

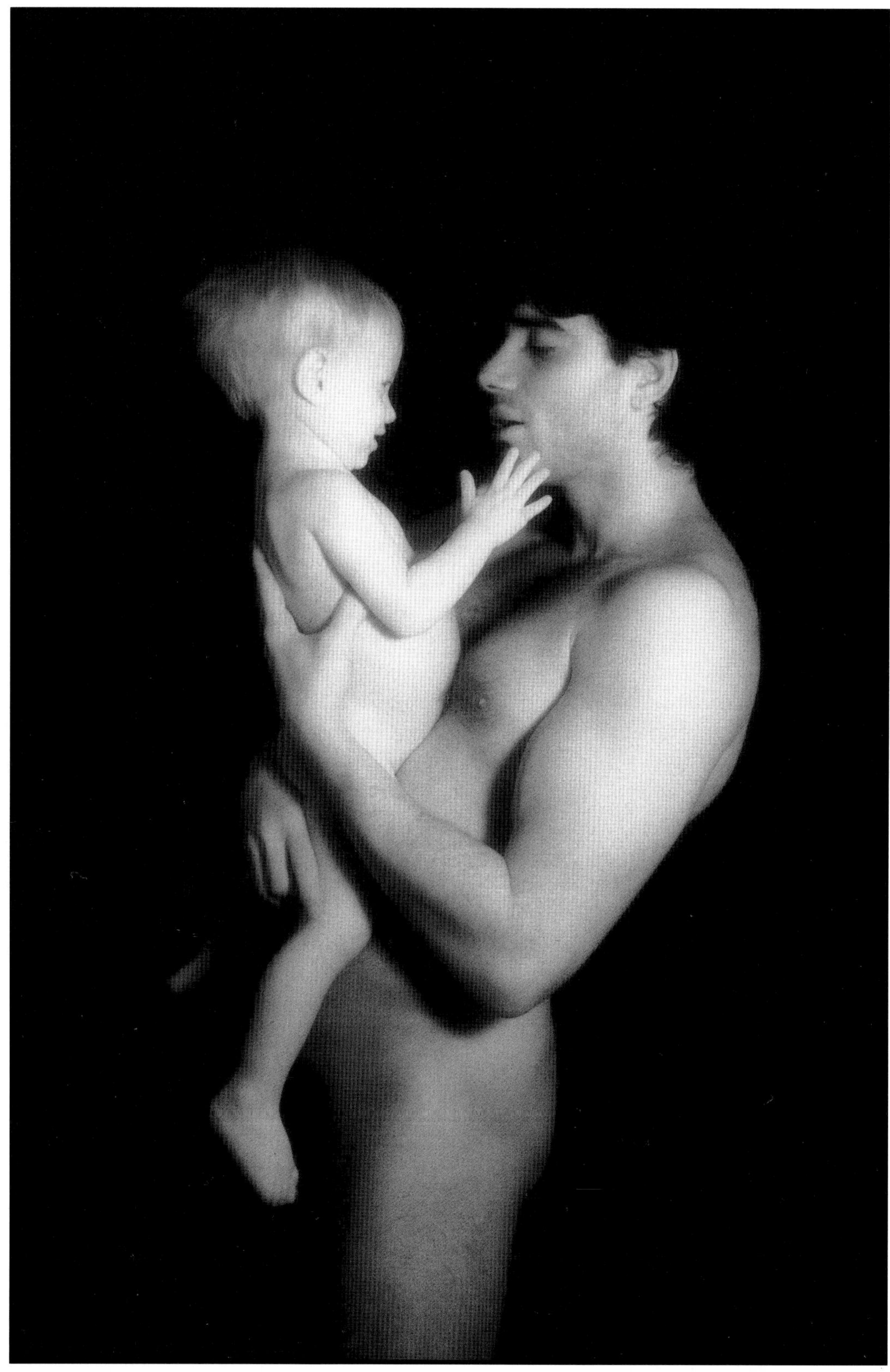

Plate 25

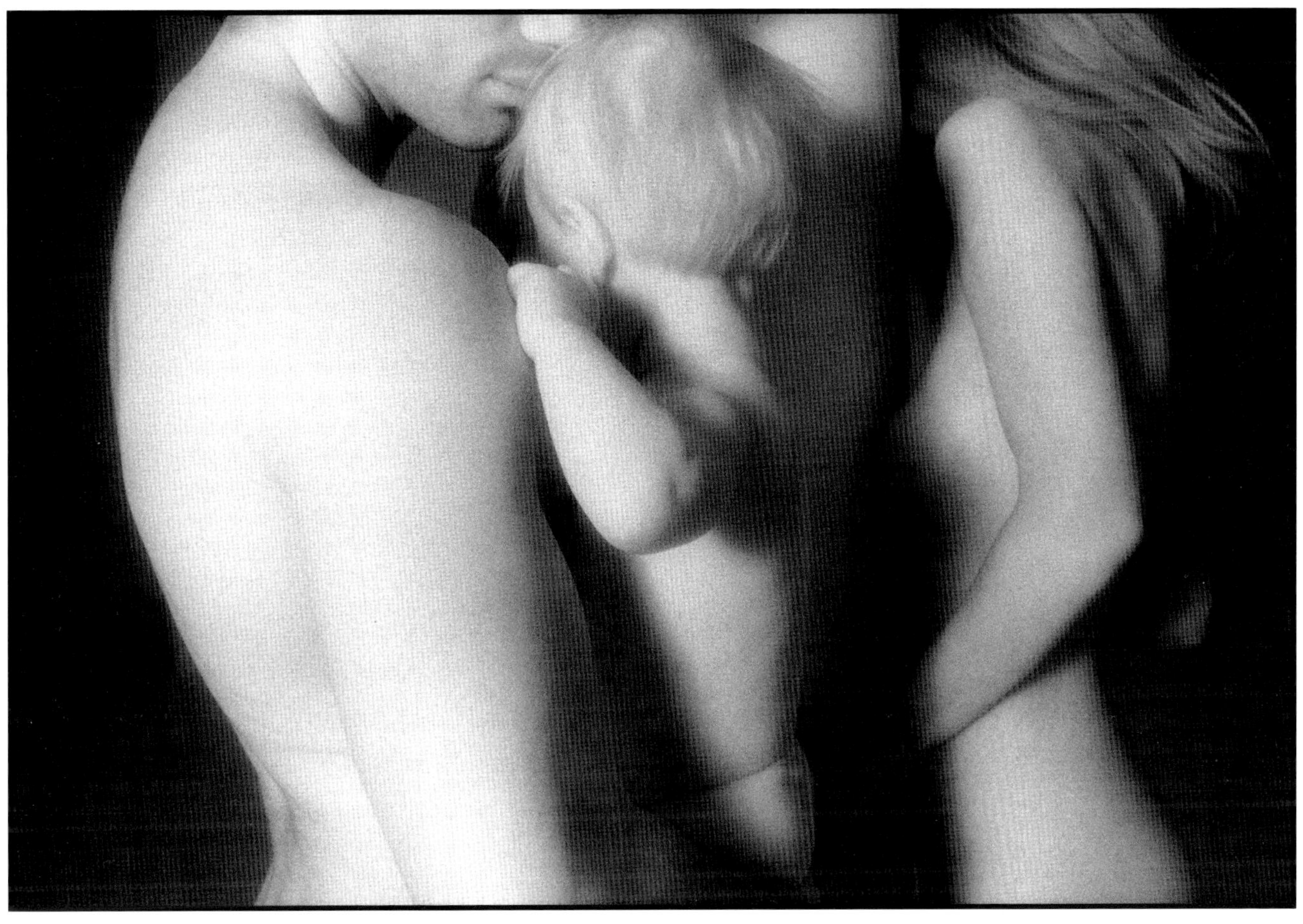

Plate 26

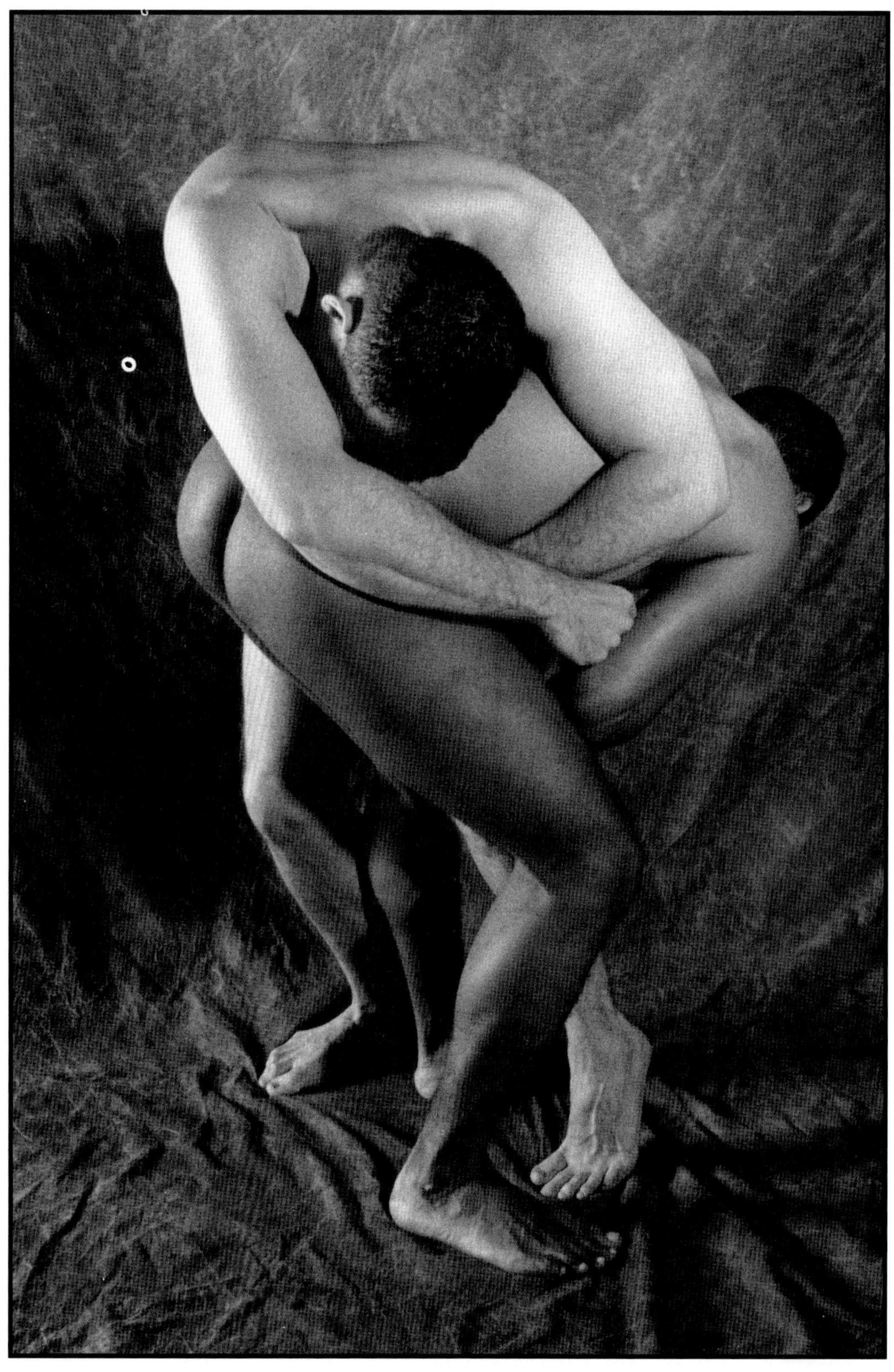

Plate 27

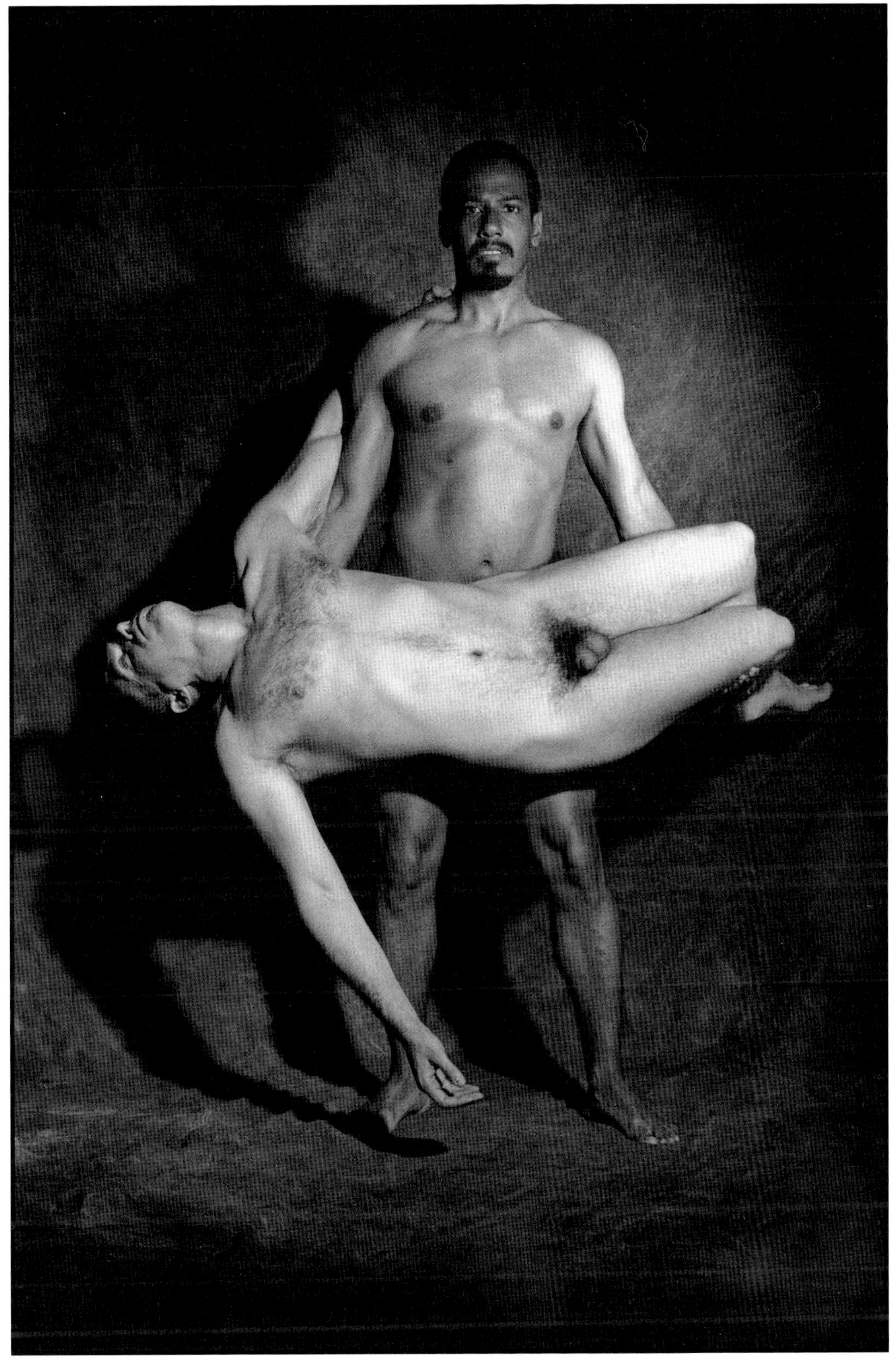

Plate 28

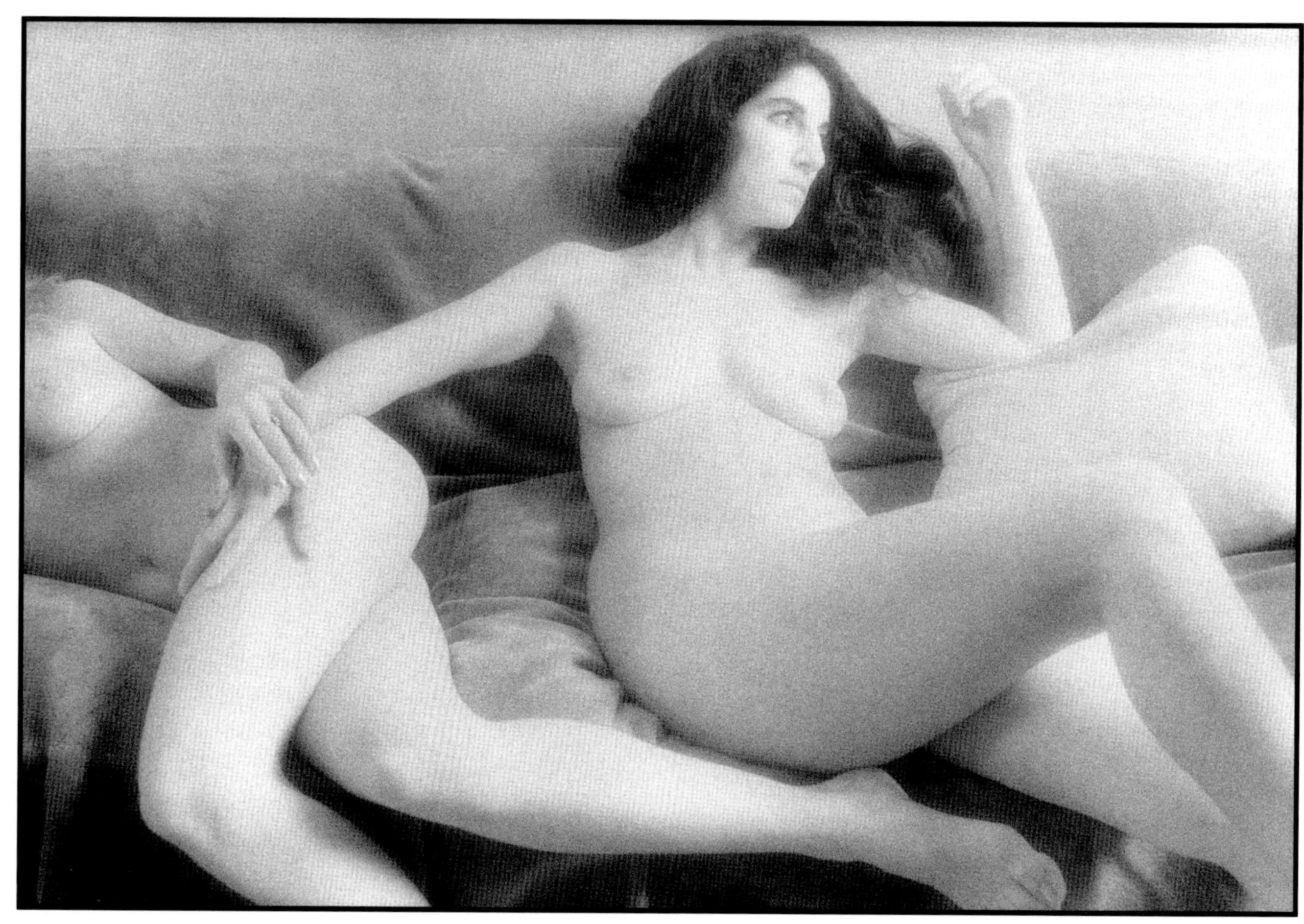

Plate 29

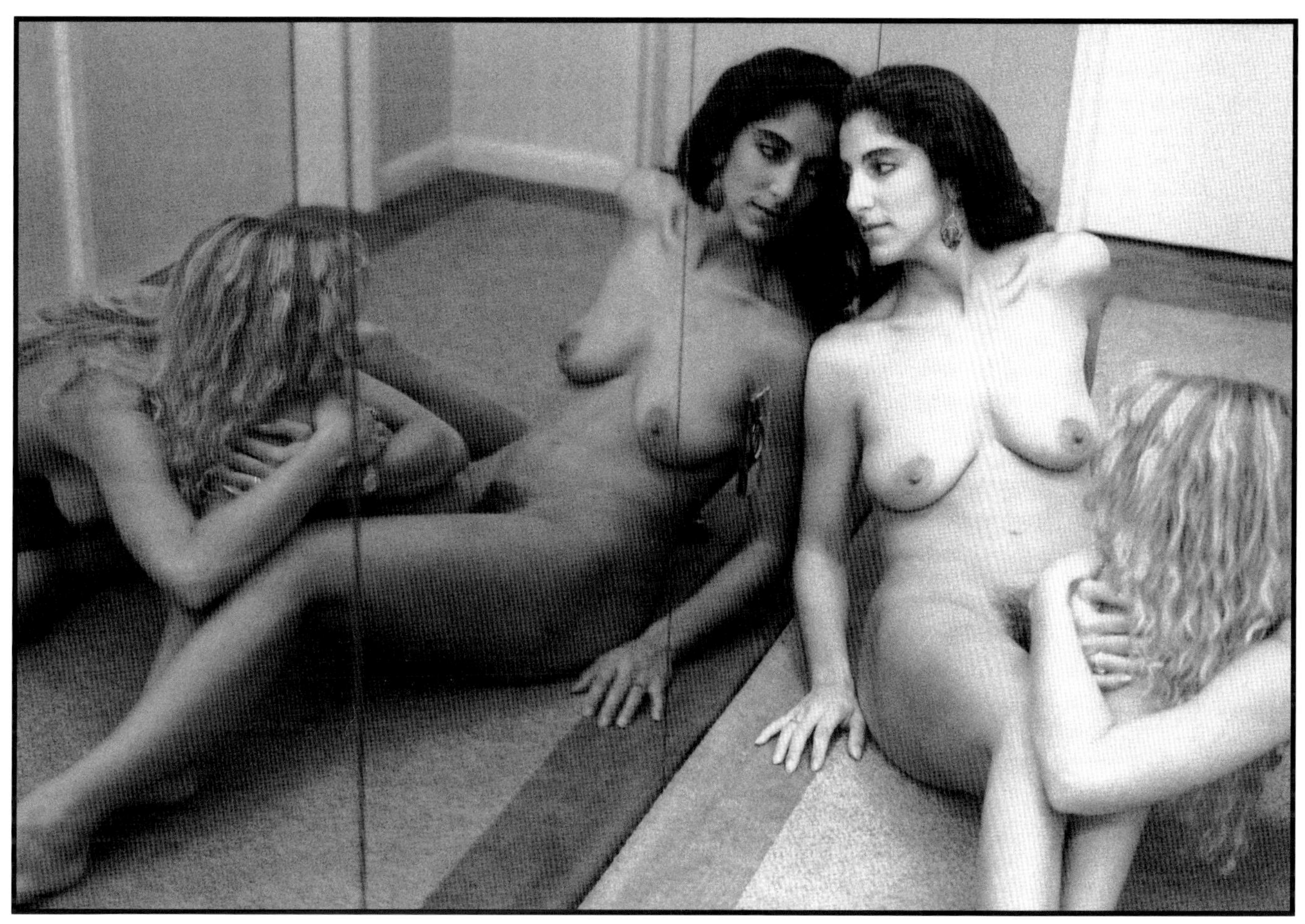

Plate 30

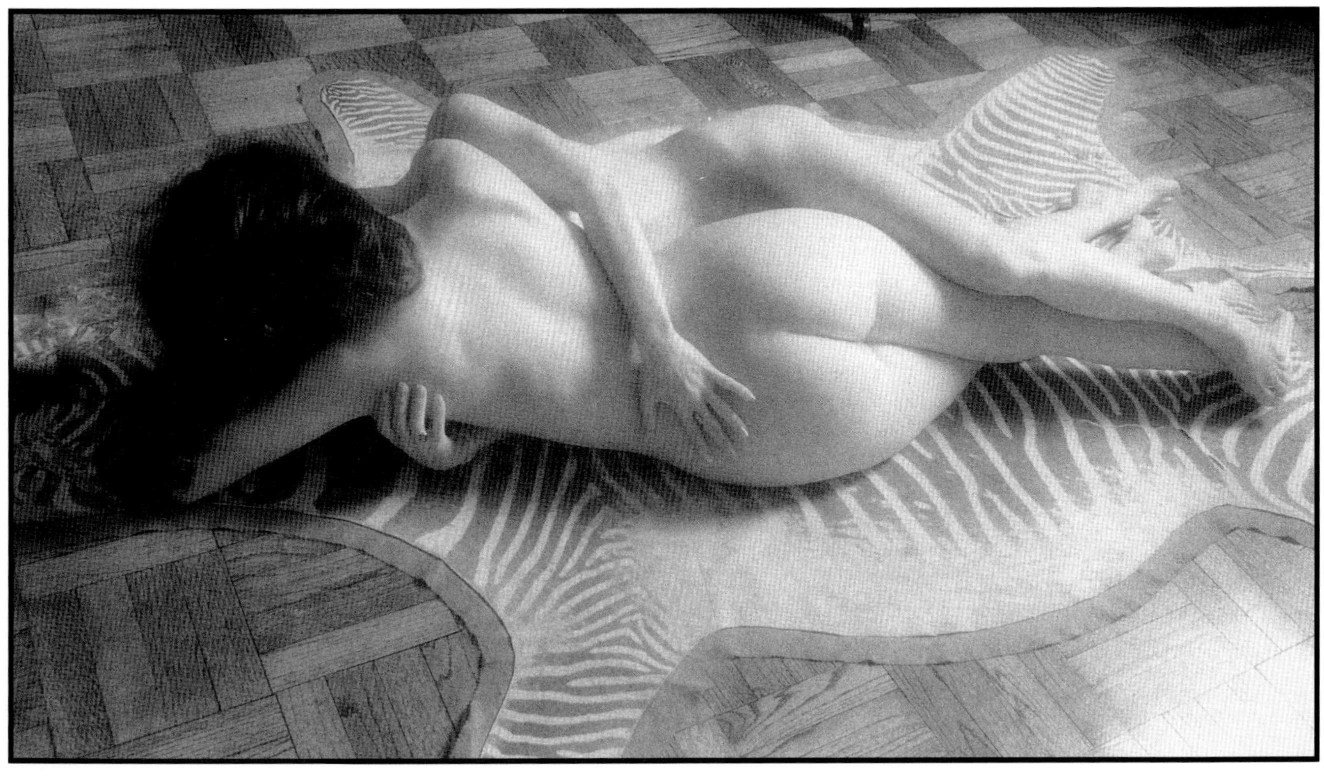

Plate 31

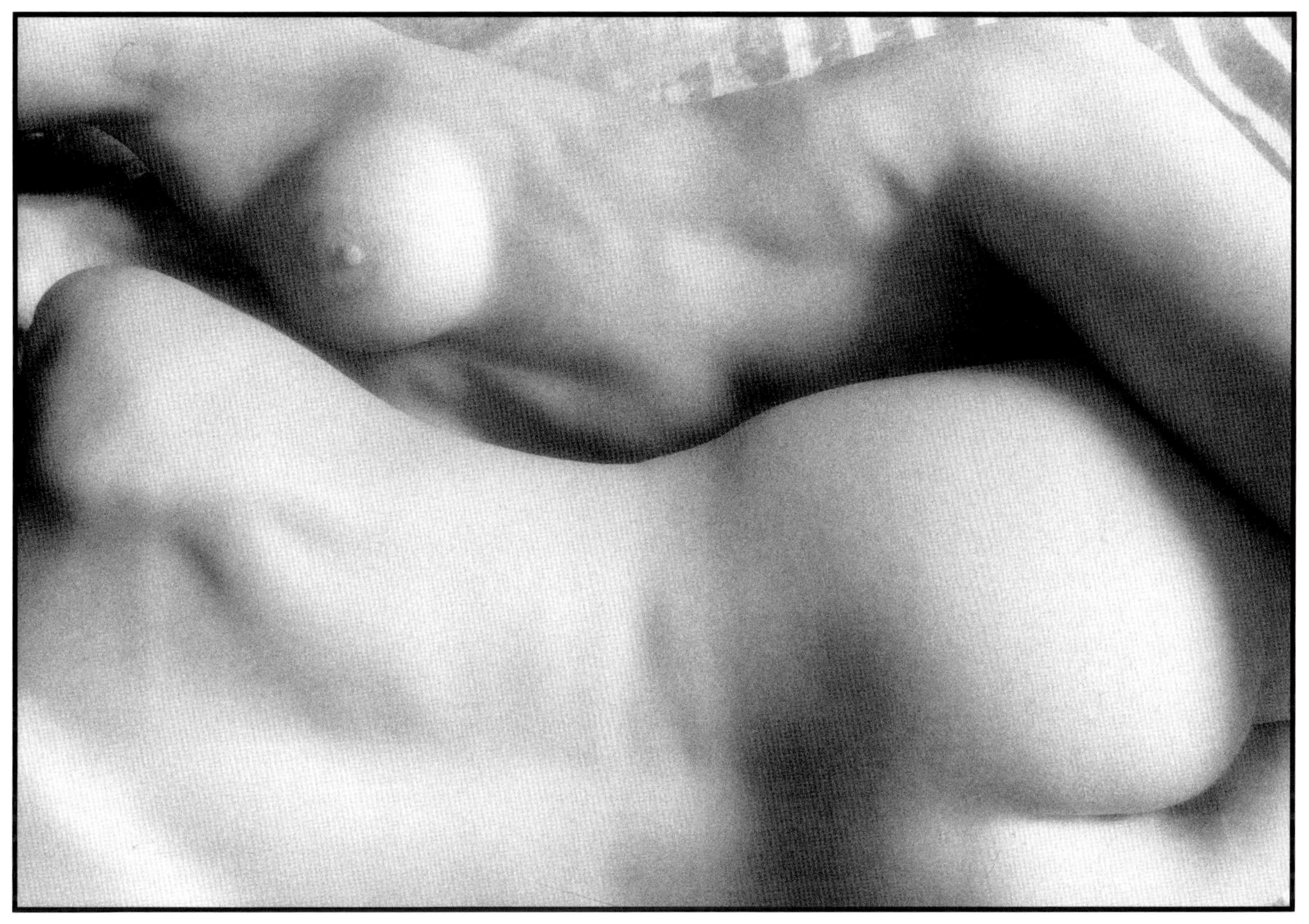

PLATE 32

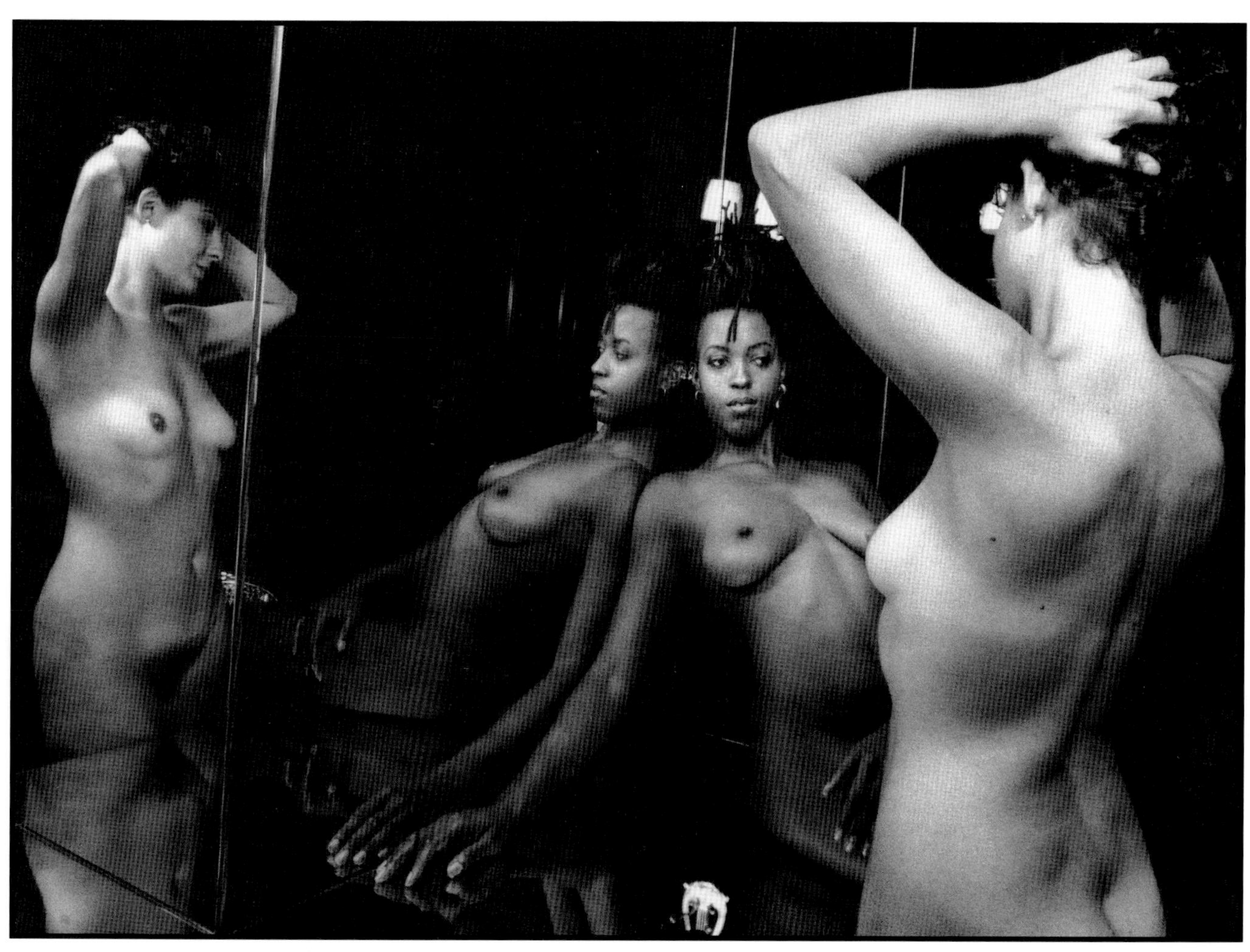

Plate 33

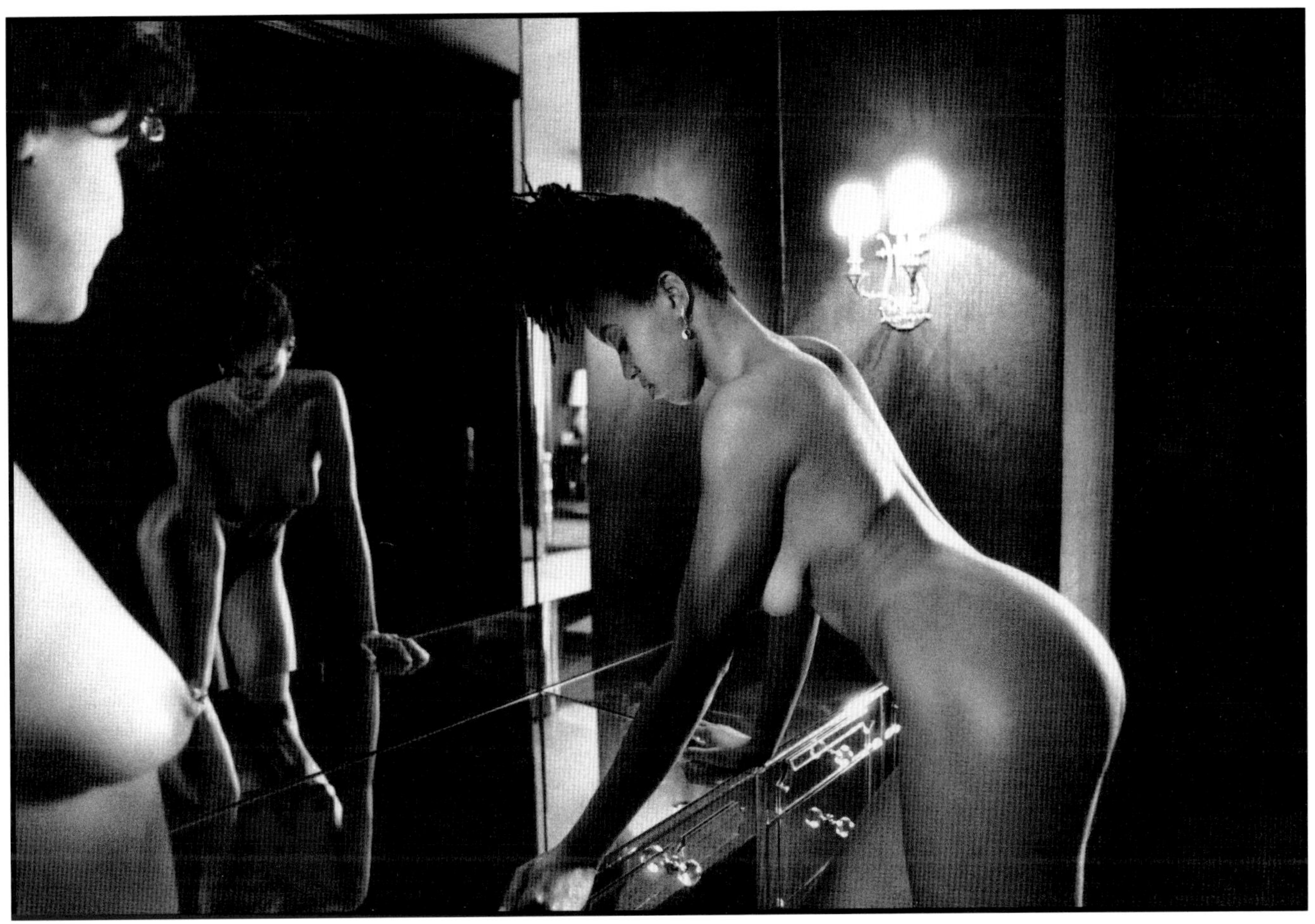

Plate 34

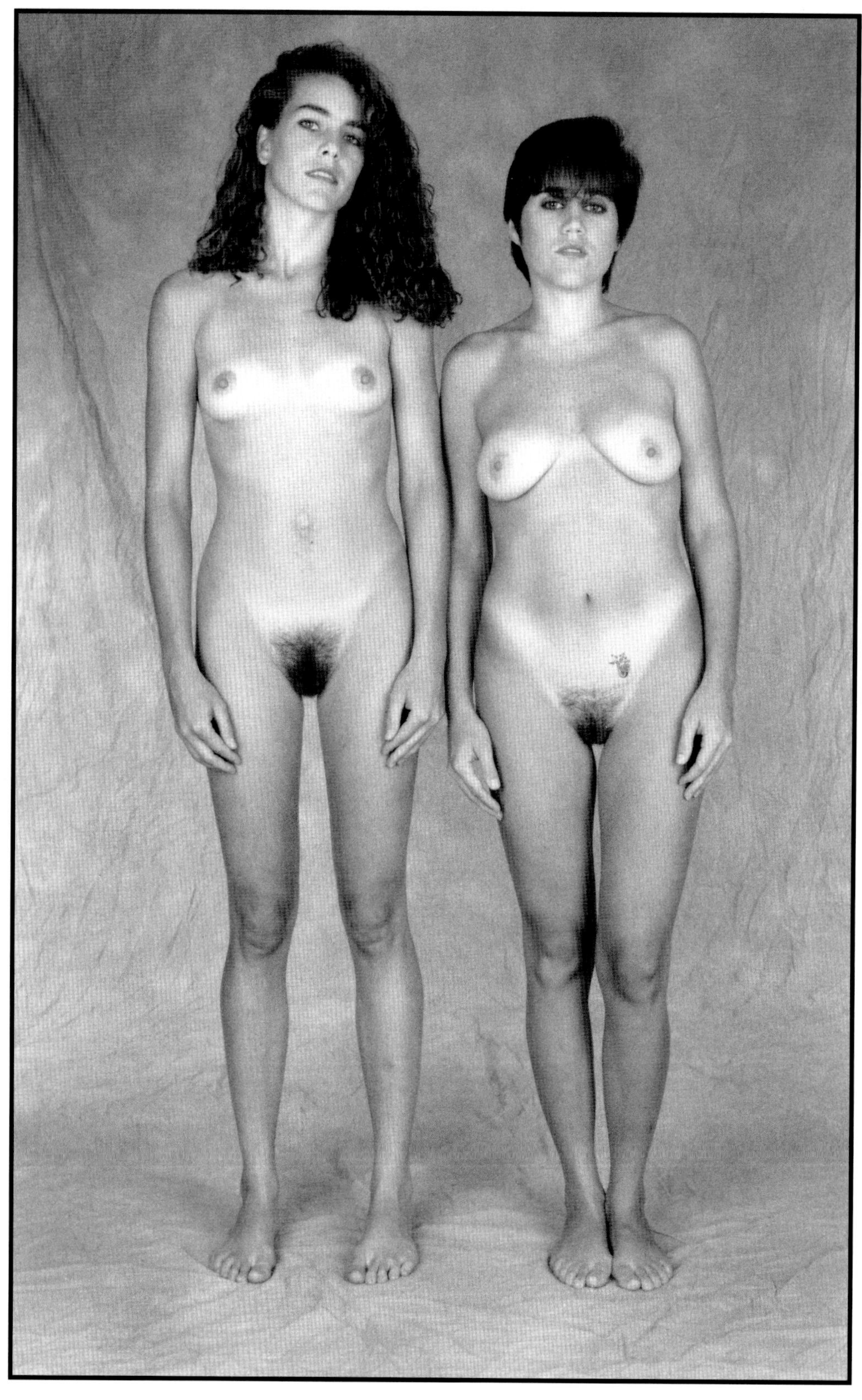

Plate 35

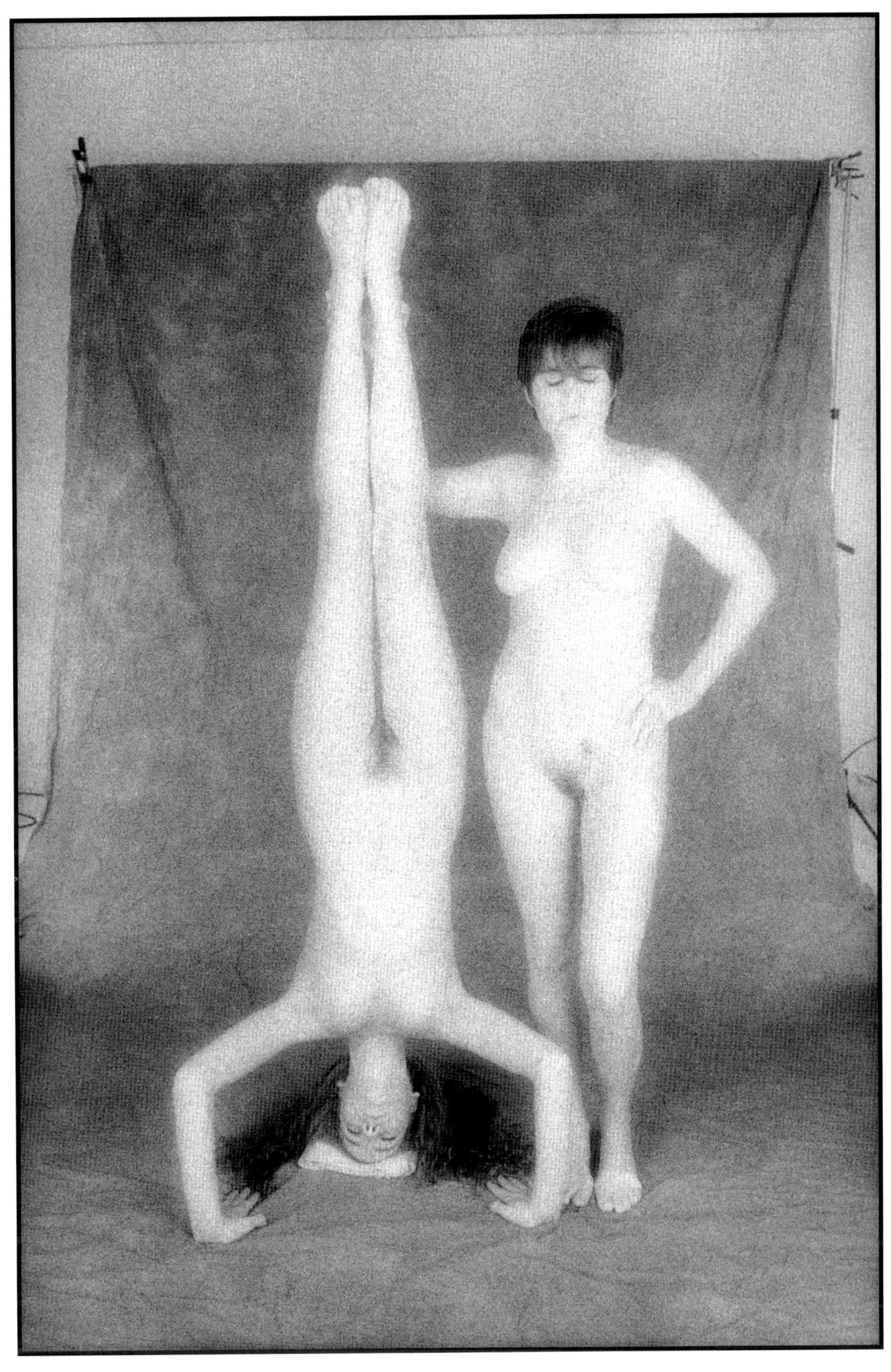

Plate 36

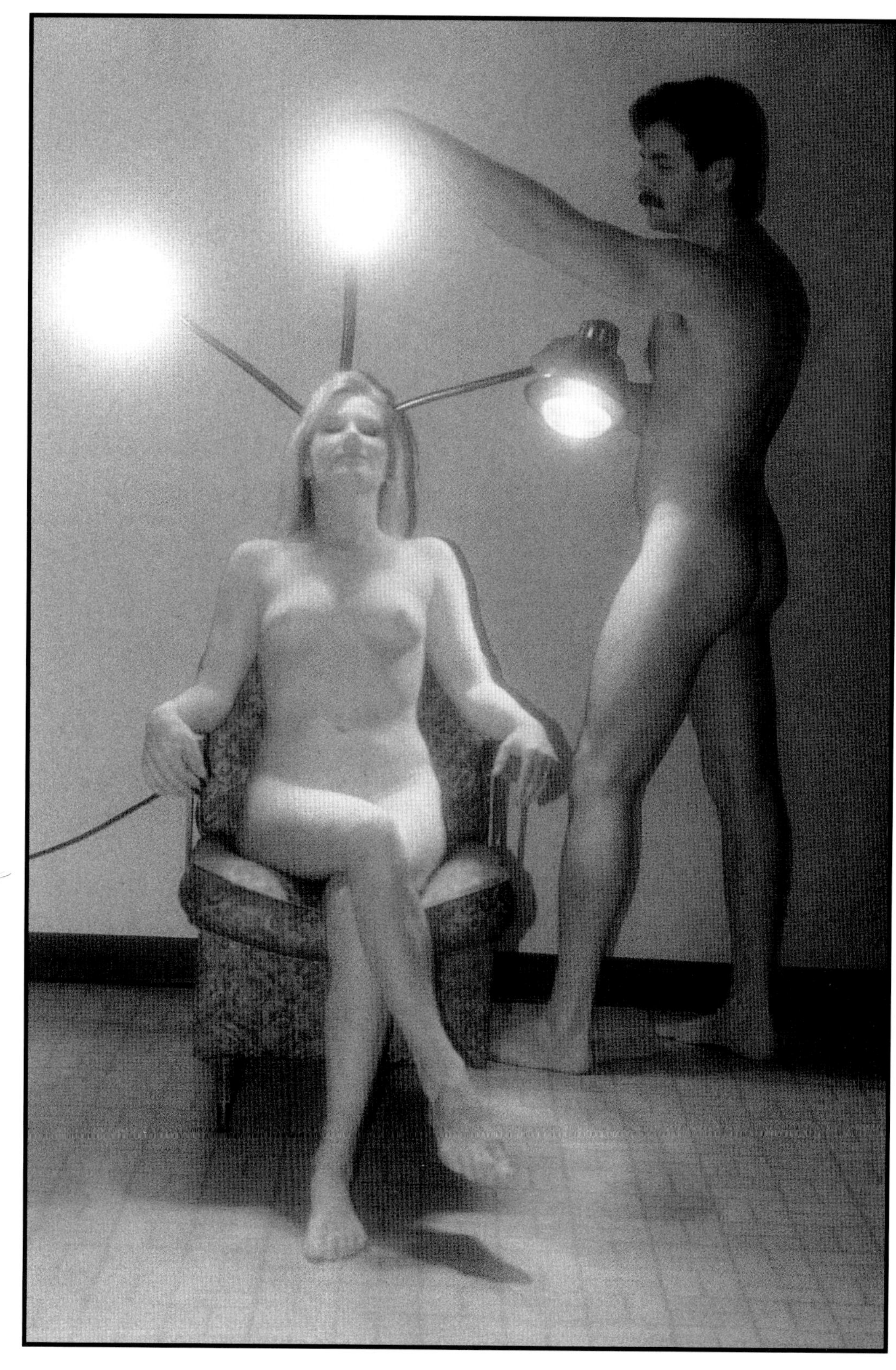

Plate 37

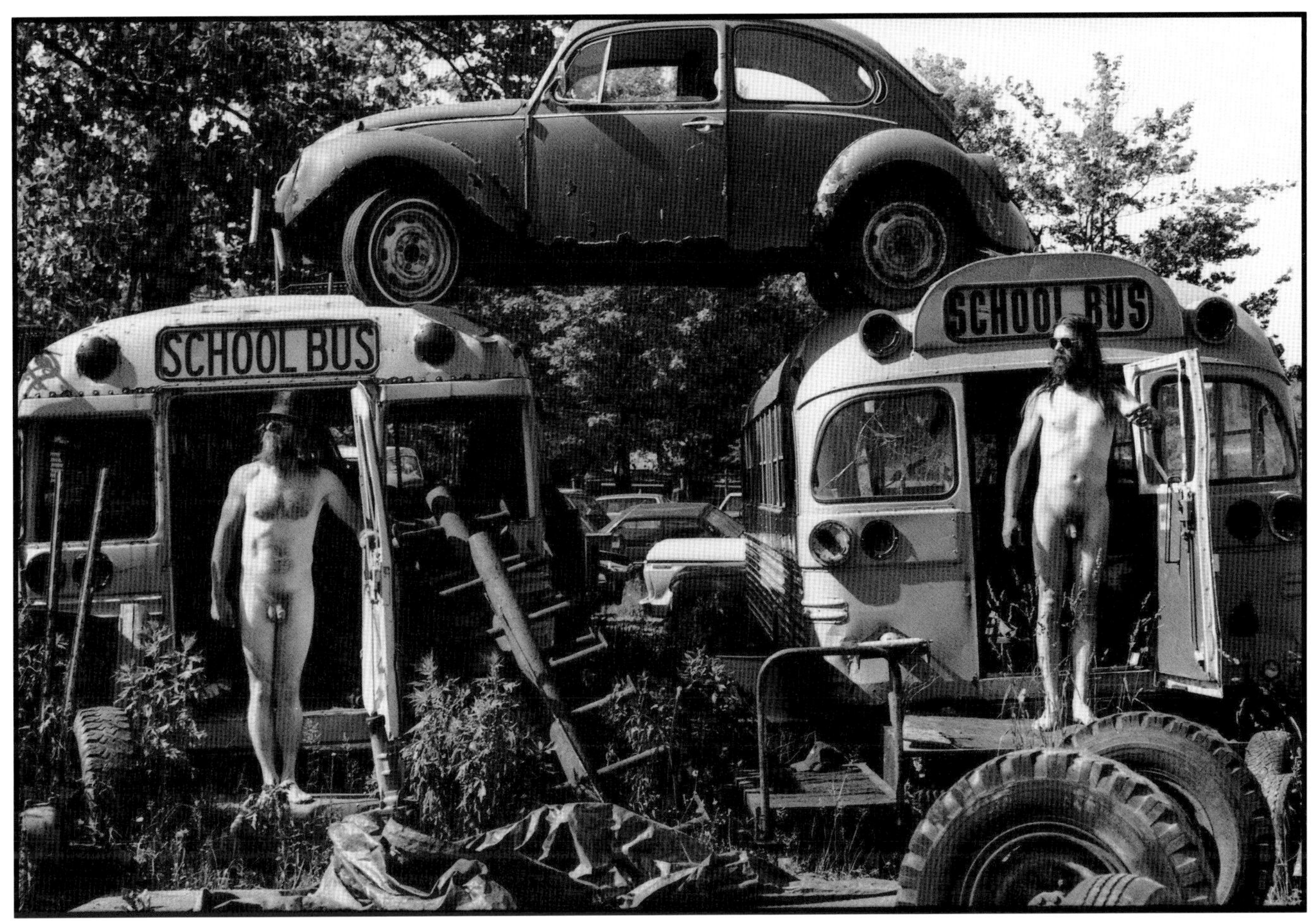

Plate 38

THE BODY UNUSUAL

I've always been attracted to the unusual. At any given moment, something I see might trigger an idea or a somewhat crazy idea will simply come to me, and I'll want to execute it. Often, however, I put the idea on the back burner until all the right ingredients come together. I enjoy touching upon and sometimes crossing those imaginary boundary lines that everybody sets up for themselves. I also enjoy having the freedom to express who I am.

Whenever you photograph the nude, keep in mind that the unfamiliar can be either emotionally stimulating or disturbing to viewers. This doesn't mean, however, that as a photographer you should be bound by limitations. You should photograph what you see. Life is filled with some rather unpleasant realities, and I choose to document them. Viewers might have to force themselves to see with a broader sensibility. By extending themselves, they'll be able to interpret the meaning of someone else's documentation of reality in a way that enables them to understand and possibly appreciate an alternative vision.

As a photographer, I look for beauty within the bizarre, as well as for elements that might shock viewers. And because a given moment often isn't repeatable, I photograph what I can while I have the chance and think about it later. Furthermore, the unusual or the bizarre can't necessarily be planned in advance. When they aren't planned, they can surprise or even repel you, the photographer. But when they're planned, they can be regarded as the photographer's deeper expressions. Whether unusual or bizarre images are planned or unexpected, viewers might find such pictures to be disturbing, if not outright frightening.

Besides shooting unusual portraits of nudes in black and white, I use the human body to portray graphic abstraction. In these images, the face disappears. Shadows create wonderful shapes across the body, as well as a wide range of shades of gray that selectively reveals parts of the body and at the same time produces abstract forms. This interplay of lights and dark tones makes the visual possibilities and expressions seemingly endless. At first glance, viewers might not think that some of the resulting lines, curves, and shapes are parts of a human body. In such pictures, the photographer renders the body's individual features virtually unrecognizable in order to convey an abstract, formal idea.

Although nude models are sometimes blessed with great bodies, I can find fascinating abstractions within the natural curves and shapes of both "perfect" and "imperfect" bodies. An abstraction can be a composition formed by the juxtaposition of light and shadow. The result is a graphic image that initially appears to be one thing, and only upon deeper observation reveals itself to be an abstract representation of the body or, as I call it, the body unusual. For example, the combination of the curve of the buttocks and the curve of the spine makes a compelling abstraction.

When a detail of an abstraction is blown up into a large photograph, the impact of the abstraction is even greater. Shooting several detailed features together can produce interesting abstract images, which can be more powerful than a single image. For example, couples wrapping arms and legs around one another and two torsos locked in an embrace create fascinating forms. Then there are individuals who move in such a fluid way that they create sculptural forms that are graphically pleasing to the eye. Within these unusual configurations, I look for folds and creases, and concentrate on details, such as a large belly, a nipple, or an armpit. When a line or abstraction absorbs my vision, I photograph it without being bound by any rules.

My photographs of the body unusual depict the mysterious, the peculiar, the wild, the imaginary, and the untamed. An element of fantasy defines these pictures, and within each image a part of recognizable reality blends with elements that aren't easily explainable. The models appear in unusual settings, react peculiarly, and aren't who they seem to be. These images raise questions and play tricks on viewers but leave the solutions up to the viewers. Viewers must interpret the situation as they see it. As a photographer shooting the body unusual, you must be aware of sculptural elements of the human body and must allow your creativity to take over. Be free. You must learn to communicate visually what you conceive in your imagination.

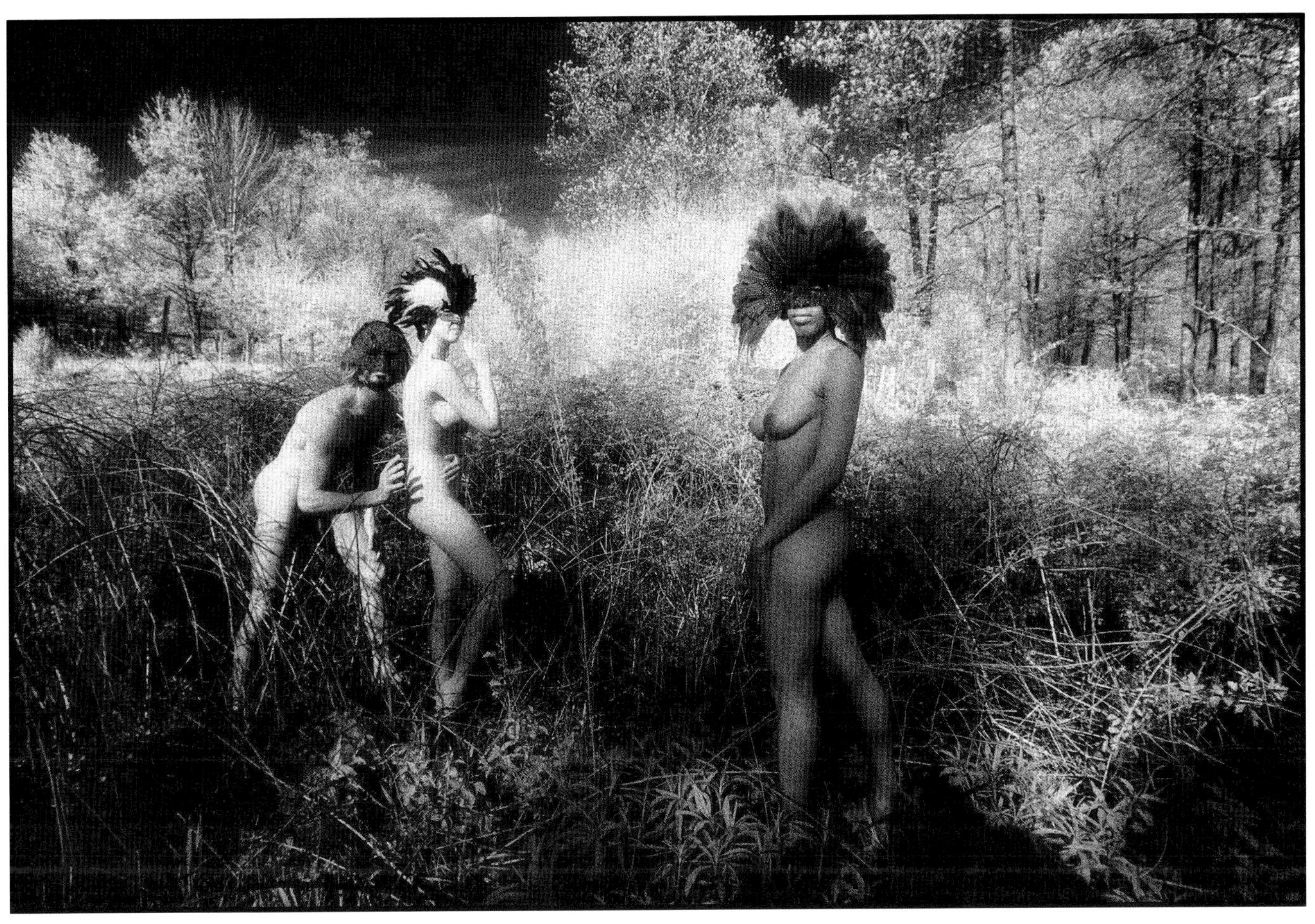

Plate 39

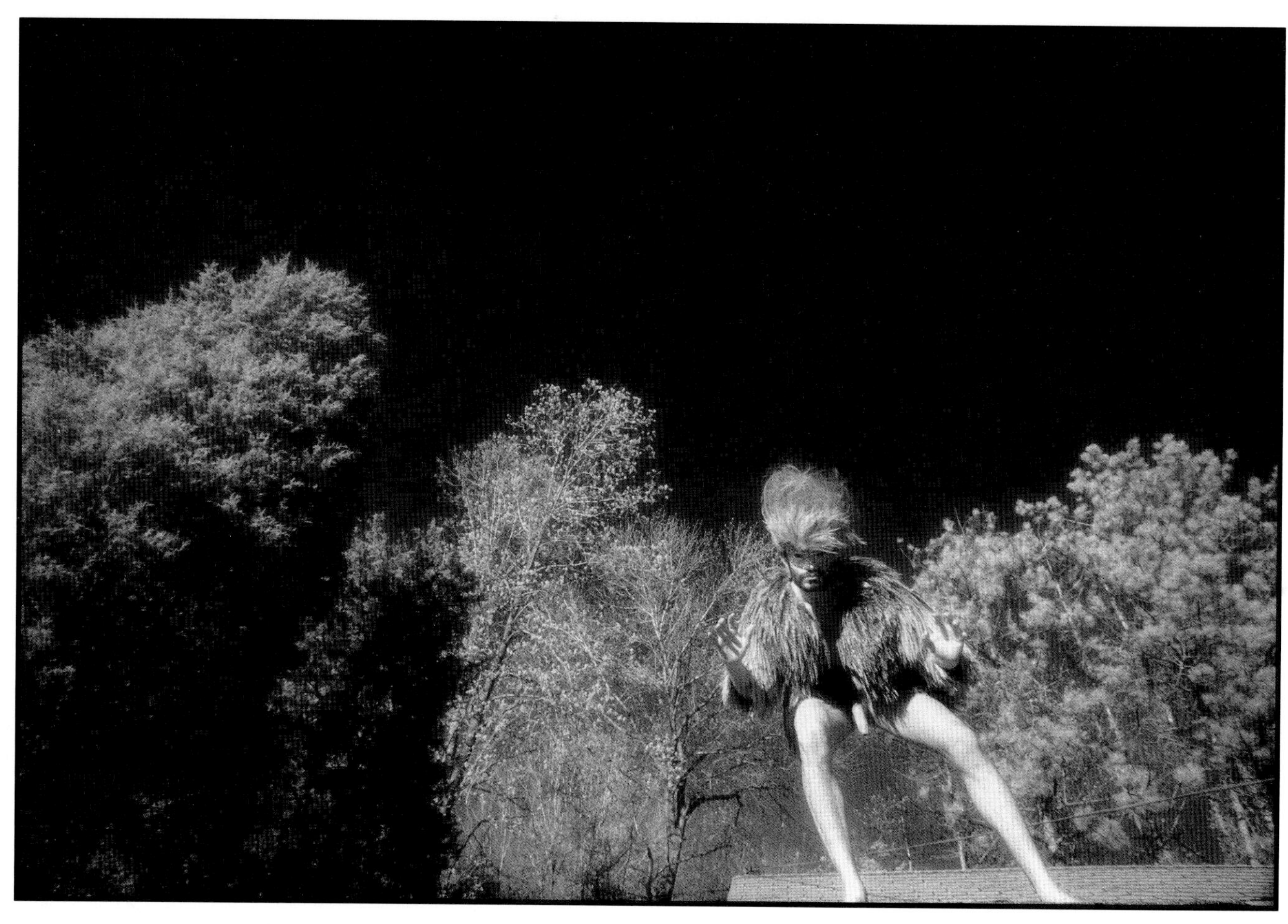

Plate 40

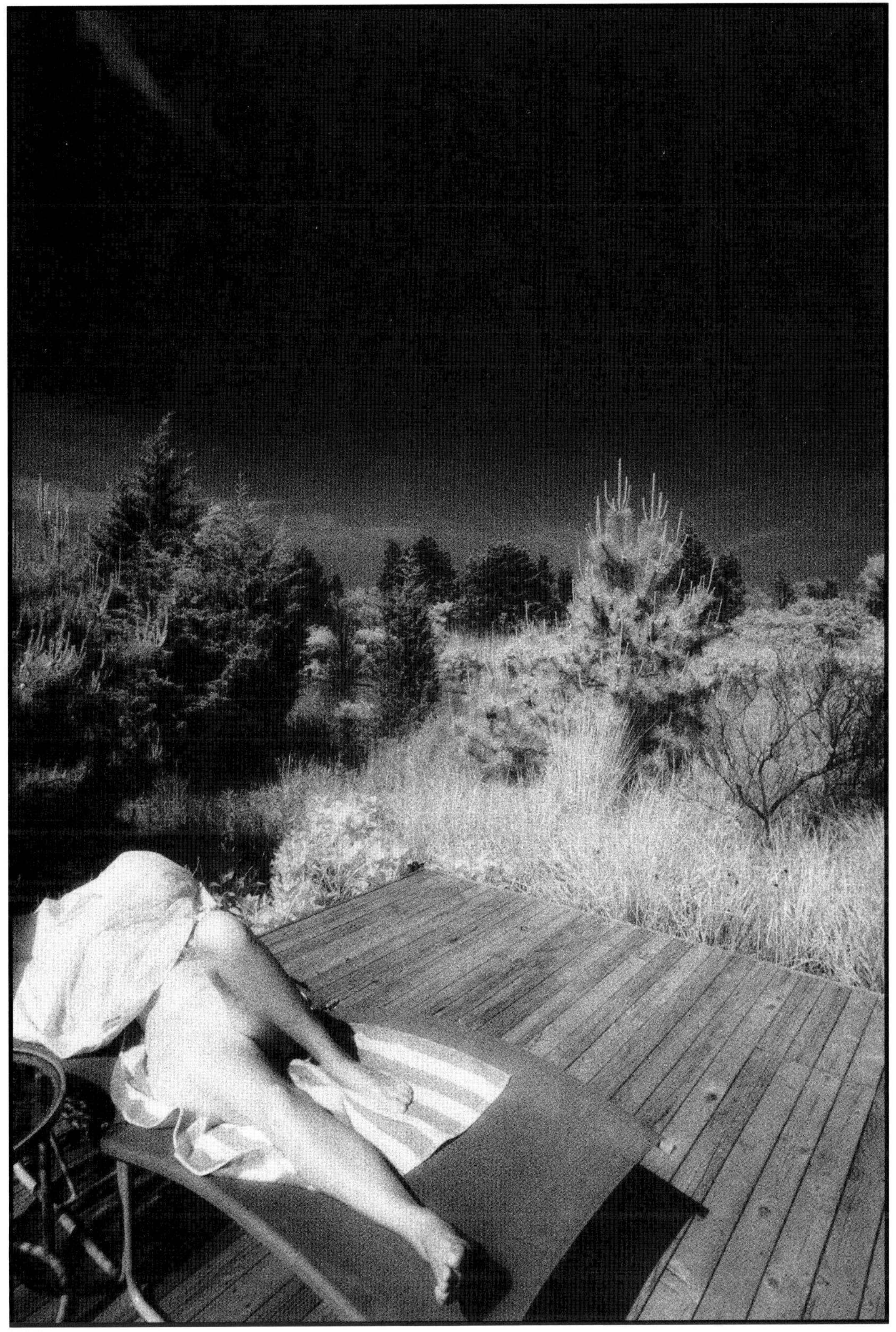

Plate 41

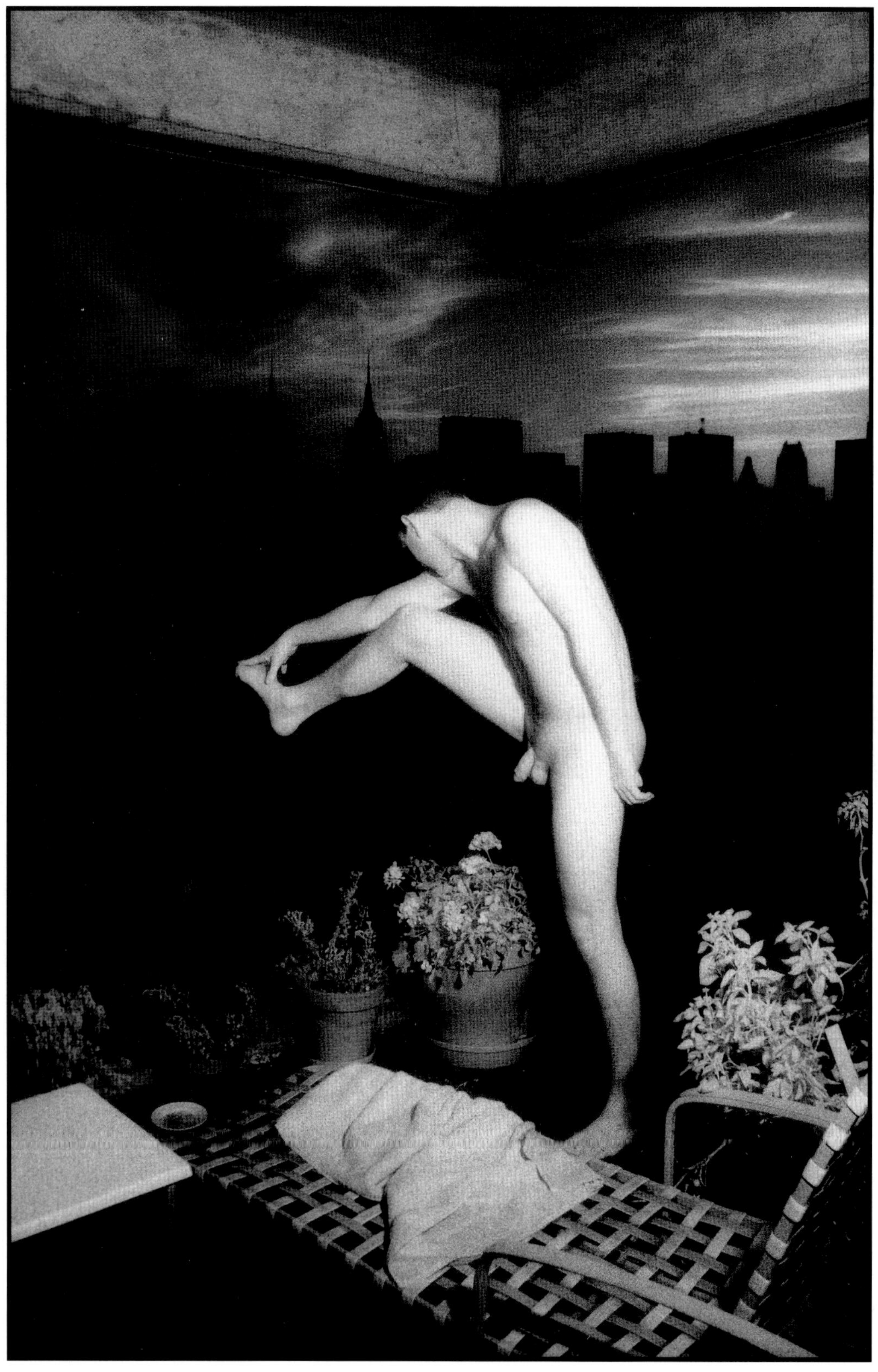

Plate 42

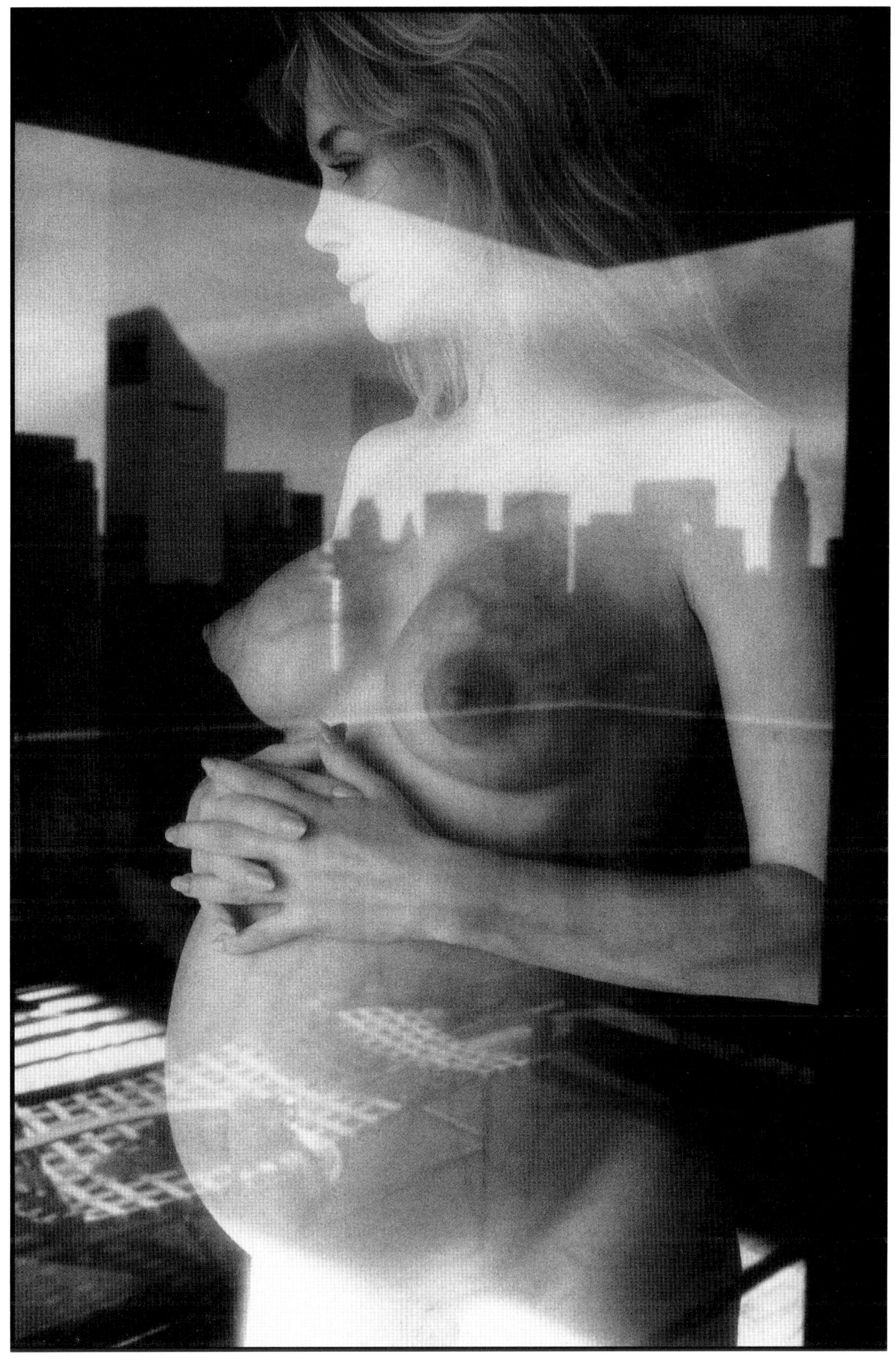

Plate 43

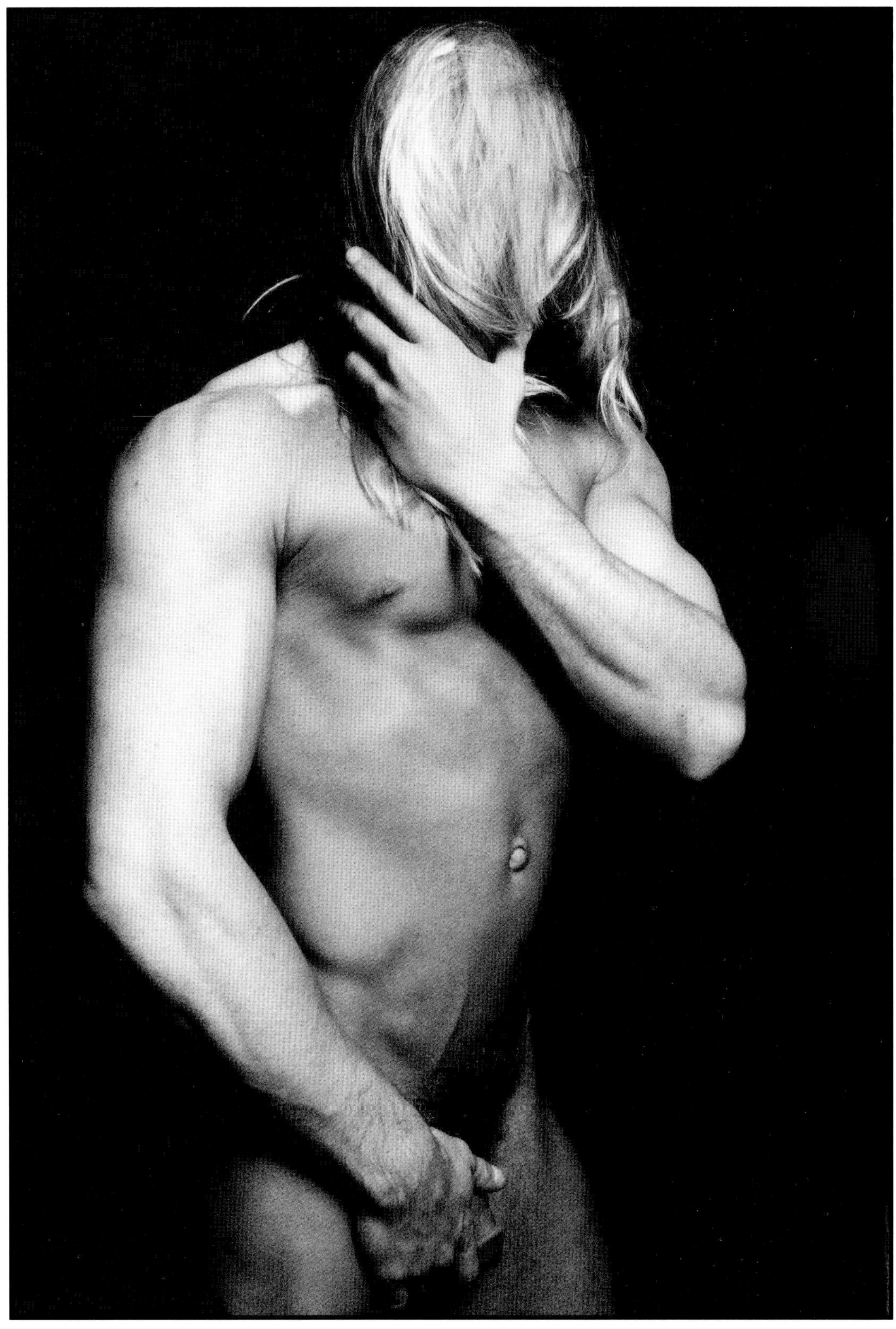

PLATE 44

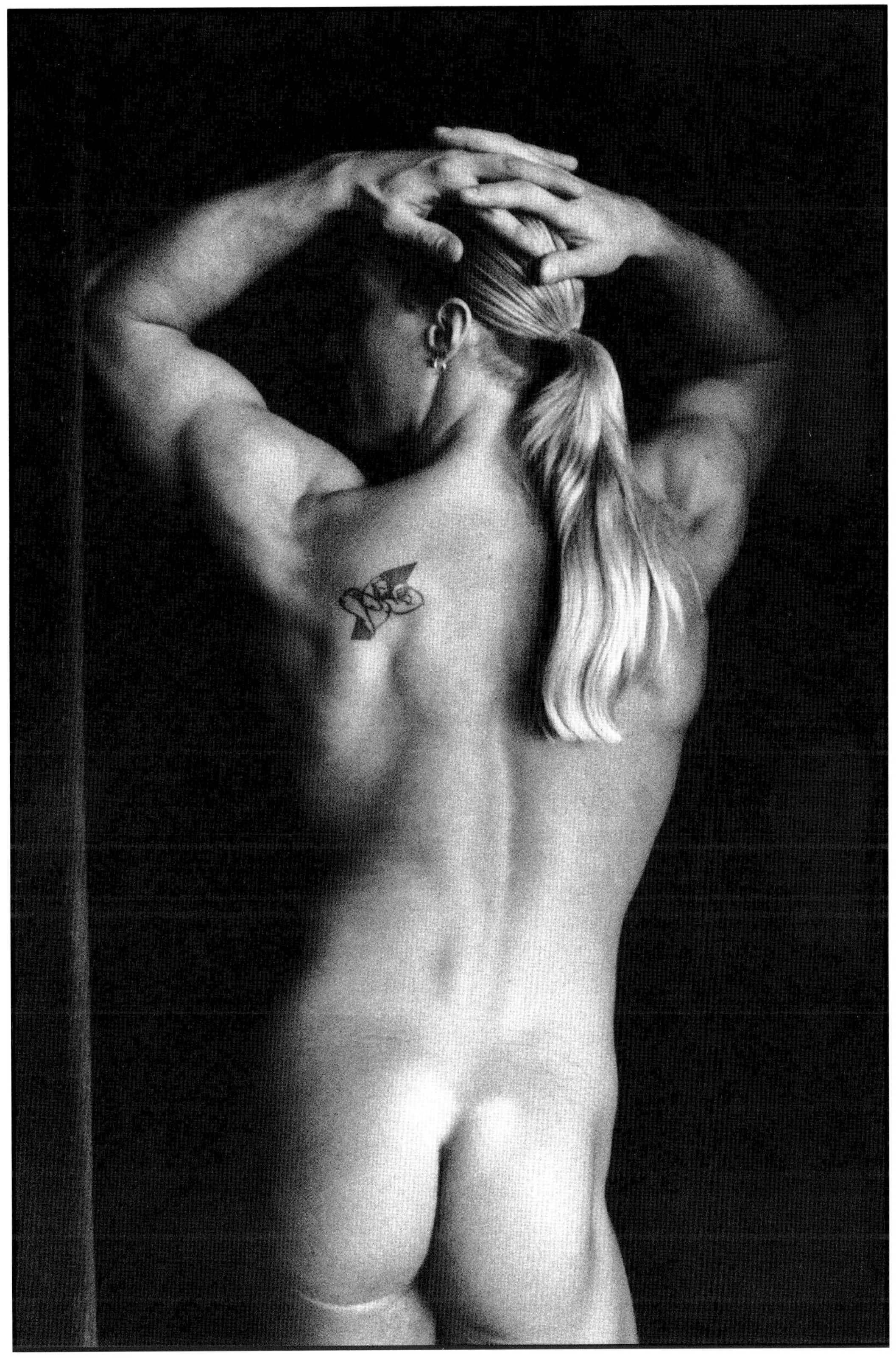

Plate 45

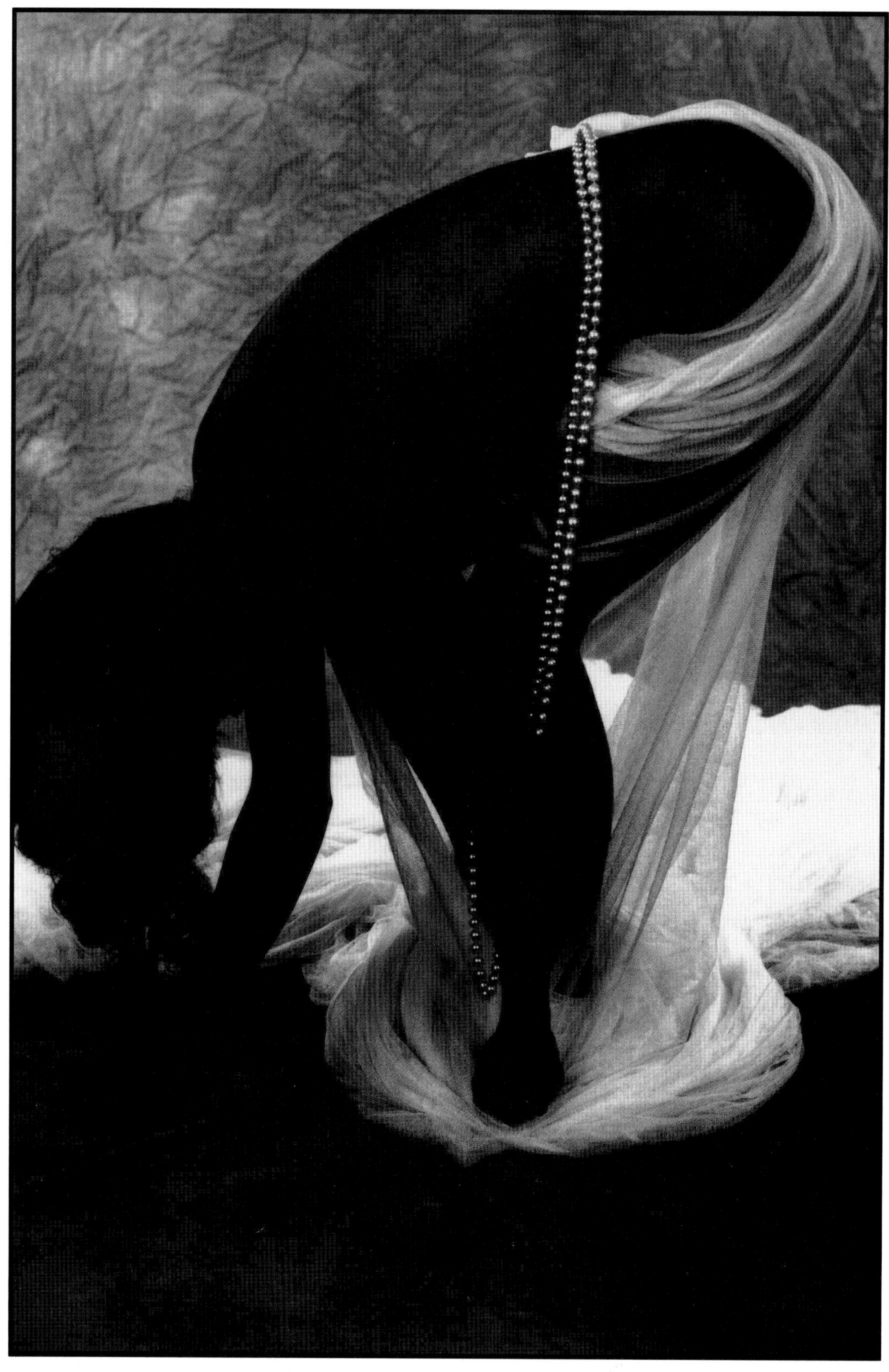

Plate 46

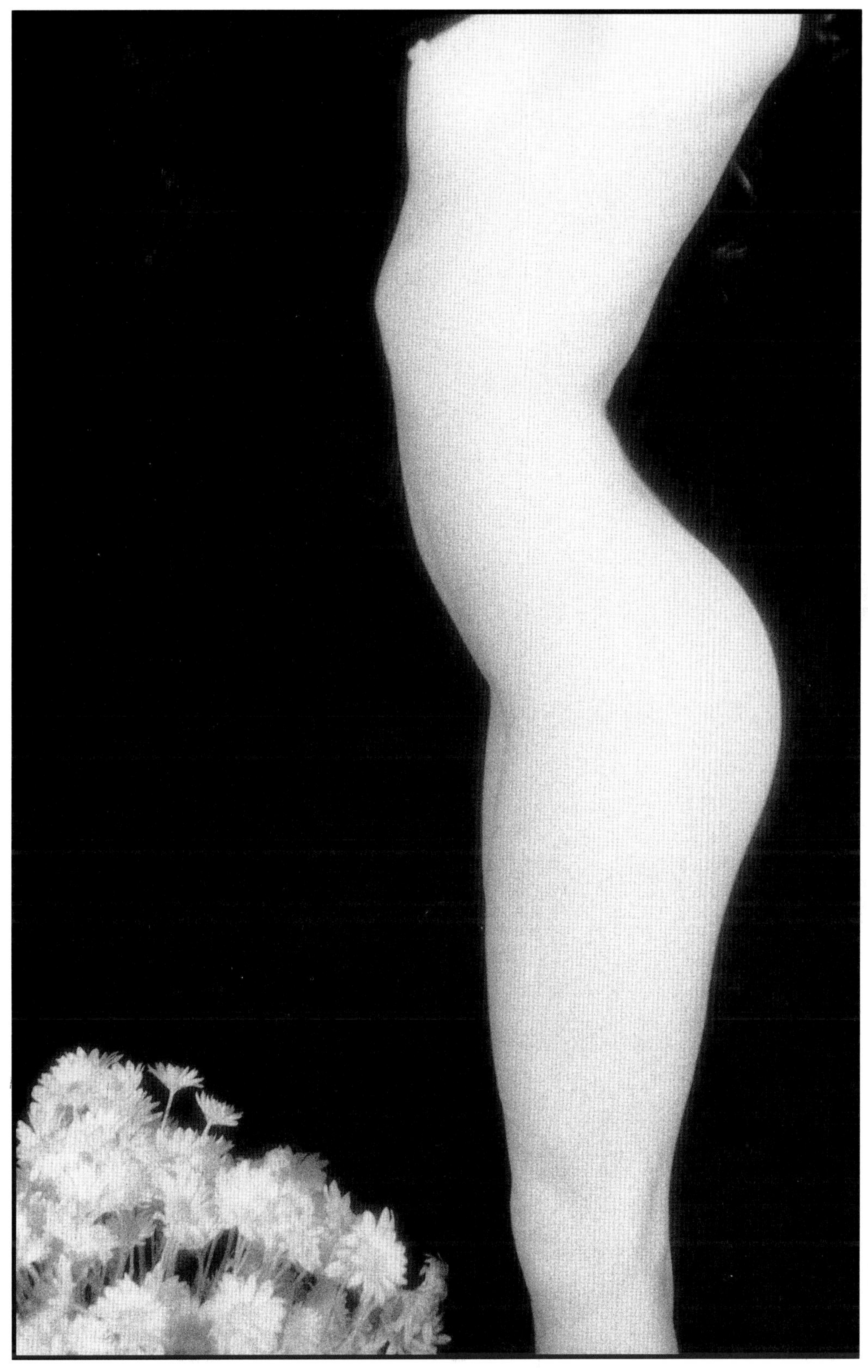

Plate 47

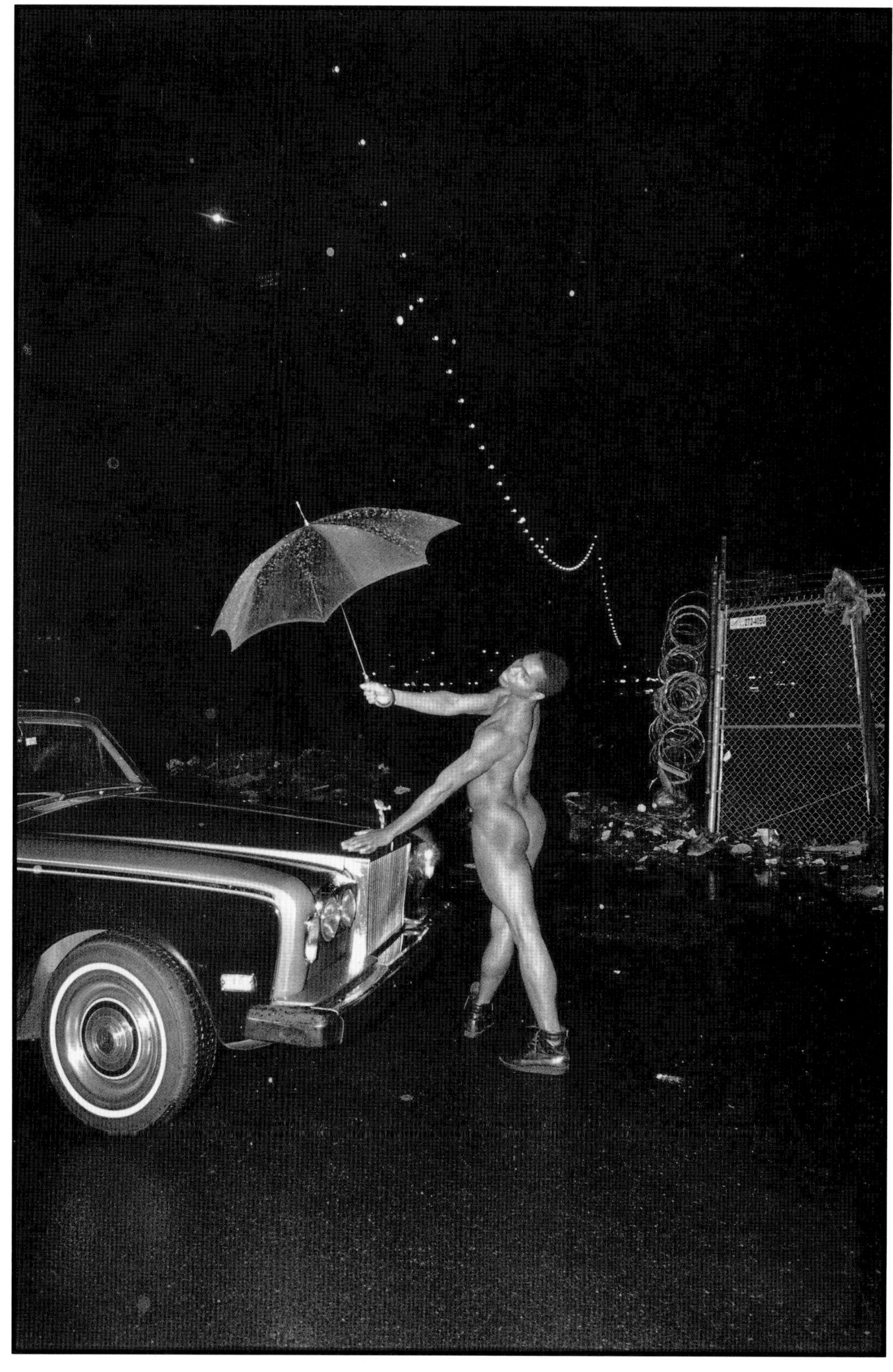

PLATE 48

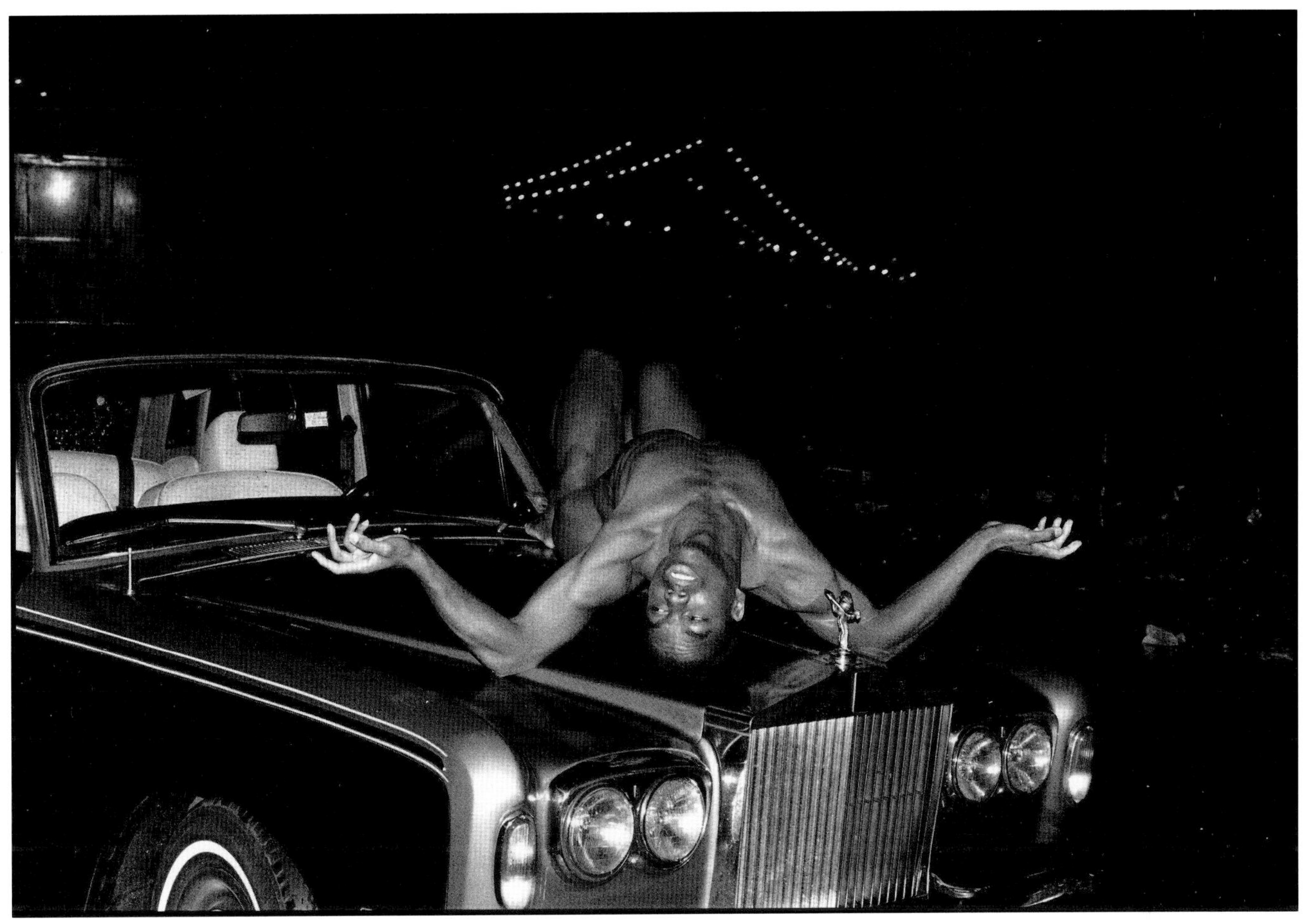

Plate 49

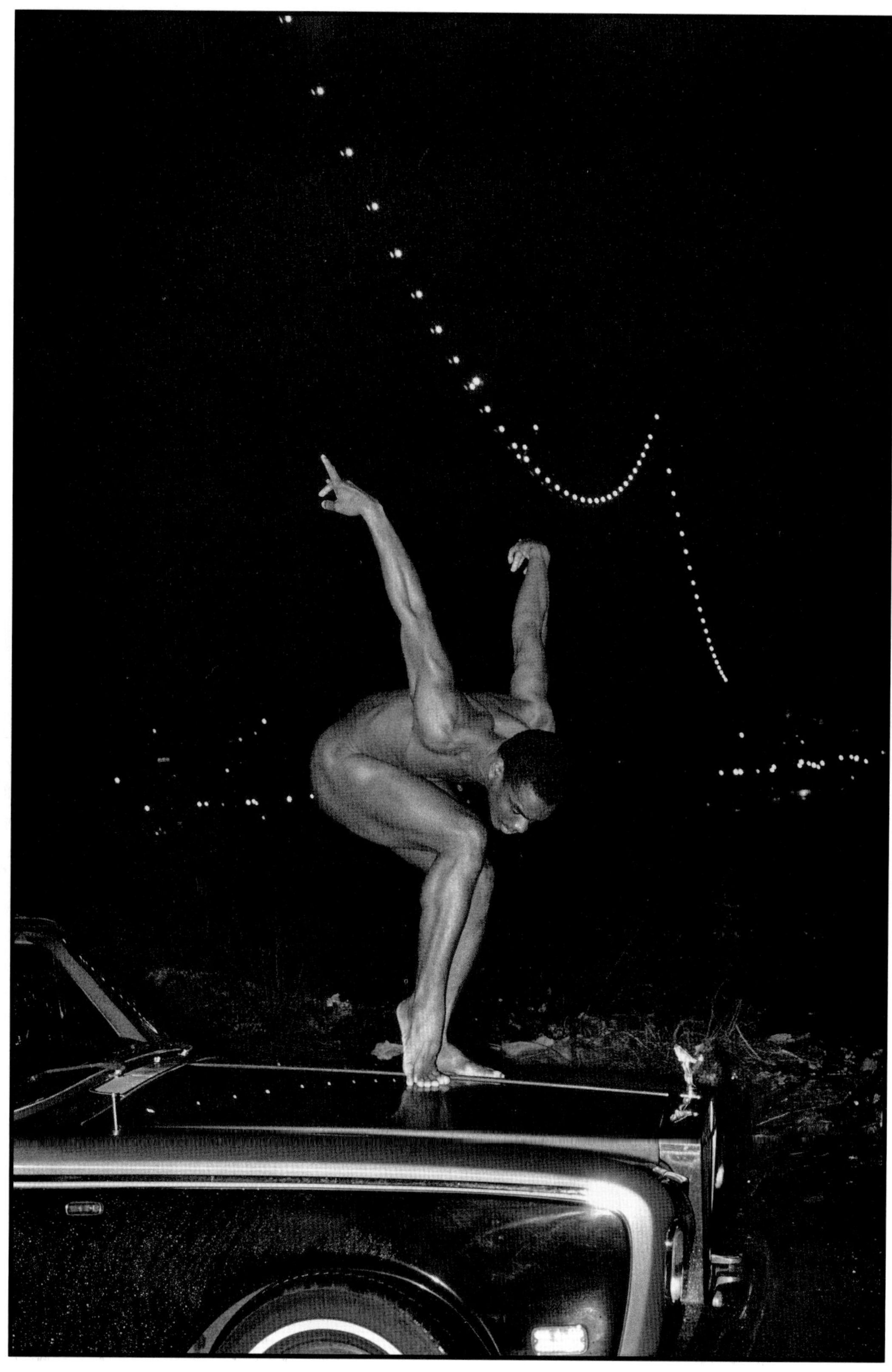

Plate 50

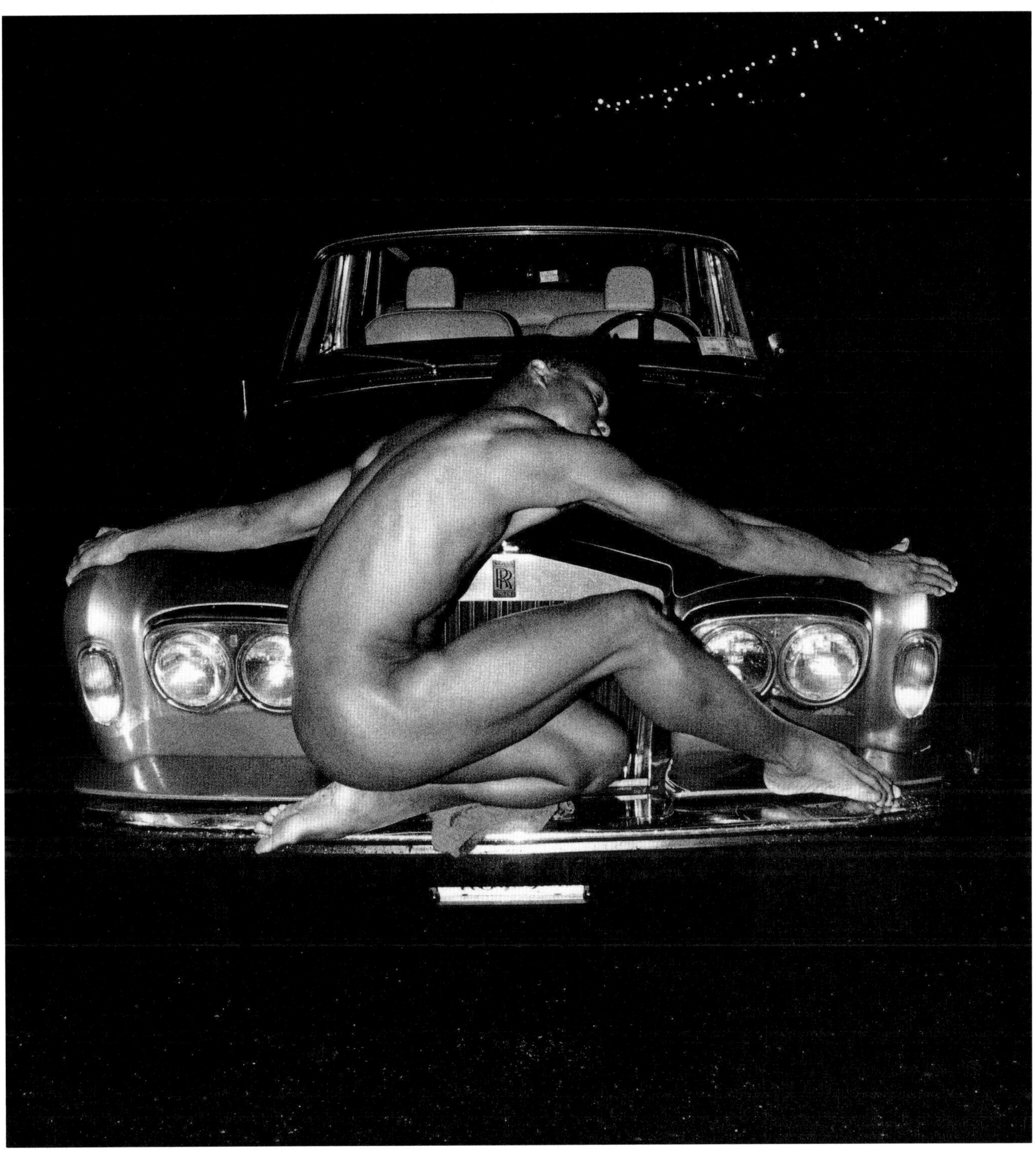

Plate 51

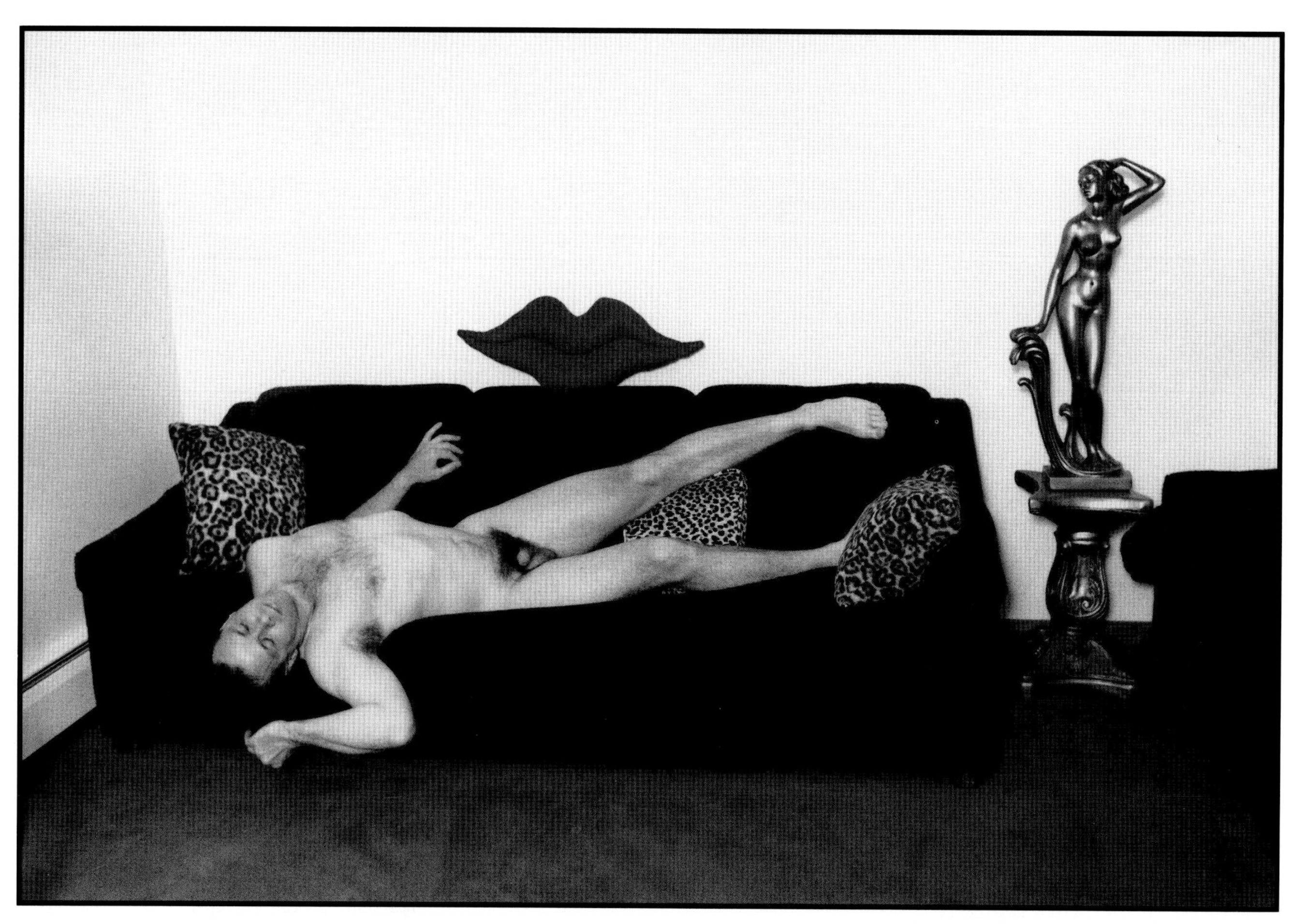

Plate 52

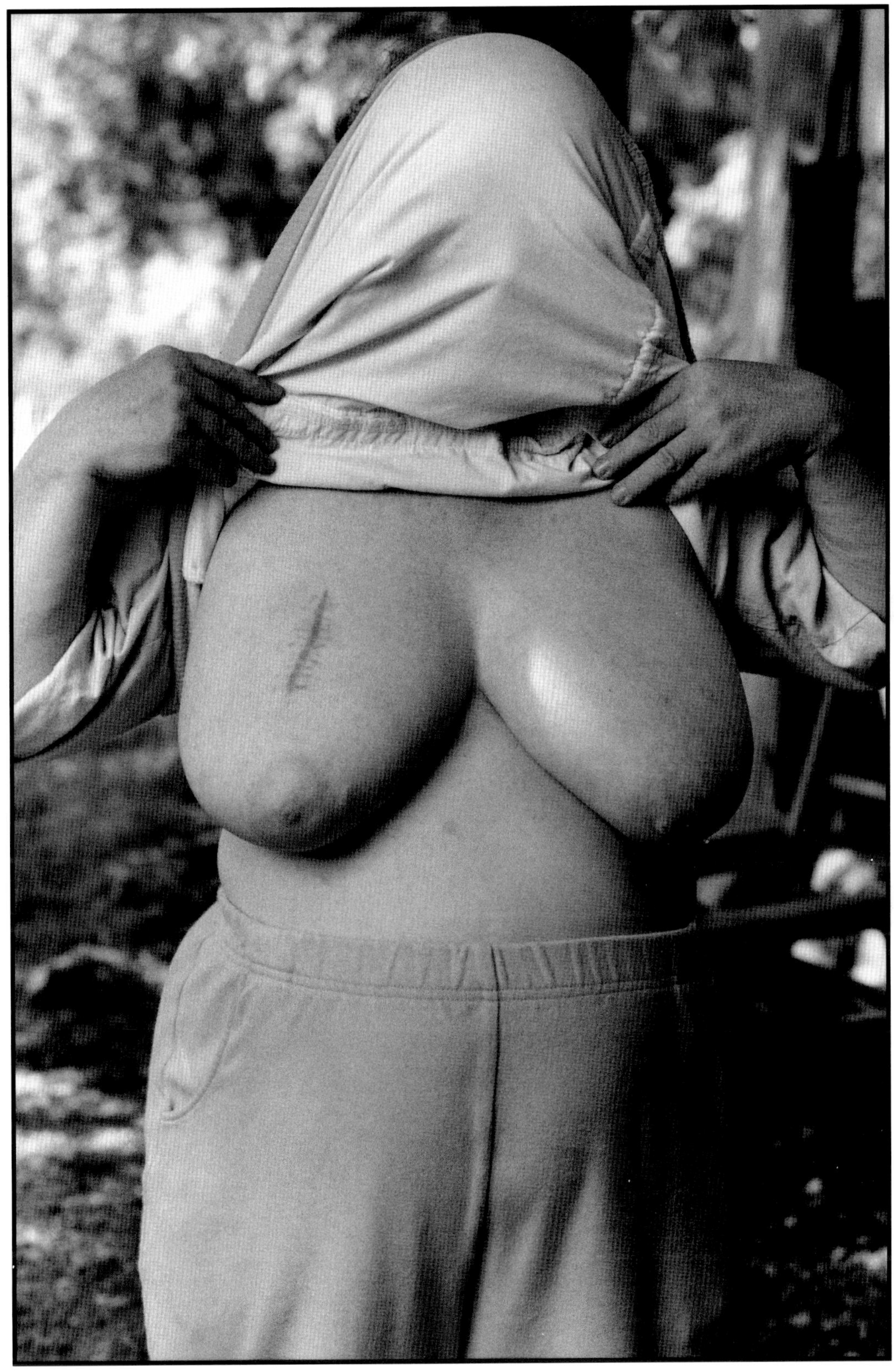

Plate 53

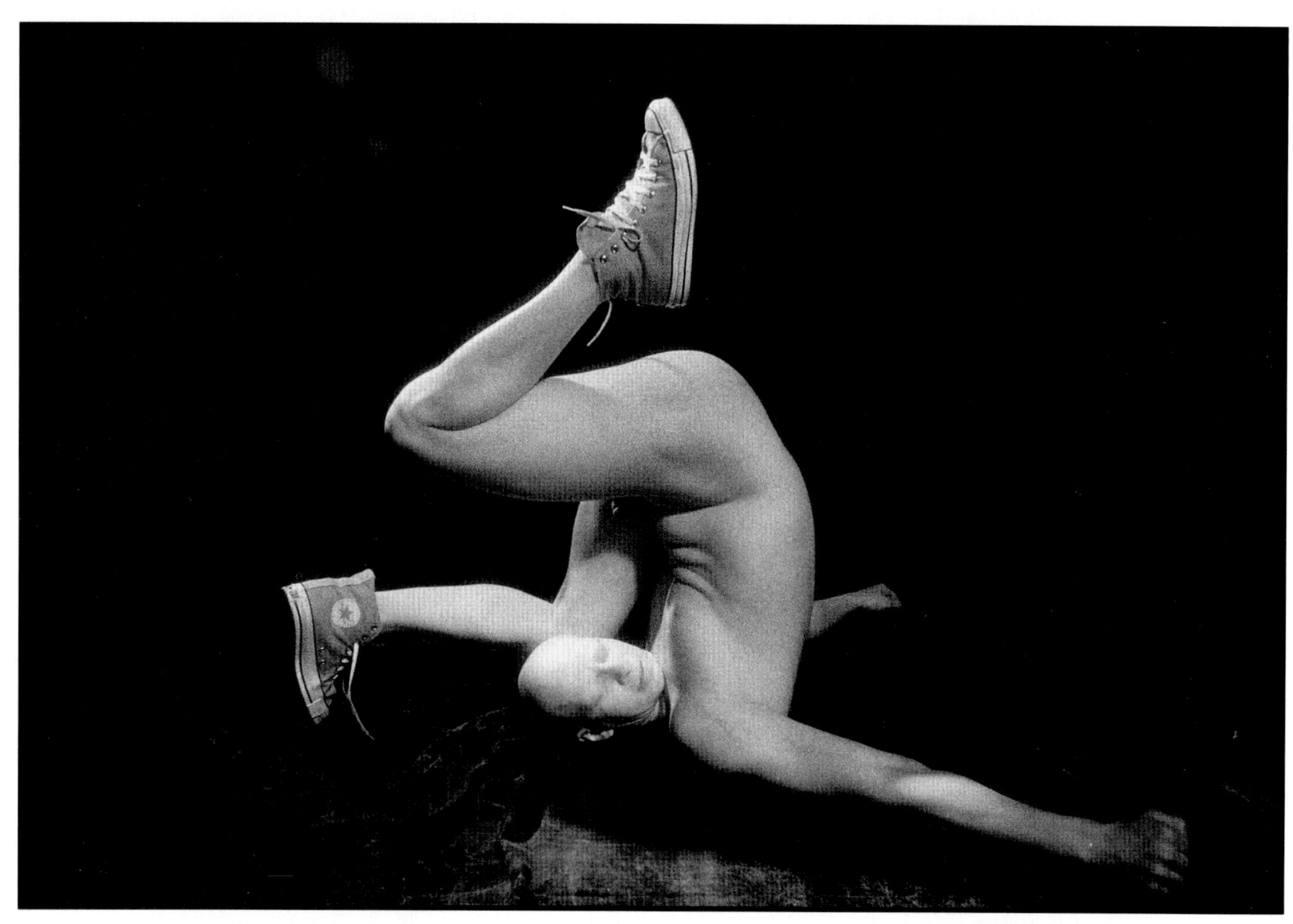

Plate 54

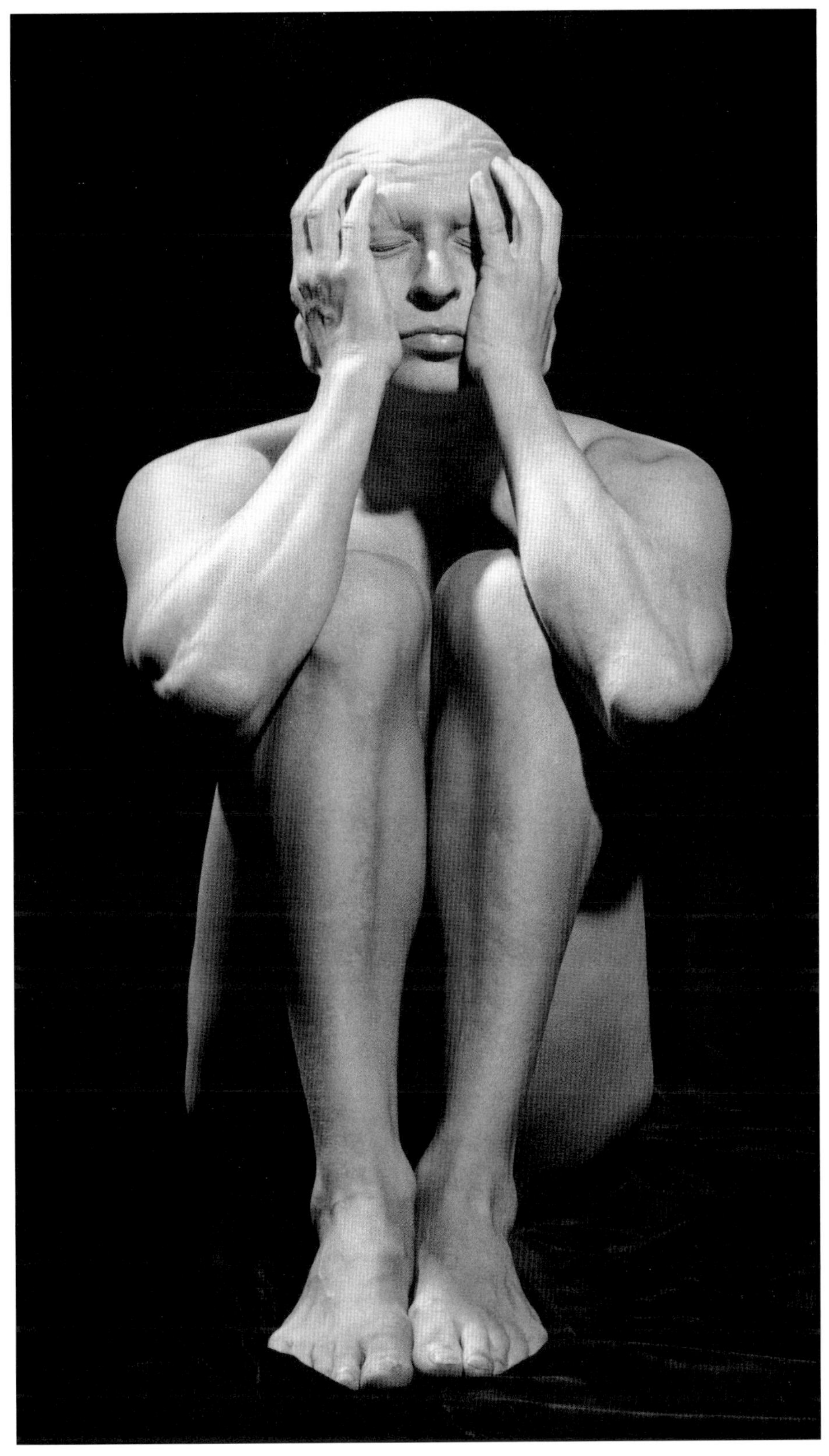

Plate 55

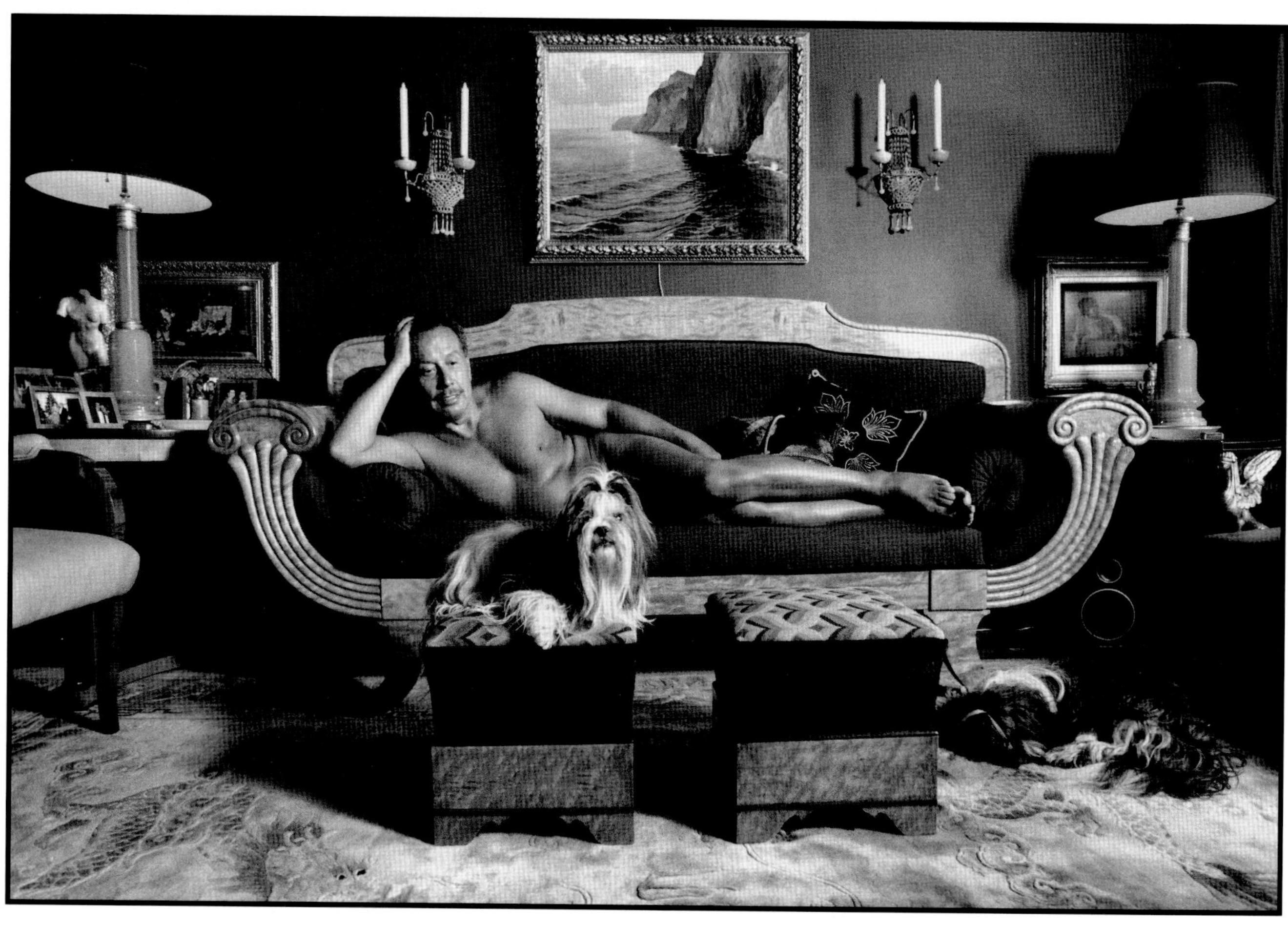

Plate 56

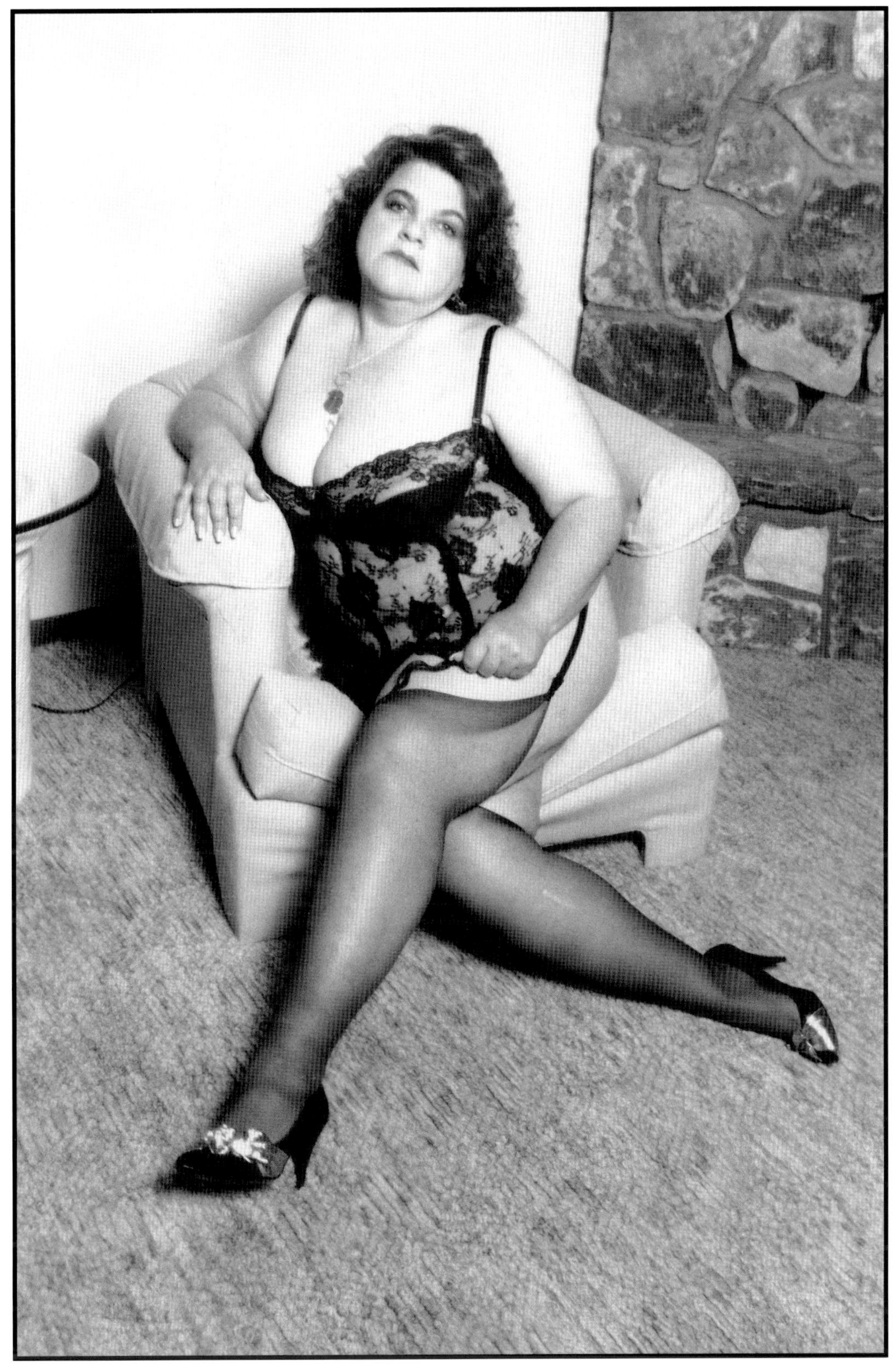

Plate 57

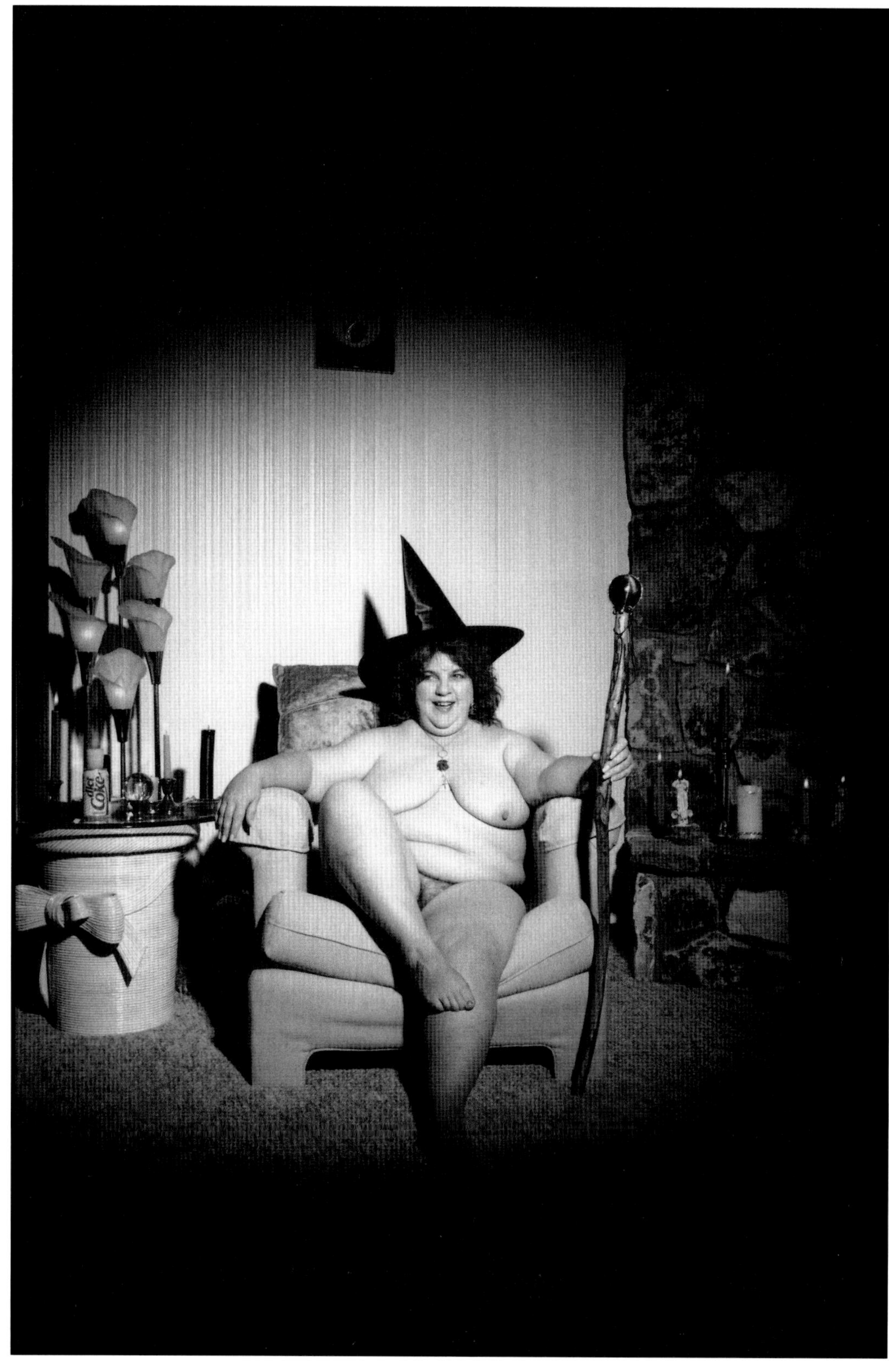

Plate 58

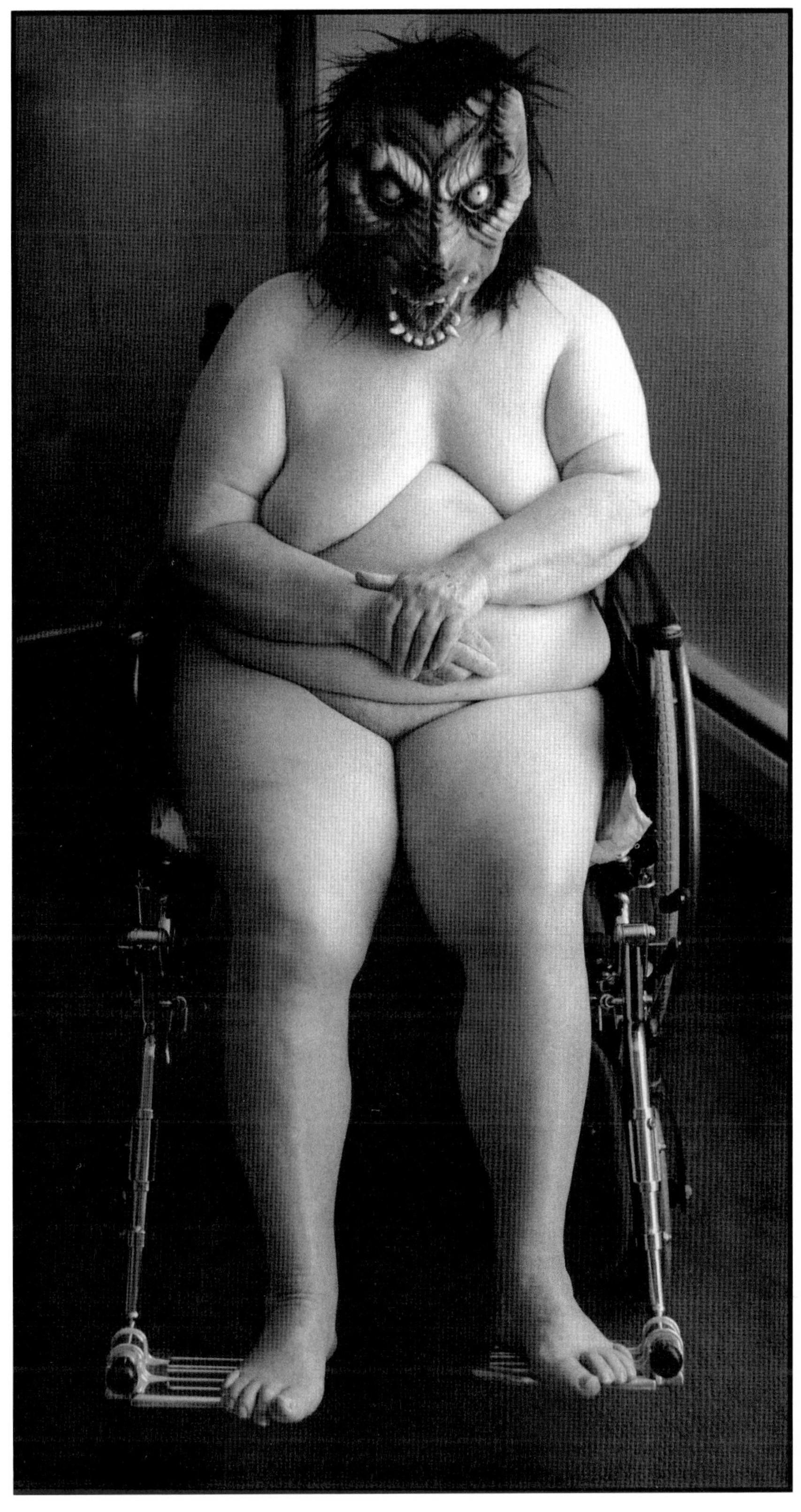

Plate 59

THE BODY NEARLY NUDE

Sensuality is enhanced by the teasing enticement of partial nakedness. When subjects are nearly nude, they are more comfortable with themselves and their physical realities than when they are completely naked. This feeling of ease comes in part from the fragment of cloth that somewhat conceals and protects them. The subjects are revealing themselves at the same moment that they're holding back.

The clothing itself plays a role in the seduction of the viewers. It provides a tangible sense of security that models can literally hold on to. At the same time, clothing is the very fabric of intrigue; it is an alluring device to engage the viewers' attention and imagination. A piece of clothing or lingerie or a draping fabric can also stir the emotions of many onlookers much faster than the naked body can. This extra element gives viewers the opportunity to explore their own fantasies and to read a version of what they see or would like to see in that image. The mystery created by the simple presence of a fragment of cloth can arouse viewers' sexual desires.

For example, Victoria's Secret lingerie-and-clothing catalogs are very successful with both men and women because they show attractive models striking seductive poses in alluring, sometimes minimal, garments to entice buyers. The potential customers' eyes and minds race, trying to unveil the "secret." As with all images depicting partially nude subjects, the inherent mystery is what brings these catalog shots to life; it frees the viewers' imagination to enjoy an array of fantasies. Once the secret is revealed, the mystery is over.

When photographing partially nude subjects in black and white, try to utilize the psychological associations that these colors inspire. Black represents the daring and the provocative, and white represents innocence and purity. You can infuse your compositions with a soft, ethereal quality by using a great deal of white and pastel colors on the set and choosing garments in similar pale shades and white. A light, airy black-and-white photograph, complete with diaphanous fabrics, can evoke a sense of the celestial and spiritual world. A dark, shadowy black-and-white shot, on the other hand, might suggest the nether world, wildness, animal magnetism, deception, drama, and danger.

In the commercial market, the demand for shots of nearly nude bodies is greater than that for shots of totally nude bodies. For this reason, you won't want to eliminate this category from your portfolio. However, I offer you a word of warning. When working with a garment, you and your stylist must always be aware of its movement and its relationship to the model's body. Light, skimpy garments slip and slide easily and can destroy your preconceived image. But, of course, this may be exactly what you have in mind.

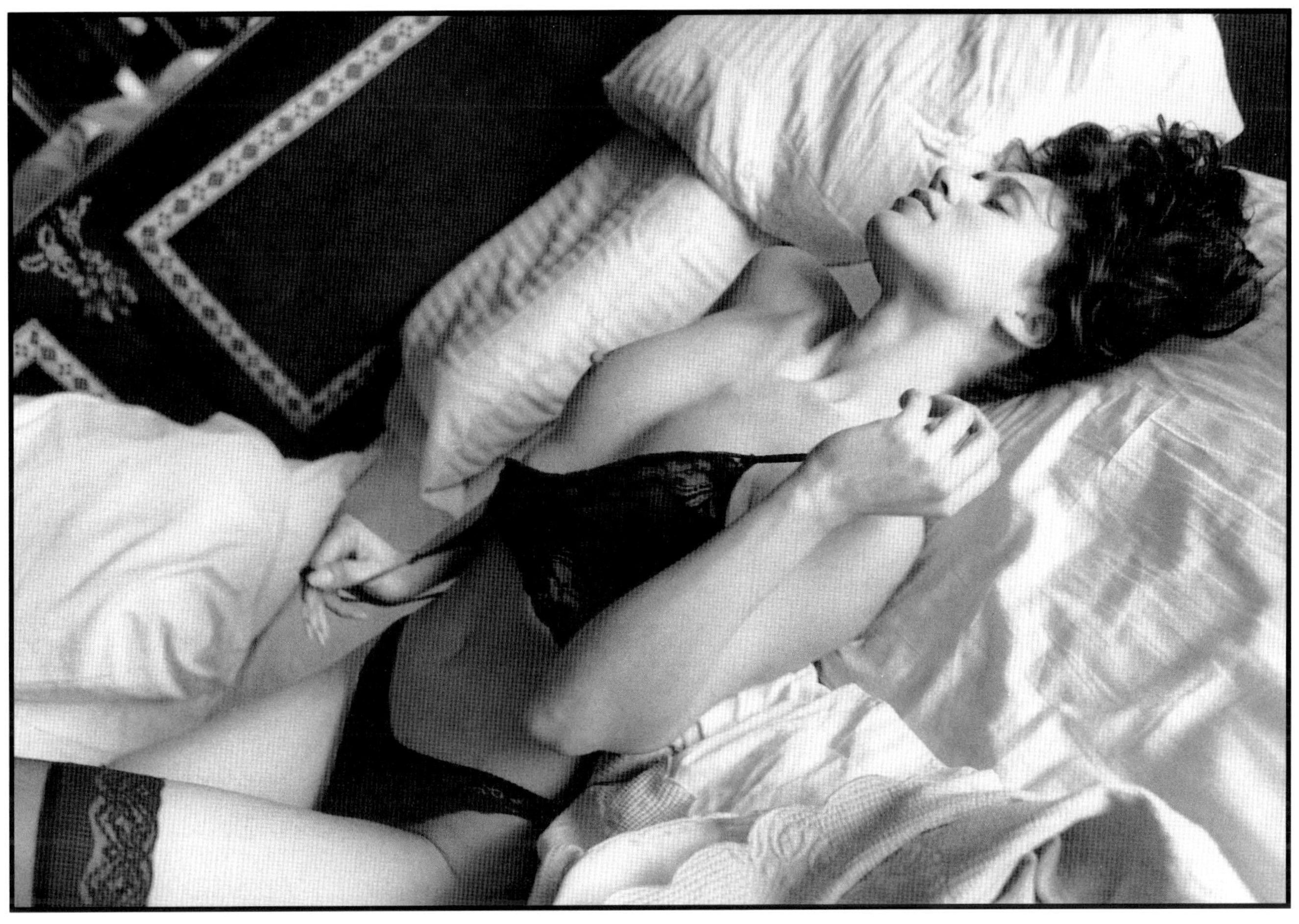

Plate 60

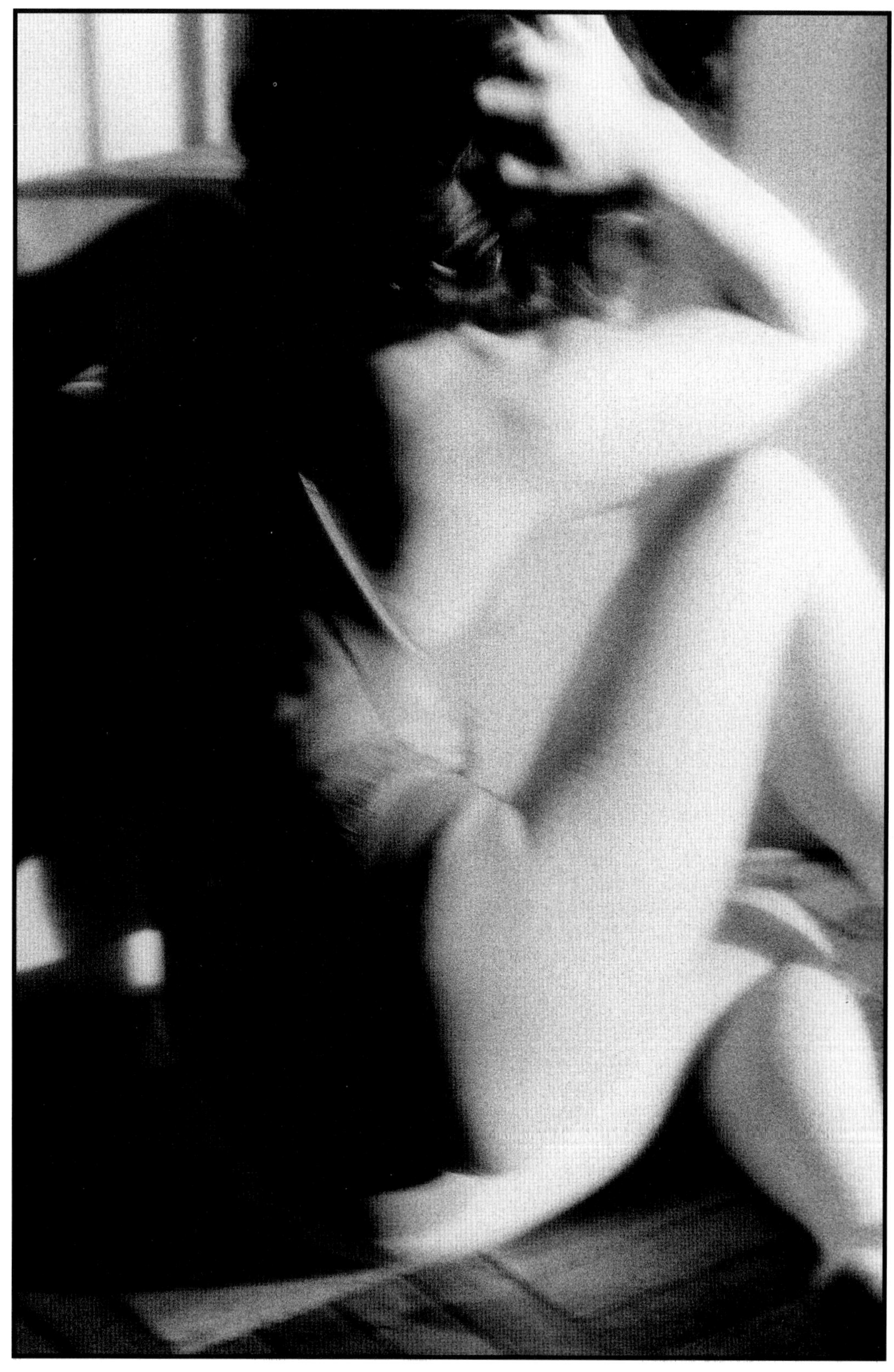

Plate 61

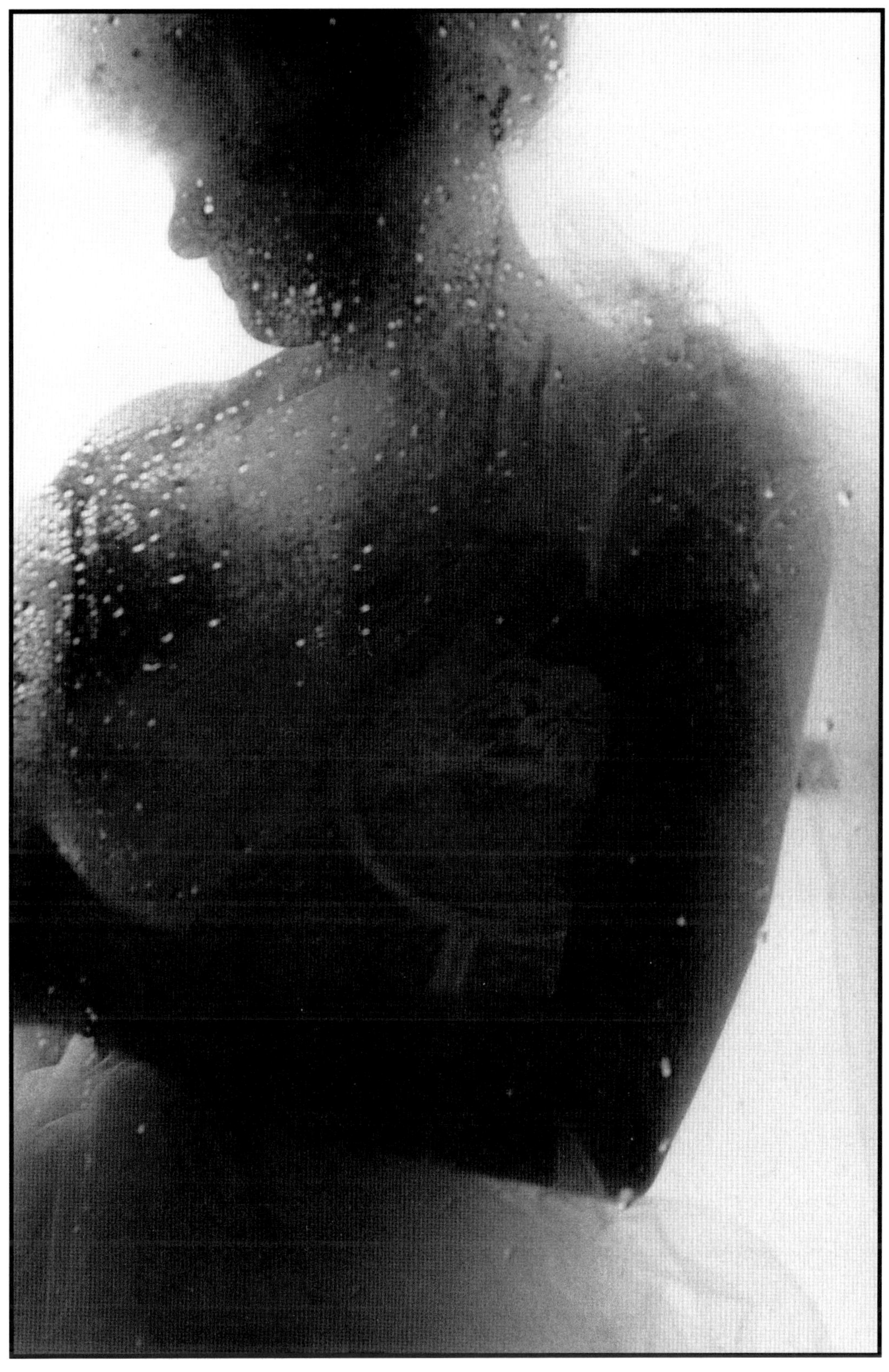

Plate 62

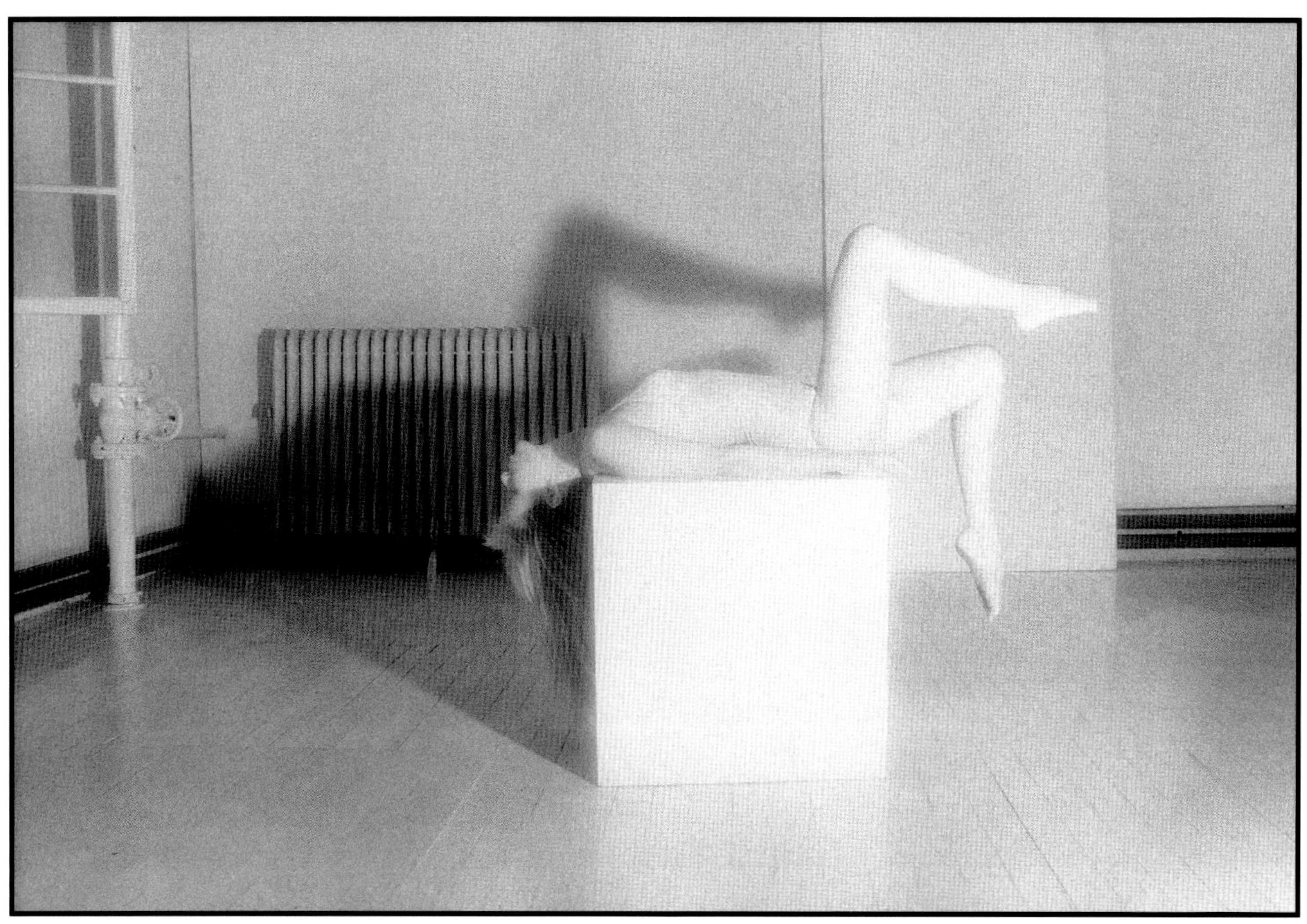

Plate 63

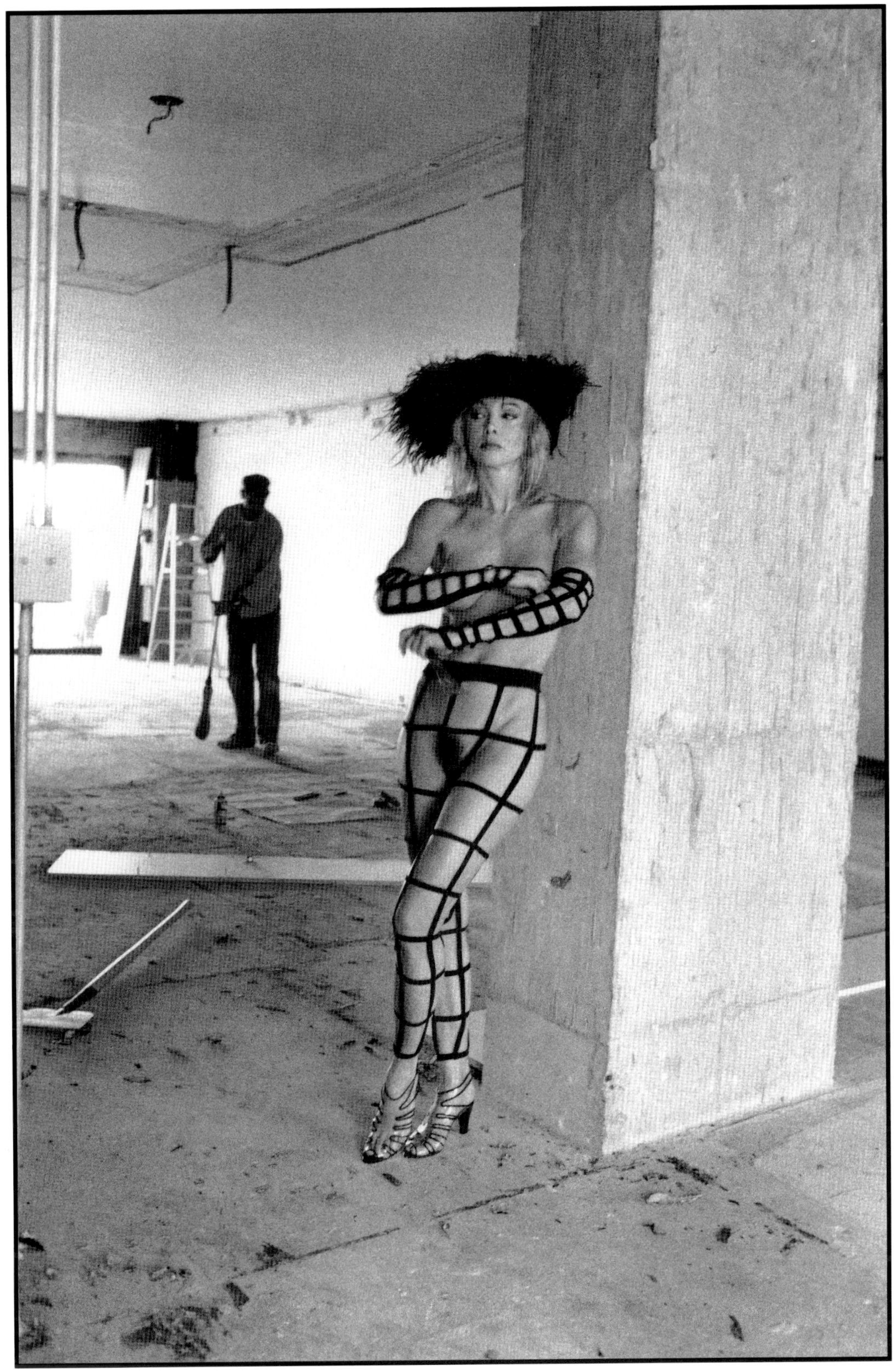

Plate 64

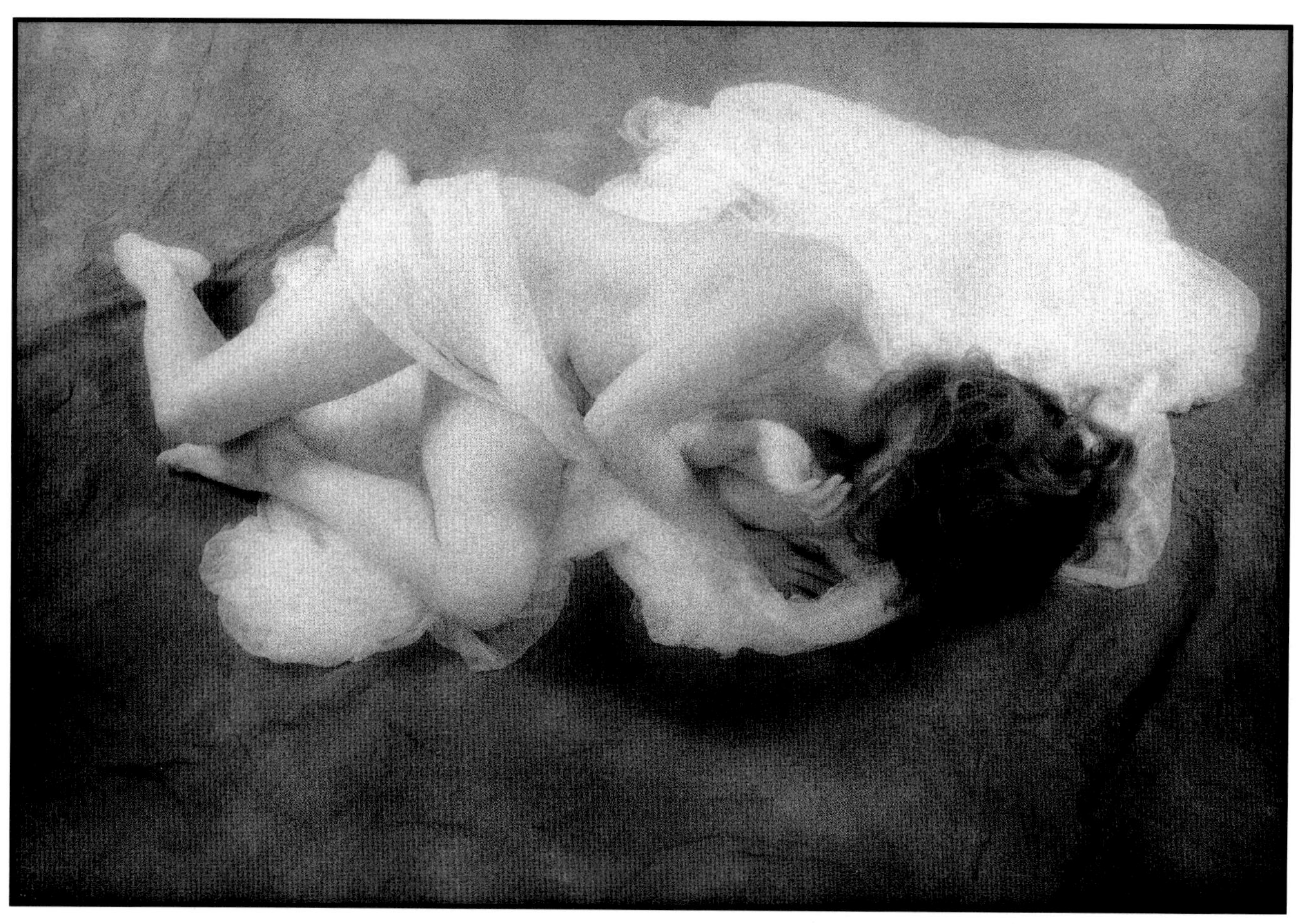

Plate 65

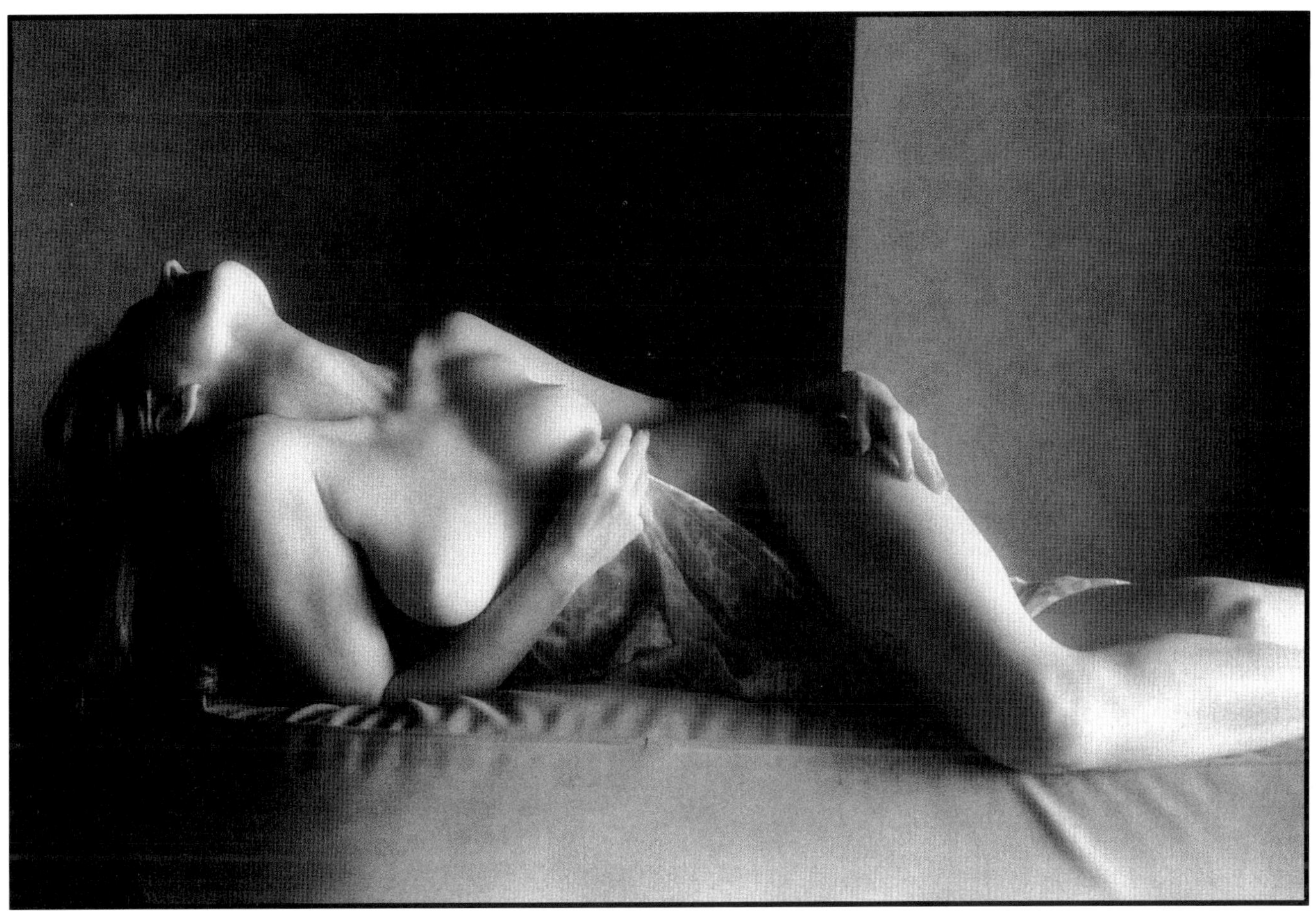

Plate 66

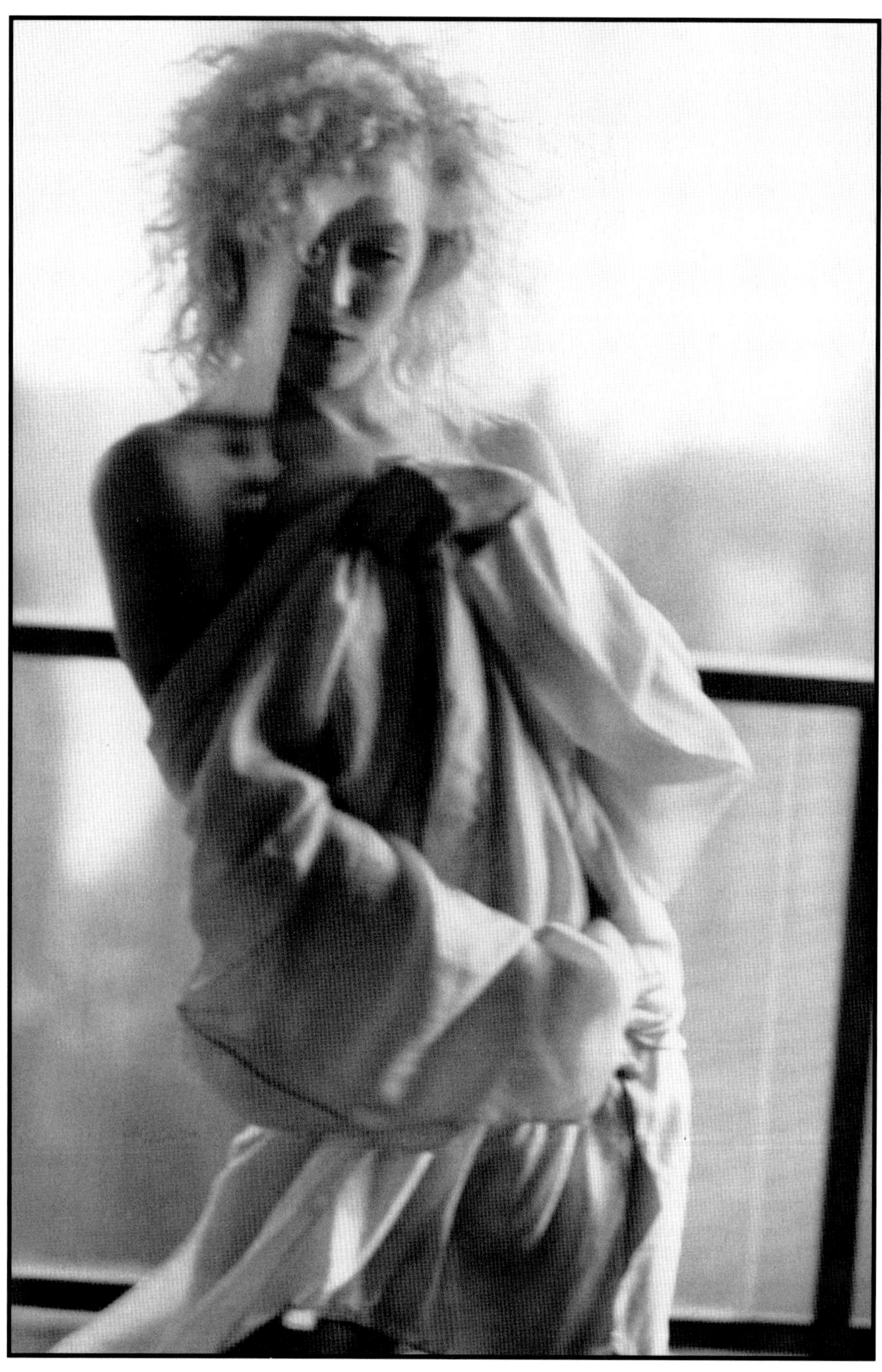

Plate 67

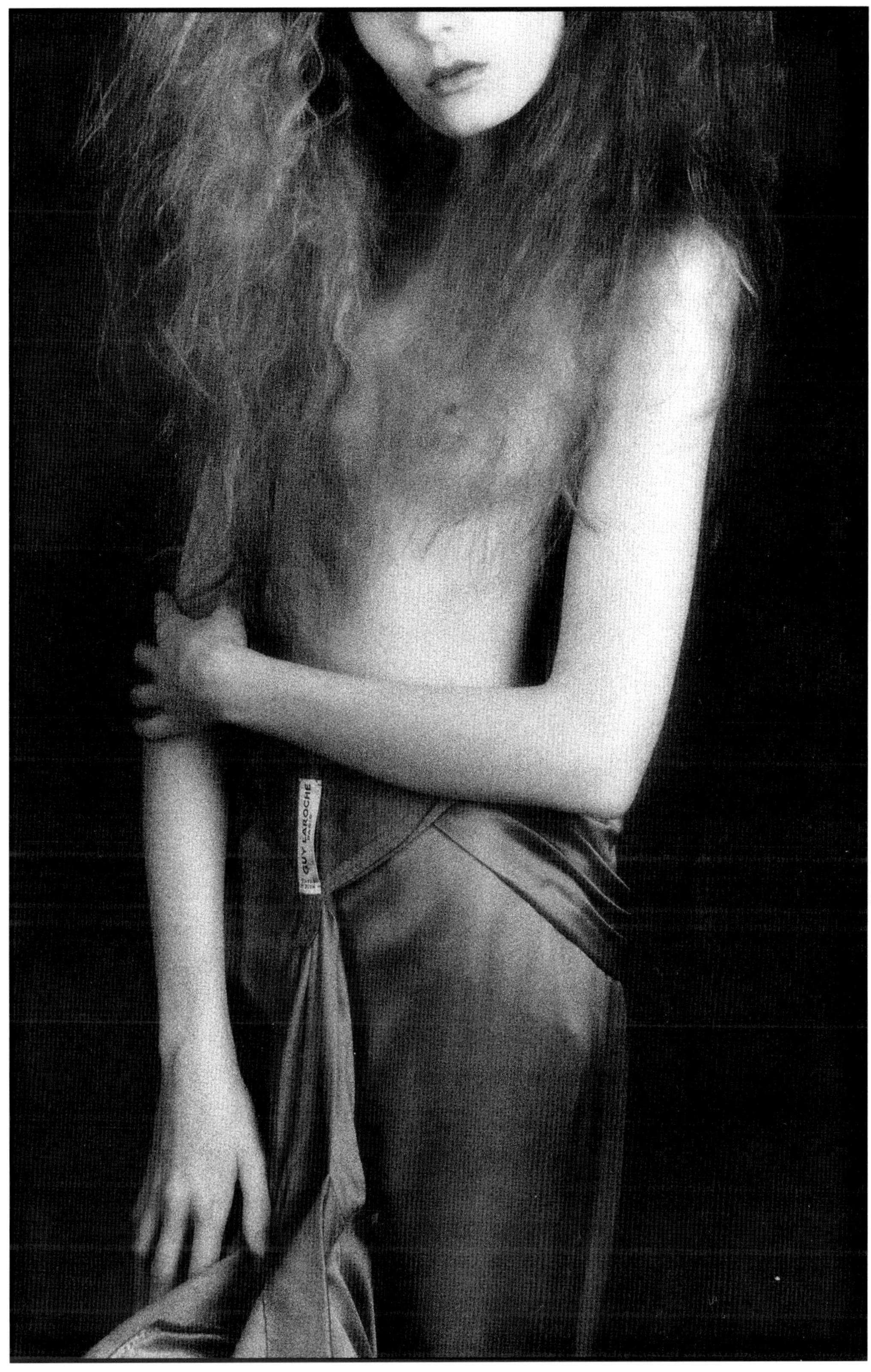

PLATE 68

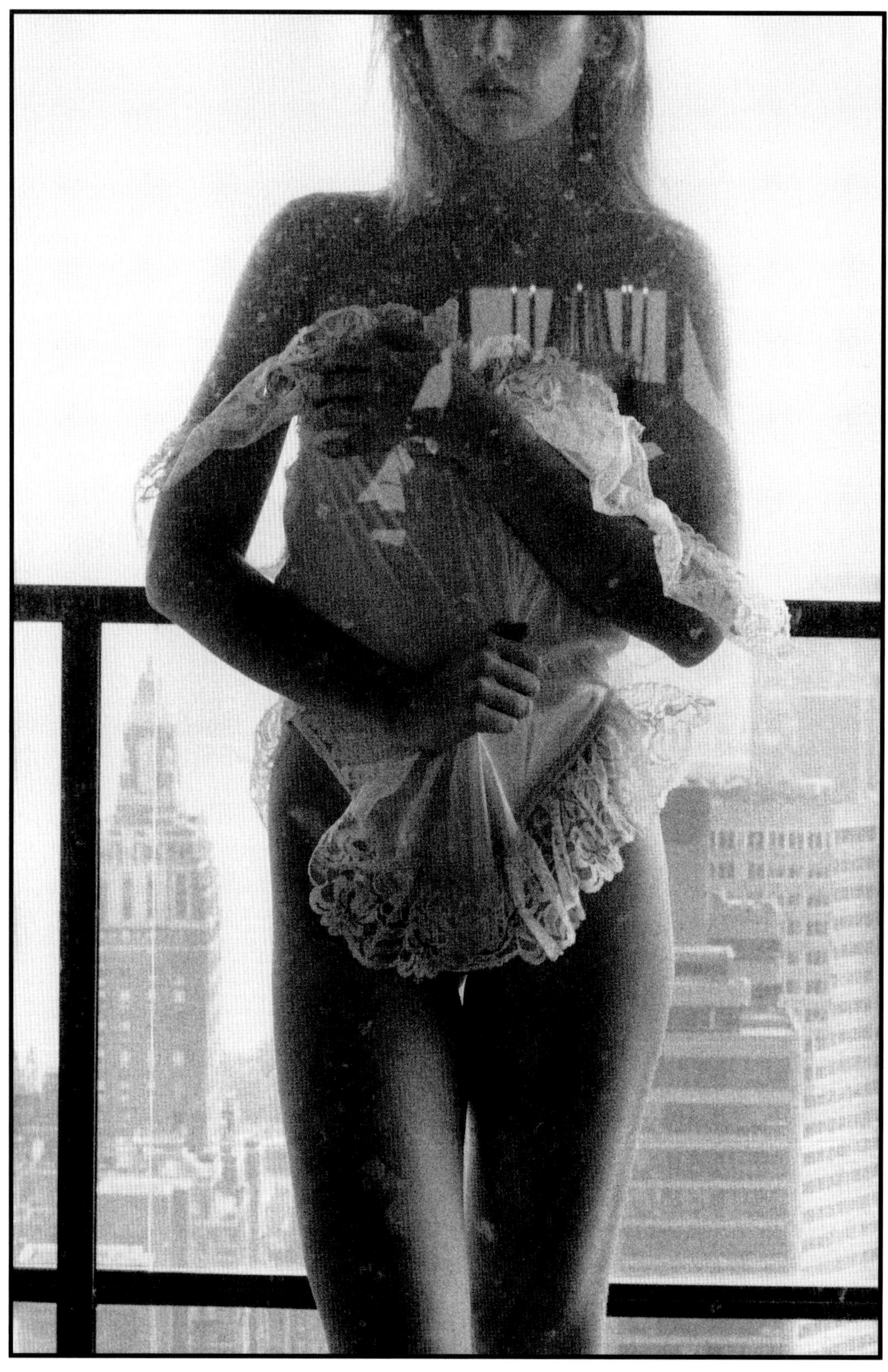

Plate 69

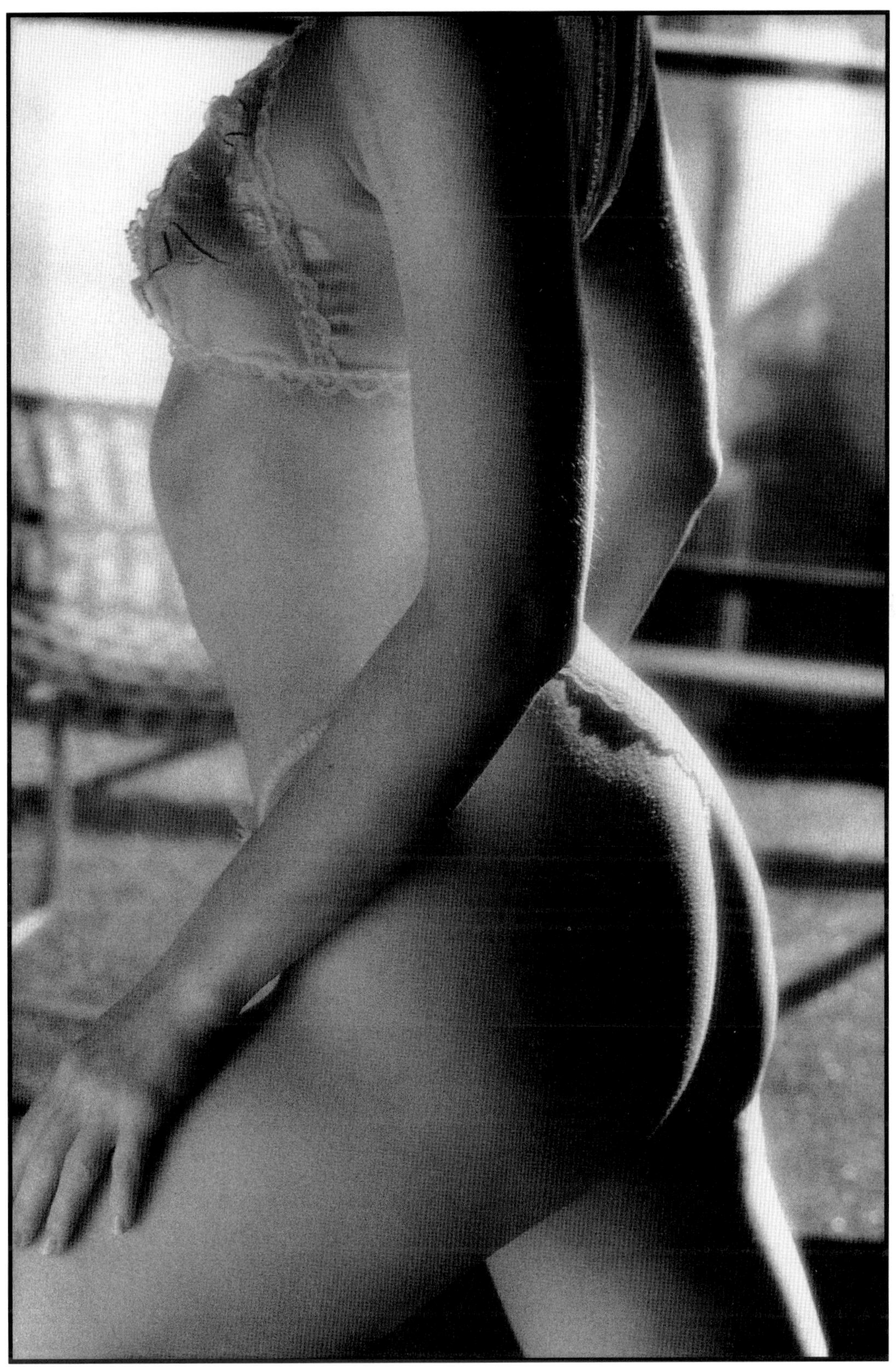

Plate 70

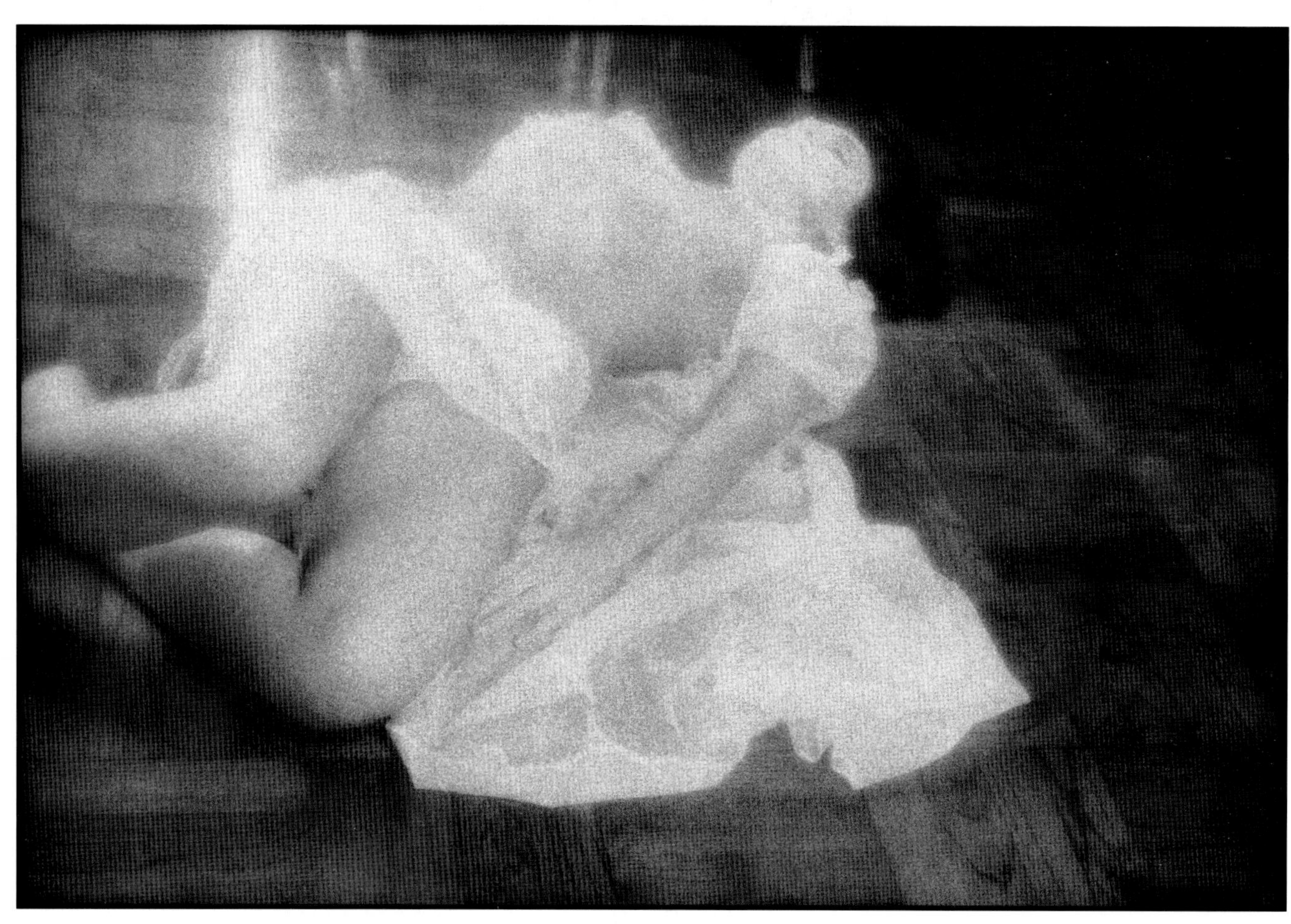

Plate 71

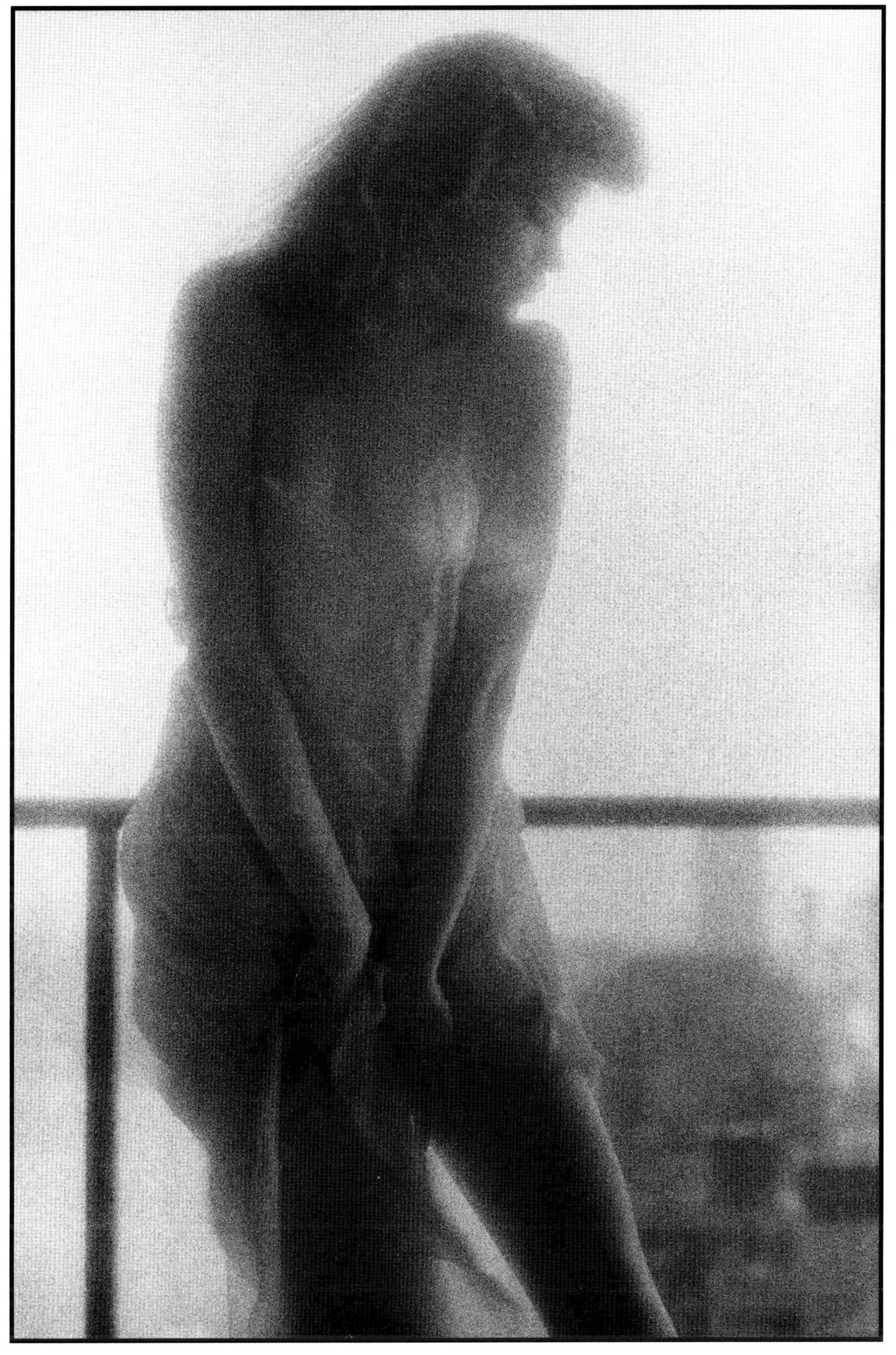

Plate 72

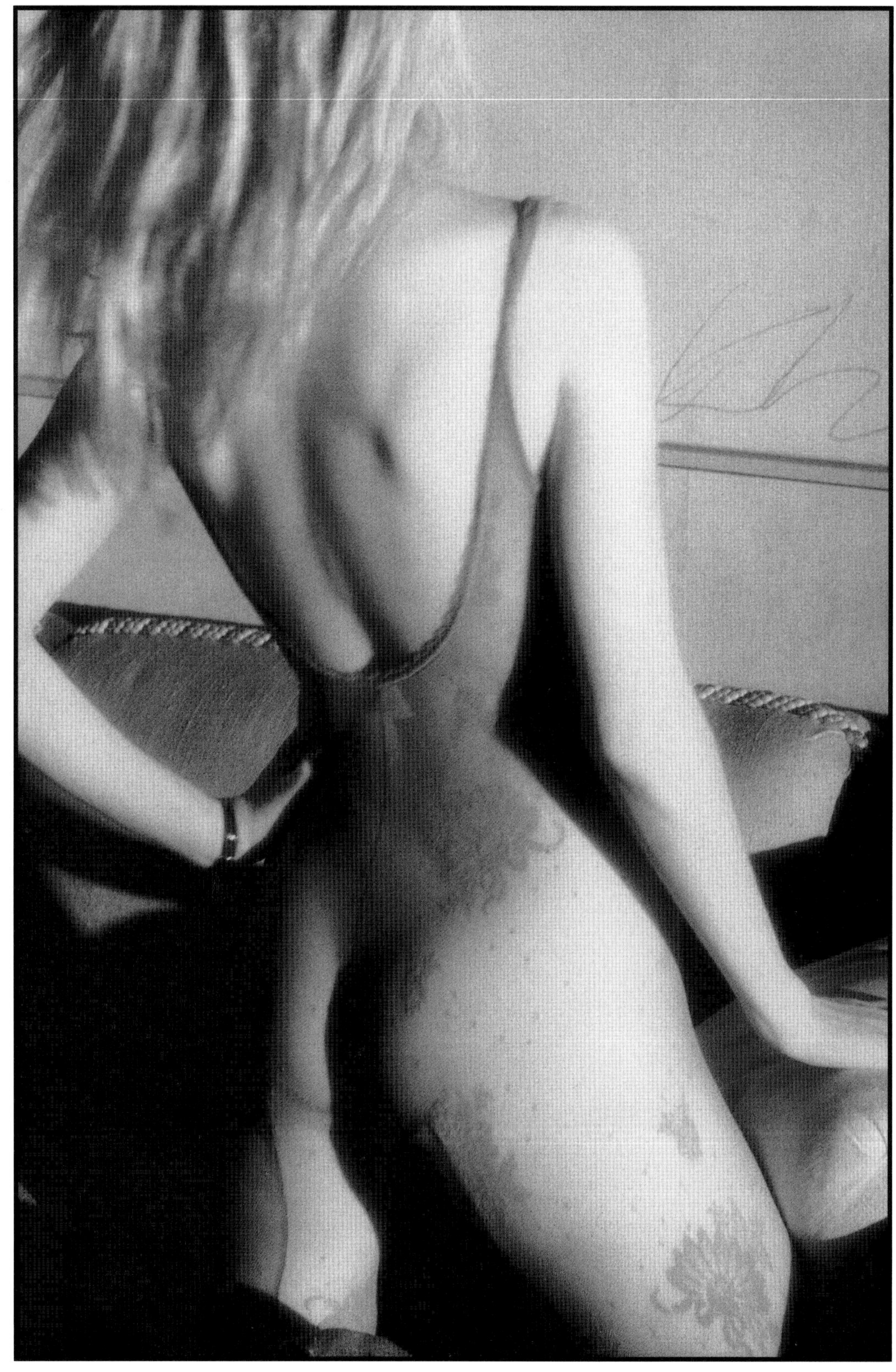

Plate 73

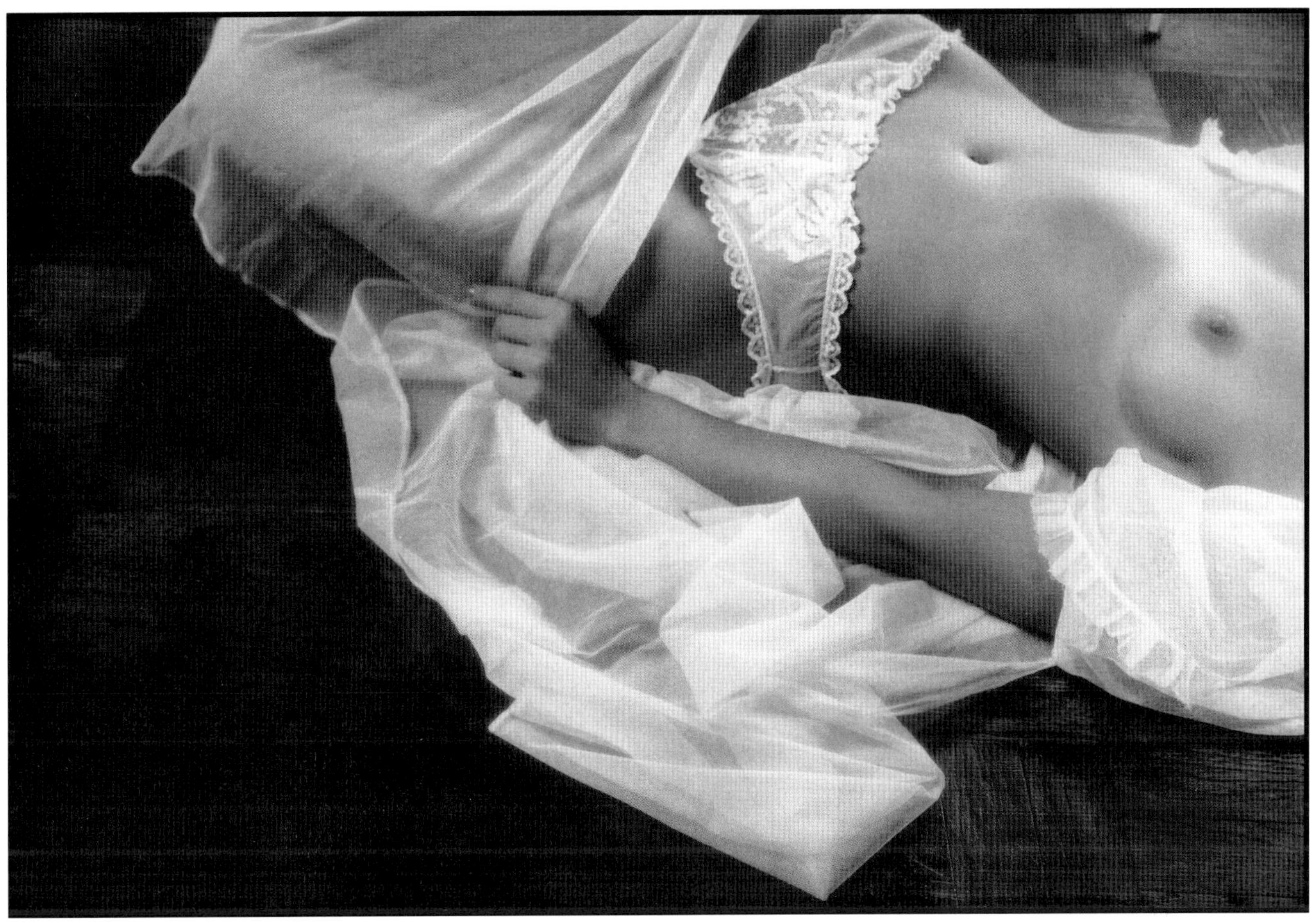

Plate 74

THE PROCESS

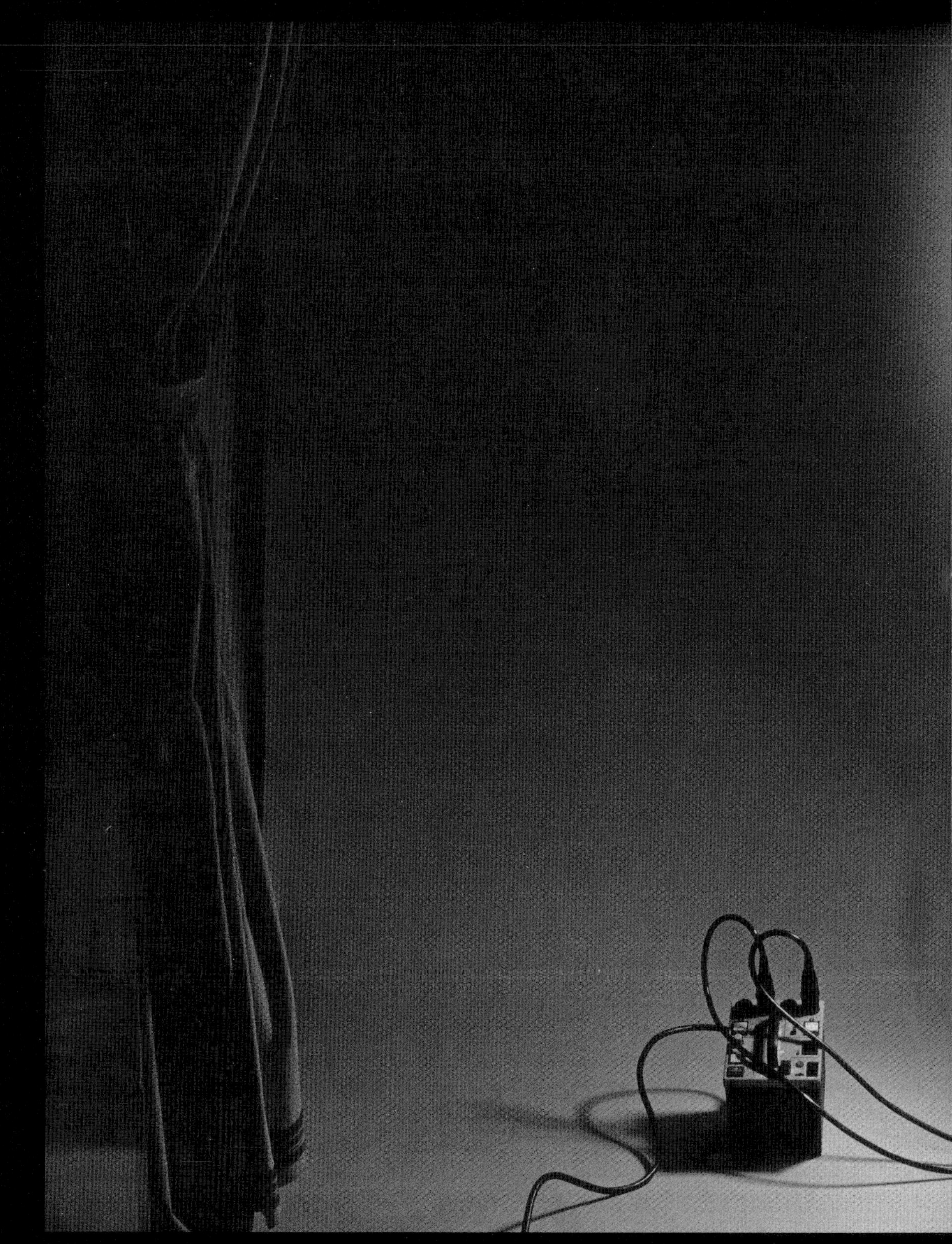

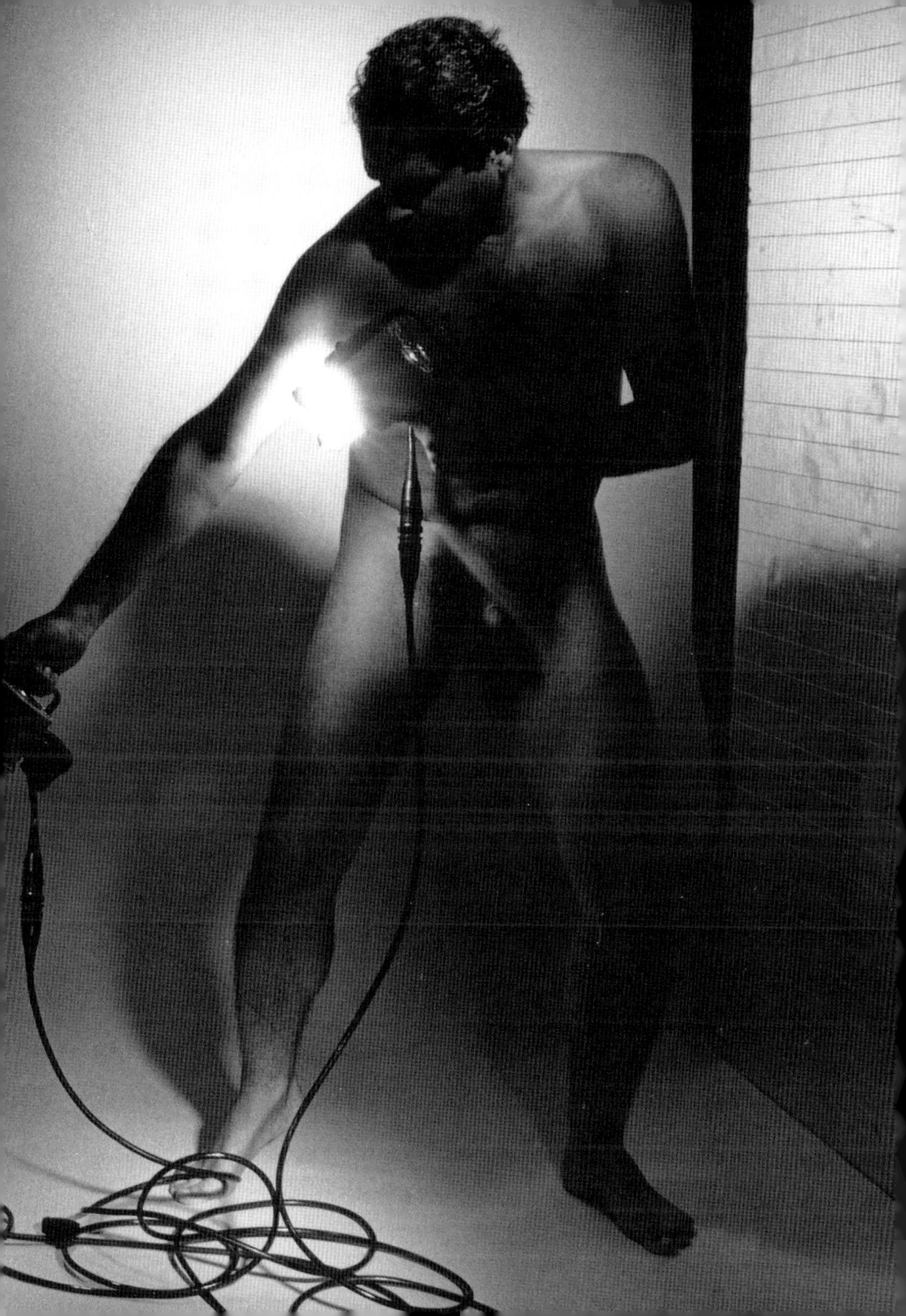

CAMERA EQUIPMENT

The first question I'm often asked is, "What type of equipment and film do you use?" For some reason, photographers seem to think that this is what really makes the difference in photography. Actually, it is the photographer and his or her eye behind the camera that are of ultimate importance. Today, with the many new advances in cameras and other pieces of equipment, you have a lot to choose from. As a result, finding the right system for your individual needs and preferences shouldn't be a problem. The various autofocus cameras on the market, which are available with a number of different lenses, make photographing a breeze for amateur photographers. Any good 35mm camera or medium-format camera, such as a 2 1⁄4, can capture extraordinary pictures. But the fact remains: the camera is only as good as the photographer behind it.

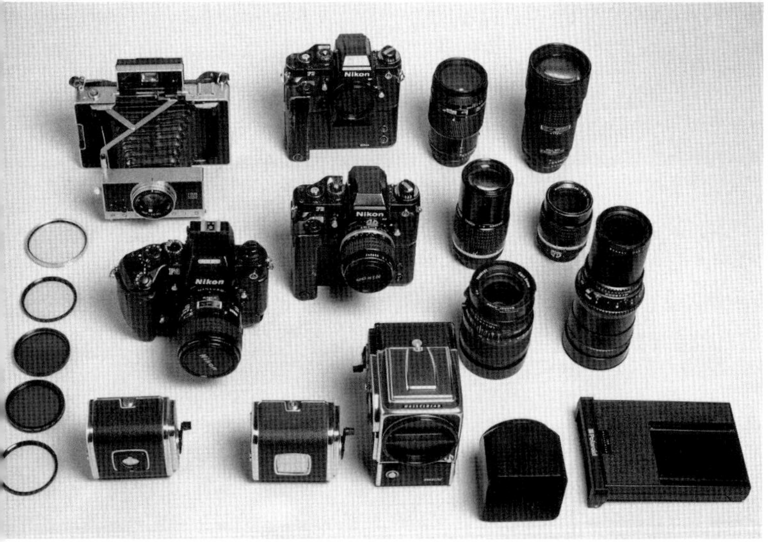

This is the equipment I use for my black-and-white nude photography: a Polaroid 195 camera; two Nikon F3 Highpoint cameras; a Nikon F4 camera; Nikkor 35mm–70mm zoom, 35mm, 60mm, 85mm, and 105mm lenses; a Hasselblad 500 ELM body; three Hasselblad filmbacks; Hasselblad 150mm and 250mm lenses; a Polaroid back for the Hasselblad camera; a reflector shade; and a variety of filters, including a polarizing filter, a red filter, a soft diffusion filter, and a skylight filter. I like to move around and try new angles when I shoot, and my Nikon 35mm cameras give me a great deal of flexibility. But when I use a seamless background, I enjoy working with my Hasselblad 2 1⁄4 camera.

I use Nikon F3s with motor drives and a motorized Hasselblad 2 1⁄4 ELM camera in the studio. I recently bought a Nikon F4 for street shooting. When I'm hired for a project, I always ask the art director up front which format he or she desires. Some art directors prefer 35mm, while others like 2 1⁄4. When I have to move quickly from angle to angle during a shooting session, I opt for one of my 35mm cameras since their size affords me much more flexibility.

The advantage of the Hasselblad is that its images can be viewed directly. The 2 1⁄4 format delivers 12 large images per roll of black-and-white film. As such, it is much easier to differentiate the pictures and choose the most appropriate one for your purposes. A roll of black-and-white 35mm film with 36 exposures provides you with 36 smaller images that are contact-printed on one sheet of paper. You must study these images carefully with a magnifying glass in order to make selections for enlargements. Both camera formats have their advantages and drawbacks. What matters most, however, is what works for you and what you feel more comfortable with.

With either format, having a motor drive can be quite helpful, especially when you're photographing a model who moves well. The motor drive enables you to capture more shots than you would without one. You can shoot many frames per second, thereby increasing your chances of capturing unusual, impromptu moments. Although using a motor drive has its advantages, it has a disadvantage, too: you'll shoot much more film, which can be costly. You can, however, minimize this potential problem when you work with 35mm cameras. Simply set the motor-drive knob to "S," which stands for single shot. You can now lift your finger after each shot. This is different from the "continuous," or "C," mode, in which the camera keeps shooting frame after frame as long as you hold your finger on the button. This mode can be good for very fast action shots, but it can use up a lot of film.

When I work on a job, I always have backup cameras with me, and I switch camera bodies after each roll of film. I suggest that you do the same; I've seen mechanical crises happen too many times. You never know when something mechanical might go wrong, so you need to protect yourself from unexpected disasters. When you have extra cameras on hand and switch them, chances are that you'll capture something similar on one roll of film if you have a mechanical failure while shooting another roll. A camera can malfunction at any point, even if it was recently repaired, so it is also a good idea to have your cameras and equipment checked periodically. This added insurance is well worth the cost.

I also bring along my Polaroid 195, an old camera that can still be found in used-camera stores. This model has *f*-stops and shutter speeds on the lens, just like a 35mm camera, which permit me to test the lighting and exposure. When I shoot with my Hasselblad, I attach an optional Polaroid filmback to it. You can now have Polaroid filmbacks made to fit 35mm cameras. By using a Polaroid camera or filmback and Polaroid film, you can see lighting effects and determine exact light ratios before you shoot the final images.

Choosing which lenses to buy in today's marketplace can be confusing and a bit overwhelming. You'll find that 35mm cameras usually come with a standard 50mm or 60mm lens. On 2¼ cameras, the standard lens is the 80mm. I recommend working with the standard lens until you feel you've mastered it. Shoot for a brief time with only one lens as an exercise, and then experiment with another lens. Rent each lens for a week or weekend and just shoot, shoot, shoot. Study the results. Do you like the final images? Which perspective did you prefer? Was the lens too heavy for you to carry around for everyday use? Would you be satisfied with being able to use it only once in awhile? You should ask yourself these questions, especially when finances are a consideration.

As you try different lenses, you might find that you'll need a particular lens, such as a 500mm lens, only occasionally. Rather than buy an expensive lens that you'll use infrequently, I suggest that you rent it for specific shoots. I prefer the 35mm lens and the 105mm lens for my Nikons, but I do use a 60mm and an 85mm; I don't use my 200mm lens often. When I am in the mood to try a new lens, I rent one for the weekend. The prices for rentals are quite reasonable.

After trying several different lenses, you'll automatically gravitate to the lens that you feel most comfortable with. This is part of the process of interpreting reality and discovering your photographic vision—and yourself. The focal length of the lens you choose will largely determine your results. You can also use a lens to control what a final photograph will look like. To emphasize a particular part of a nude subject, simply focus on the area you want to call attention to and choose a large aperture. The rest of the image will appear blurry because depth of field will be very limited. Conversely, if you want to show the entire figure and the background in sharp focus, stop down until you get to a small aperture.

In 35mm photography, standard lenses, which are generally considered to be in the 50mm to 60mm range, provide a perspective that is close to that of the human eye. Obviously, then, these lenses minimize distortion and provide a true representation of reality. Wide-angle lenses, on the other hand, have a much more noticeable impact on the outcome of your pictures. The most popular of these lenses range in focal length from 24mm to 35mm. You can use a wide-angle lens to distort images or to add exaggerated lines to them. Such distortions can enhance the artistic quality of your final images; however, if you don't manage them well, they can be just that—distortions.

You can create another perspective with the environment and the human body by extending the lines and angles. Slightly tilting your wide-angle lens will enable you to emphasize your subject and achieve interestingly bizarre results. Another advantage to using a wide-angle lens is that it lets you capture more of the ambience or setting around your subject than a standard lens does. This is the beauty of a wide-angle lens: It offers extensive depth of field.

Medium-telephoto lenses, which range in focal length from 85mm to 135mm, are ordinarily used for portraiture. These lenses permit you to be farther away from your subject and capture a truer perspective than standard and wide-angle lenses do. If you were to use a wide-angle lens close to a face, the subject's chin and nose would be out of proportion, thereby distorting the whole look of the face. If, however, you were to use a medium-telephoto lens, the result would be an ideal, distortion-free likeness.

Long lenses, such as the 200mm and the 300mm, have flattening effects. They narrow the fields of view and must be used at distances of at least 7 or 10 feet. Long lenses bring your subject closer to the foreground and the foreground closer to the background. This capability produces a loss of perspective and depth. The advantage is that if you can't get close to your subject, you can bring your subject close to you via the use of long lenses.

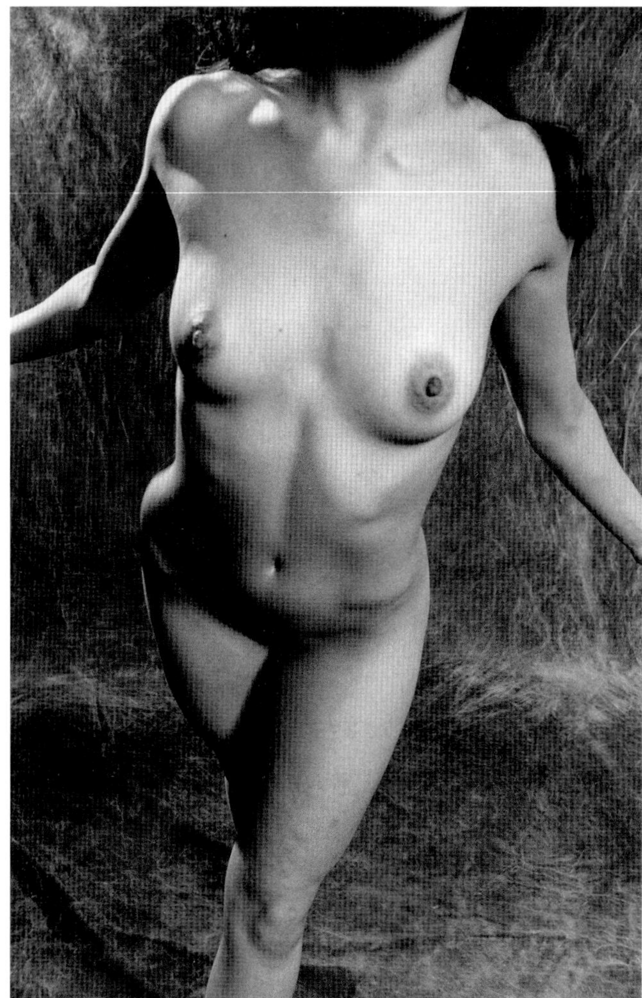
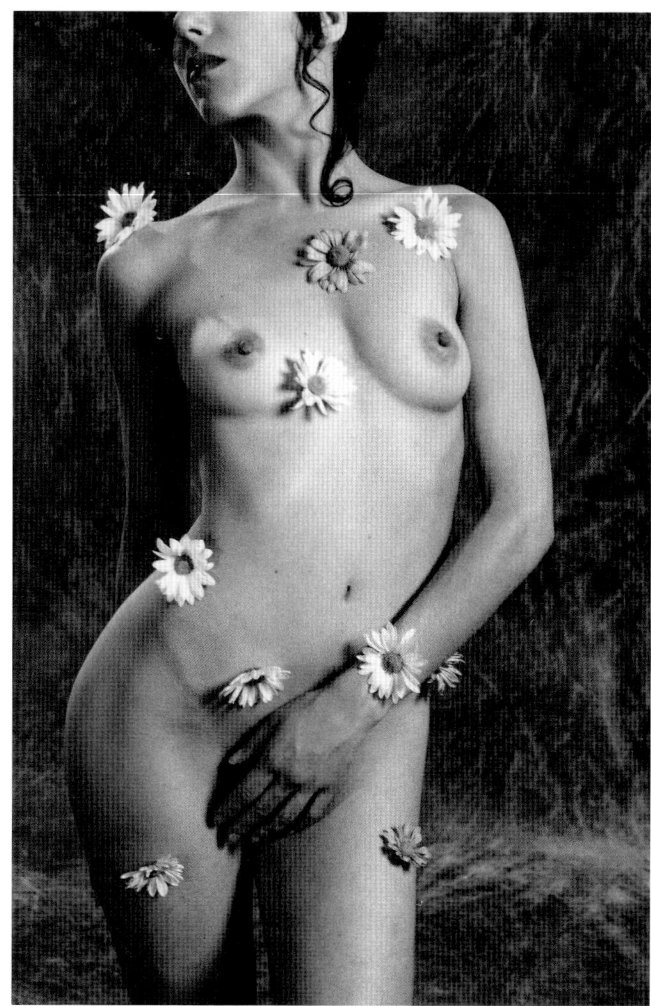

I tilted a 35mm wide-angle lens purposely to distort the model's figure (left). Although some distortion works well visually, an excessive amount can result in disturbing images. Then I switched to an 85mm lens to close in on my subject without distorting her or the background (right).

Zoom lenses come in a variety of focal-length combinations and are quite popular with many photographers. Nevertheless, the lenses have two drawbacks. They are large and heavy, and more important, they sacrifice sharpness for convenience in many instances. They are almost as sharp, but not quite as sharp, as fixed-focal-length lenses. Still, many photographers are willing to make this sacrifice in order to have intermediate focal lengths at their immediate disposal. By using a zoom lens, you can save time and prevent the possibility of missing a good photograph since you don't have to stop, change lenses, and move to a new perspective. Whenever you shoot, your goals and sense of aesthetics will determine which lenses you'll use to achieve the desired effects. Eventually, however, you'll gravitate to your favorite lenses, and the resulting look will ultimately become your signature.

In addition to cameras and lenses, you need to think about what kind of lighting equipment to buy. When I started shooting professionally, I bought three strobes and two powerpacks. I recommend this basic collection for any beginner. If finances are a consideration, start with one powerpack; Dyna-Lite's 1000-watt unit supplies enough power for a good start. Today, I own about 10 heads and five powerpacks. I can very easily use two to four strobes to illuminate a background, one strobe to light the subject's hair, and two or three strobes to light the foreground. And just as I do with my cameras, I make sure that I have backup lighting equipment on hand. All of a sudden in the middle of a shoot, a powerpack might lock and be unable to produce a flash. Although the problem might be something as minor as a blown fuse, it is much easier and considerably less distracting to simply switch units rather than fiddle with the malfunctioning unit. Determine the problem and solve it after the session is over.

For me, weight has always been a major consideration when I choose lighting equipment. Occasionally, I work without an assistant and must be able to lift equipment and light a set on my own. For this reason alone, I prefer Dyna-Lite equipment, which is lightweight, compact, and simple to pack. Since I shoot so many jobs outside the studio, perhaps at someone's apartment where space might be a problem or on location where space isn't a problem, I find that the lighter the equipment, the easier the operation.

I like to change the lighting frequently. Using the same lighting setup over and over again is boring. I might use a softbox as my main light with a shoot-through umbrella for fill, or I might use two direct strobes with grids as my main lights, which would cast shadows on the background. A softbox is a box with a piece of translucent material in front of it. The illumination it provides is quite diffused because the light travels inside the box before hitting the subject. When I use available, or existing, light, I might decide to aim a fill light set at a very low flash output into a shoot-through umbrella. The resulting illumination is enough to fill the shadows but not enough to overpower the existing light.

Every photography student is curious to know what type of light and lighting equipment well-known photographers use. Although studying the lighting techniques of other photographers is important because it makes you aware of just how many options are available, you must determine what works best for you. This, in turn, will enable you to develop your own style.

To get started, work with one light as your main light in order to see what this type of illumination can do for you. Once you've mastered using a single light, add another, perhaps as a fill light. Learn how to balance light ratios, which are the differences in light output between strobes. When you feel comfortable using two lights, you can venture even further by adding a third light as a backlight or hairlight, or to highlight a particular body part.

I like strobe light, but many other photographers prefer tungsten light. One major advantage of working with tungsten lights is that they don't require powerpacks. Keep in mind, however, that they throw off a tremendous amount of heat and provide less illumination than strobes. As such, you're giving up speed and spontaneity when you opt to use them. For color work, tungsten light requires the use of tungsten-balanced film. Strobe light arrests motion and captures the moment, while tungsten light may translate the action as a blur. Of course, this look can add to the aesthetic appeal of a photograph.

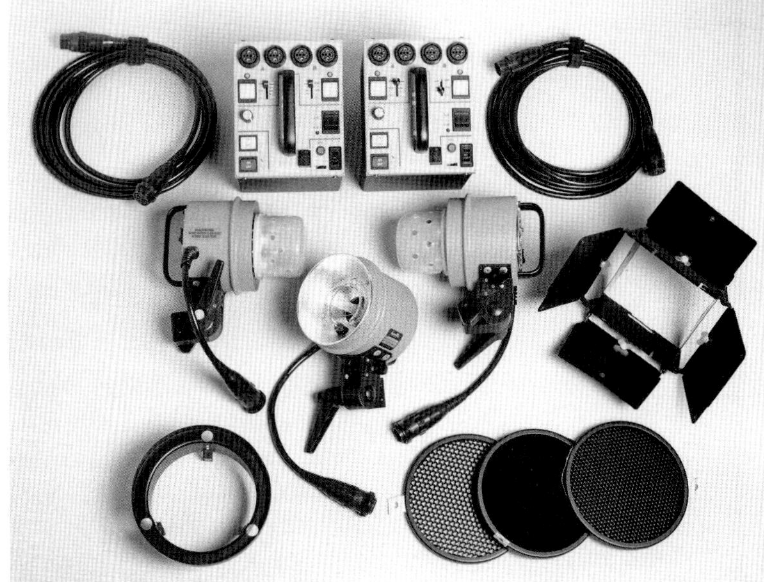

The lighting equipment I recommend when you start doing black-and-white nudes consists of two Dyna-Lite powerpacks, three strobe heads, powerpack cords, and a grid holder that attaches to the strobe head to support the grids and barndoors. Grids and barndoors control the angle of light and can completely change the mood of an image. The spread of light is controlled by the sizes of the holes on a grid; these vary from small to large. If you use two grid-covered direct lights as your main lights, the resulting harsh light and shadows will be quite dramatic, and the light will fall in a circular pattern. If you use two direct lights without grids, the resulting illumination will again be harsh, but wide open, not concentrated.

Two regular photographic umbrellas, which are white on the inside and black on the outside, and one or two translucent shoot-through umbrellas are recommended when you're just starting out. Eventually, you'll want to add a softbox and a few grids to your collection of lighting equipment. You should have one stand for each light head that you own, as well as a few extras. You should try to choose lightweight stands for portability, but the size and weight of each stand are dictated by the size and weight of the unit it must support. Your supplier should recommend the correct stands for your strobes. Extra stands serve other useful purposes, too. For example, a 30 x 40-inch reflector board clamped to a stand can bounce light back onto your subject, and a black card can be positioned to act like a shade or gobo, preventing any main light from reflecting back into the camera.

Next, you have to figure out which accessories to get. Walk into a camera store, and you'll see racks and racks of accessories to choose from. What do you actually need to buy? I keep my accessories to a minimum, and I recommend that you do the same.

Of course, I have the basics, including a tripod; as far as I'm concerned, this accessory is an absolute necessity. Suppose that you're shooting in a low-light situation and must use a slow shutter speed. Using a sturdy, durable tripod will prevent camera shake. And if you're using a medium-format camera, such as a Hasselblad, a tripod is suggested because the camera may prove too heavy to support by hand. If you attempt to use a medium-format camera without a tripod, accidental camera shake will be virtually guaranteed. Shooting with a long lens on a small camera, such as a 35mm, also requires the use of a tripod to eliminate camera shake. Don't skimp when you purchase a tripod. A solid, heavy-duty tripod helps ensure fine results, while an inexpensive, lightweight one will inevitably let you down.

Reflectors are another accessory that you should always have available during photo shoots. You never know ahead of time how necessary or handy they can turn out to be. They help control the degree of shadow in an image by reflecting or bouncing light into the shadow area. Fold-up reflectors shaped like circles are compact and can fit into most equipment cases. An alternative is to buy 30 x 40-inch sheets of double-sided reflector board. These come in a variety of color combinations, such as shiny silver on one side and dull silver on the other, white on one side and black on the other, and gold on one side and white on the other. And most studios keep 4 x 8-foot pieces of foamcore on hand, which can serve as large reflectors.

A reliable exposure meter is yet another essential accessory. Because you depend on your meter, knowing that it is "on the money" relieves you of any unnecessary stress. I recommend getting a meter that

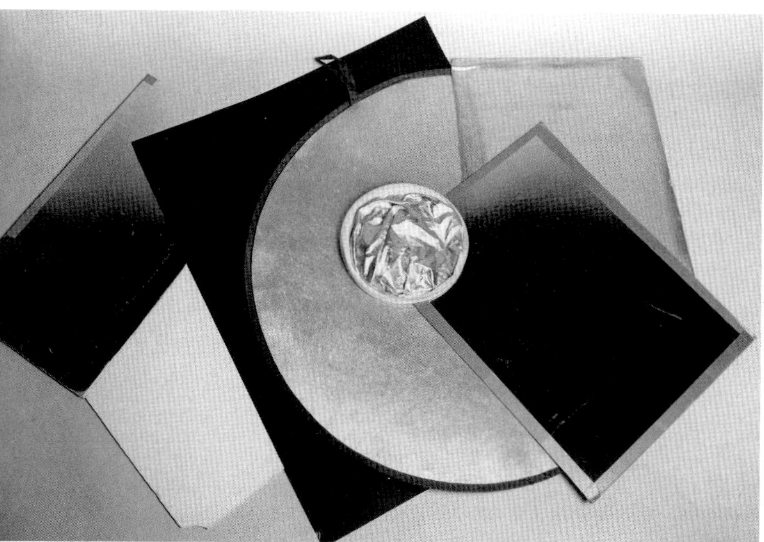

When photographing nudes, I like to vary the illumination. I have at my disposal two folding reflectors, a few 30 x 40-inch double-sided boards that are white on one side and black on the other, another board that is silver on one side and white on the other, and several gold-on-gold smaller boards. I use a reflector to bounce daylight or strobe light onto subjects and/or shadow areas to soften the shadows, as well as to distinguish details that otherwise wouldn't appear in the final image.

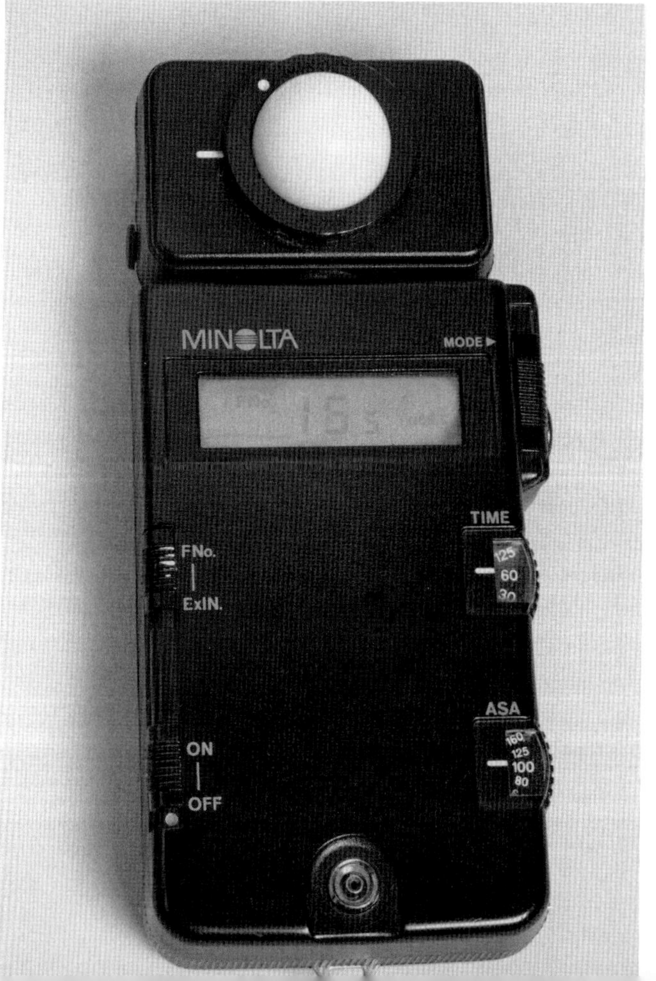

My Minolta III flash meter isn't the latest model on the market, but it is very reliable, which is precisely what a meter must be. Its various modes enable me to successfully shoot in available light, as well as with strobe light with or without the use of a sync cord.

reads both strobe light and available light, such as the Minolta III strobe meter. Even though shooting black-and-white film affords you more latitude than shooting in color, accurate meter readings are still critical.

So when you or your assistant takes an exposure reading of the light falling on the models during shooting sessions, you should have the meter in the exact place your subjects will be located. It is your assistant's responsibility to watch carefully while you're shooting and advise you if the models move too close to the camera or too far behind the designated mark. If your subjects move, you must meter again or direct your subjects back to their original location. Otherwise, when the models move closer, too much light falls on them and your pictures will be too light. Conversely, when the models move back, not enough light reaches them, so your pictures will be too dark. In either case, you can lose some great shots.

To prevent these problems, check the exposure by taking meter readings several times in between shots during the course of the shoot. After you've gone through a lot of trouble putting the shoot together, why leave anything to chance? If there are any background lights, take a meter reading of them first. You can then control the amount of light falling on the background and the amount of light falling on the subject. When you work with tungsten lights, the light you see on the set will be the exact light you'll see in your final photographs. Strobe lights, on the other hand, look one way to the eye but record differently on film. Shooting a Polaroid lets you see what the final outcome will look like, as well as saves you a great deal of time and money. You can make any final adjustments or changes to the lights if you don't like what you see in the Polaroid.

When buying accessories, you'll probably want to get some filters. Although the many filters available on the market today create a number of effects, I find most of them to be too gimmicky for my taste. With black-and-white film, however, I sometimes use contrast filters, as their name implies, to control contrast and to emphasize certain tones. For example, red, yellow, green, orange, and blue filters, which come in various intensities, can increase or decrease the amount of contrast in your pictures.

The standard rule is that a filter will lighten its own color in the final image. A yellow filter absorbs excess blue, thereby darkening a blue sky and accentuating the clouds. An orange filter darkens a blue sky more than a yellow filter, and a red filter creates even more dramatic results. In black-and-white photography, a green filter alters skin tones under artificial lights and is good for nudes.

However, you must consider the other elements in the image, such as the props, clothing, and/or background, and the effects that various filters will have on them. Experimentation is recommended. (I don't use these filters for my black-and-white work.) Finally, when you use filters, keep in mind that they reduce the amount of light recorded on film, so you must compensate accordingly by using a larger lens opening.

I do, however, think that a polarizing filter, or polarizer, is a must. Polarizers create effects that other filters can't, and are the only filters that don't change the actual color values of images recorded on film. For example, a polarizer intensifies—that is, darkens but doesn't change the color of—a blue sky and causes clouds to appear separate from it. However, you lose almost two stops in exposure.

Useful both in the studio and on location, polarizers enhance shadows, thereby producing stronger forms. You can also eliminate unwanted highlights in an image simply by moving a polarizer in a circular motion. As you do this, you can actually see reflections and glare disappear.

I shy away from most special-effect filters. And on the rare occasions when I want an image in soft focus, I like to create my own soft-focus "filter." Sometimes I stretch a nylon stocking across a filter ring. Covering a clear filter with a light layer of either hair spray or petroleum jelly is another way to mimic the effect of a soft-focus filter. Unlike actual soft-focus filters, these alternatives enable you to control both the extent of the diffusion and the size of the area that you're softening. But whichever method you choose, don't put the diffusing material directly on your lens. This could conceivably ruin it. So always put the diffusing material on a clear or skylight filter. Any damage that occurs will affect only the filter, not your more expensive lens.

Finally, unless you work in a large studio where you can use auto-poles to hang seamless paper, you'll need a set of portable background poles to hold the seamless in place or to drape the canvas over the cross bar. These poles are also handy for location work. Obviously, there is no limit to the amount of equipment and the number of accessories you can choose from. I suggest that you start with a basic unit, experiment, and then expand according to your likes and needs.

FILM

Working in black and white provides you with many options that shooting in color doesn't. You translate what your eye sees into shades of gray, so you can record tonal nuances. You can vary the control and processing of your black-and-white film, thereby discovering your own unique style. Being able to interpret a single negative in many different ways can be quite exciting. I find that black-and-white film is more artistic in both its application and the resulting images than color film is, and its wider acceptance in the fine-art world seems to confirm this.

When you start looking into different black-and-white films, you'll notice that today's films have a great deal more latitude in terms of film speed. For example, Kodak T-Max P3200 Professional film is an incredibly fast film with a coarse grain structure. With an ISO rating of 3200, the film's very fast speed enables you to use it in low-light situations, whether the light is artificial, available, or a combination of the two. You can rate Kodak T-Max P3200 Professional film at 6400 for even more grain and speed; however, you must compensate for this increase in film speed, which is known as pushing film, during the developing process. The higher the film speed, the less light you need in order to shoot successfully.

If you're hired for a job, use a film that you are familiar with. If you're shooting for yourself, you can experiment with various films. Suppose that you want to record an image with very little grain. In this case, you should use an extra-fine-grain to fine-grain film, such as Kodak Technical Pan, Kodak Plus-X Pan, or Kodak T-Max 100 Professional film. For grainier images, select a film rated at ISO 400 or higher, such as Kodak Tri-X Pan, a medium-grain film. If you want even more grain, an alternative is to change the film-speed rating of an ISO 400 film to 800 or even 1600. However, each incremental increase of the film speed requires corresponding adjustment during developing. This also holds true when you pull film, or use a slower ISO rating than the film's recommended speed.

Black-and-white infrared film can be exciting to work with because you aren't always sure of what your final photographs will look like. I like the surreal quality of infrared images, and I'm always astounded by the results. You can rate infrared film at different film speeds and develop it accordingly. This type of film responds to near infrared radiation between 700 and 900 nanometers, which is a measurement of wavelength; infrared radiation; ultraviolet radiation; and visible light.

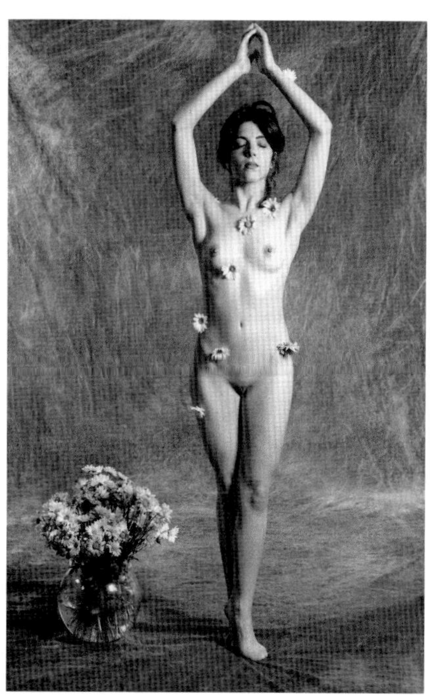

In order to achieve the soft, fine-grain effect of this photograph, I used a softbox without a fill light and Kodak Plus-X Pan film. This film is less grainy than other films, such as Kodak Tri-X Pan film and Kodak T-Max P3200 Professional film.

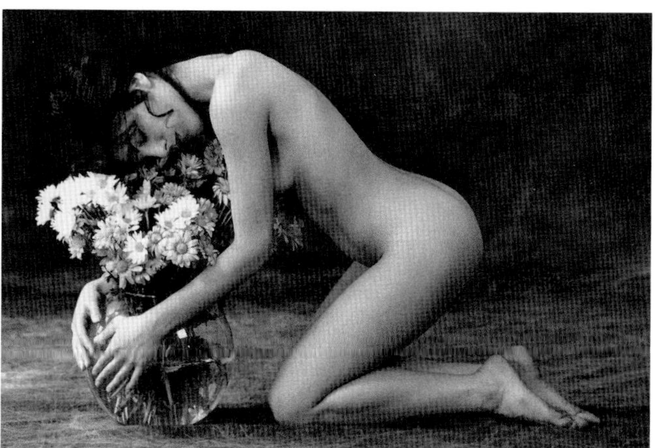

I made this photograph with Kodak T-Max P3200 Professional film, which is ideal for working in very low light and enables photographers to shoot in situations that used to be beyond the capability of any other film. I placed one tungsten light high to my right and another light to my left and then angled both downward. Not much light is needed with this high-speed, coarse-grained film.

When using infrared film, you must use a filter on your lens, such as a 25 red filter. Blue skies will appear a dramatic black, and foliage will appear white with beaming highlights. You can also experiment with a 29 dark red and either a 12 or 15 deep yellow filter. Like the 25 red filter, the 29 dark red filter blocks out visible light, thereby enhancing the infrared effect. To use these filters properly, simply focus as you ordinarily would, and then turn the lens' focusing ring until the red dot lines up with the corresponding distance. A final point about infrared film: It must be loaded and unloaded in complete darkness.

Polaroid film is used to assess the lighting setup and to observe the situation before you begin shooting the final images. Test Polaroids enable you to make final adjustments to the lights, camera position, lens selection, composition, and subject details. I use Polaroid 664 most of the time because it has an ISO rating of 100. This film speed is close to Kodak Plus-X Pan's ISO rating of 125, so I can shoot a Polaroid and have a good idea of what the final film image will look like. By checking Polaroids carefully, you'll start to train your eye to see in shades of gray. If something isn't working visually, you can quickly change it. For example, if the color of a prop isn't strong enough or registers as too strong a tone in black and white, you can switch to another color prop.

New Polaroid films include Polapan and Polagraph. These 35mm films actually permit you to shoot a situation and develop the film immediately, within five minutes, using a Polaroid 35mm Auto-Processor. Advanced Image Transferring gives you the opportunity to discover new and artistic outlets. What you're actually doing is projecting a Polapan or Polagraph image onto colored Polaroid film. You peel apart the film, set aside the positive, and transfer the dye-containing negative to a nonphotographic surface called a receptor sheet. This material can be any of the recommended surfaces, from watercolor paper to a piece of silk. Each material calls for a great deal of experimentation on the part of the photographer, but each produces its own one-of-a-kind image.

You must, however, compensate for the bluish-green tint that results when you transfer an image to colored Polaroid film. Using a blue filter gives the final image a cool, monochromatic look, while an amber filter gives the final transfer a sepia quality. You can enhance the image even further through the mechanical application of such color mediums as pastels, watercolors, and pencils.

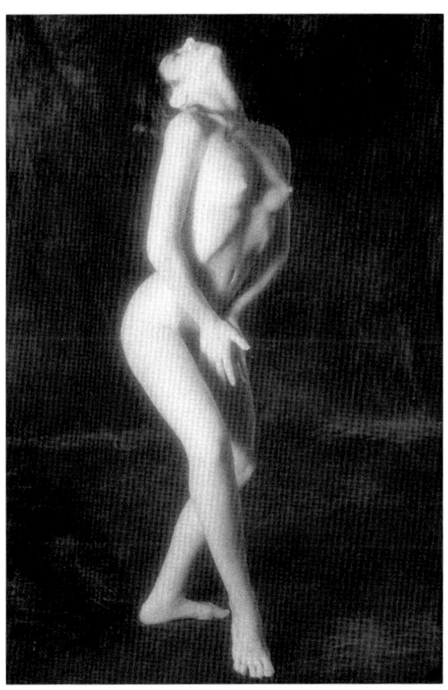

I love working with infrared film because you can never predict the results accurately. You might have a good idea of what to expect, but you might also be in for a big surprise. Infrared film can be rated at various film speeds and has its own grain structure and a moody quality. For this shot, I chose a film speed of 100 and used strobe light.

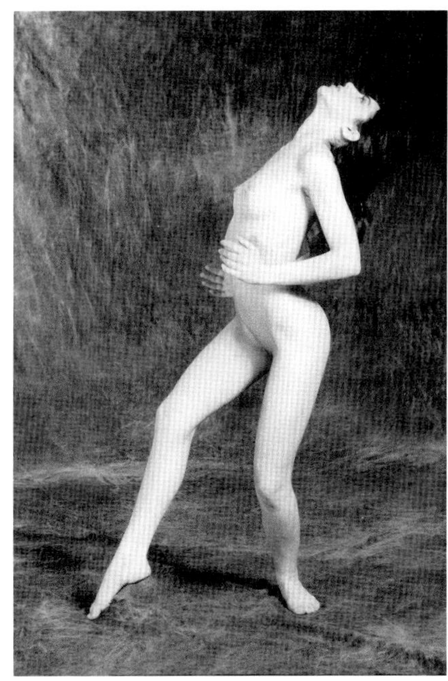

For this photograph, I decided to use Polapan. As the picture shows, your choice of film dictates the final image. One of the advantages of using Polapan is the ability to process the film and see the results instantly.

Whichever film you decide on, be sure to order enough film for your shoot. You have to estimate according to what you're planning to shoot, how long you intend to shoot, and how many different shots you'll be taking during that time frame. Always have more film than you anticipate using. I usually find that I shoot more film than planned, not less. Also, if you're working on an assignment, discuss the goals the client and/or art director want to achieve with them. You wouldn't want to give them a grainy photograph when image sharpness is needed.

PREPARING FOR A SHOOTING SESSION

Many photographers want to photograph nudes for the glamour that it represents. Others are challenged by the idea of capturing a specific image of a nude on film. Still others are attracted to the human body because of its erotic qualities and their own sexual arousal.

Before you get completely immersed in photographing nudes and planning your first session, you should ask yourself why you want to shoot this type of picture. If you want to photograph nudes in order to meet attractive models, stop right now! If you don't act in a professional manner, you'll soon be out of business. As a professional, you should never come on to your models. If you do, your unethical reputation will get around town very quickly, and you'll find that no one will want to work with you.

Never put your models in compromising situations. Sexual overtones can make models feel threatened and uncomfortable. Reassure your models about the session and the type of conduct that you feel is appropriate. How would you like to be the subject of a nude study with an unprofessional photographer? If you don't understand why models might have a difficult time with this, try putting yourself in their place. You become vulnerable when you are nude. Keep this in mind when you're photographing nude subjects, and you'll undoubtedly be more sensitive and caring.

If, however, your reasons for photographing nudes are valid, set yourself in motion. Most people have a tendency to think about what they would like to do for years and years but never get around to doing it. Once you've made your decision, put the word out. Of course, before you can begin shooting, you need willing subjects. How you go about getting models can be a bit problematic. Sometimes I have trouble finding nude models I would like to photograph. Ask friends and relatives to pose for you, and assure them that they'll feel comfortable in front of the camera. Another option is to locate the person who hires models for classes at various art schools and colleges in your area.

At this point, you should entertain the idea of using a hair and makeup artist and/or a stylist who want to build a portfolio and get a great photograph in return. This is true even if you're doing a personal shoot because the problems that arise on a location shoot for your own work can crop up on a business assignment. Having these individuals to help during the session will add a sense of professionalism and will free you to concentrate on your shooting, and watching them work will show you how to plan in advance for various potential emergencies. If you eventually decide to do nude photography at a professional level, you'll find that this experience will enable you to prepare for nude shooting sessions more effectively.

After you've chosen a model, a hair and makeup artist, and, possibly a stylist, and agreed on a date and time with all of them, you should consider working in the studio, using seamless paper as the background. Here, you can limit the number of distractions, which in turn, will allow you to get acquainted with your nude subject and to feel at ease directing him or her. You'll also be able to take control of the situation.

Once you feel confident working in the studio, you might decide to shoot your next session on location. However, working on location can pose problems that you may not even be aware of. Challenge yourself. For example, with little space in the confines of a small room you'll be forced to use a wide-angle lens, so make this part of your artistic statement. Then come up with an idea as a starting point, such as photographing your fantasies or those of others. You can make your own rules.

By studying photography as well as other avenues of creative expression, such as painting and sculpture, in person or from books and exhibition catalogs, you may find that your imagination will be triggered during your shoots and new energy will surface. These sources of creativity are stored in your subconscious mind and can manifest themselves without your realizing that this is happening. As such, when you plan your shooting schedule, you should always leave room for the unexpected.

Good photography makes a statement and reflects the conflict and the harmony within you. Remember, photography is an exploration, especially of yourself. It is about evolving and going well beyond the conscious layers of the mind to find your true direction. Where life leads you is a continuation of where you are. What do you love to do? What are you attracted to? If you involve these areas of interest and reflect your preferences in your photography, you'll start to see a trend developing in your work.

Some photographers like working with a particular type of model. This choice eventually becomes part of their overall statement. For example, you might want to photograph only muscular men with perfect bodies or females who are perfect "10s." You can, of course, take the opposite approach and photograph only overweight or imperfect bodies. Next, you have to learn how to extract movement and emotion from your nude models. Eventually you'll find the techniques that work best for you.

As you prepare for your shooting sessions, you'll discover that they involve a lot more than simply taking the photographs. This, in fact, is only one of the many steps that this process entails. You have to give some thought to the goals you hope to achieve, as well as the models, hair and makeup artists, stylists, assistants, studio sets, and locations. And in addition to the choices you have to make concerning composition and lighting, you have to consider the creative potential of film developing and printing.

CHOOSING MODELS

As mentioned earlier, when preparing for a nude shooting session, you need to figure out if you want to work with an experienced or inexperienced model. There is no "right" answer to this question. Both options have distinct advantages. But whether you're executing an assignment or experimenting for yourself, your first consideration should be the type of model you're looking for. What do you have in mind? Has your client told you exactly what the company is looking for? You also have to think about deciding between a top fashion model, experienced in nude photography, or, perhaps, a friend or a neighbor about whom you have a "vision"? These are concerns that only you can resolve.

As you make your choice, you should ask a model to disrobe for you in order to eliminate any surprises later on. For example, hairy legs, a large scar, and/or a tattoo don't belong in a soft, romantic shot. You can either ask models to shave or wax their legs or tell them that they aren't right for this particular shoot. If a model's insecurities about a specific feature surface at the beginning of the session, reassure the model that you'll look for this in the camera and choose a perspective that minimizes the unflattering angle. The key to any successful shooting session is to have your model trust you.

Booking Experienced Talent

Experienced nude models are much more comfortable in front of the camera, take direction more readily, and have a better understanding of what you're looking for than inexperienced models. Experienced models can express their ideas clearly to you and may contribute significantly to what's happening on the set. In addition, they have a variety of positions and forms to deliver to the camera; posing is second nature to them. As such, photographers just starting out in nude photography can find it advantageous to photograph these models and might even learn something from them. If you're shooting a job, an experienced model will save you time, money, and film, and, in general, will deliver more than a person who has never posed nude before. If your budget is tight, go with a pro.

Professional models carry their own calling card, which is known as a composite. It shows several different photographs of a model, usually taken by various photographers. A composite includes a body shot, which is particularly important if the model poses in lingerie and/or partially nude. Professional models who agree to pose nude for advertising purposes charge very high rates. You can expect to pay $5,000 or more for such work. Large modeling agencies are quite concerned about a model's future career and have very specific requirements with respect to the use of the photographs. A release form specifying exactly how the photographs will be used and the length of time they'll be used must be signed.

When choosing a model from a modeling agency, you should first find out whether he or she's willing to do nude photography and, if so, whether the model is available for the day and time you want to shoot. Some models specialize in body parts, such as elegant, youthful-looking hands with long fingers or slender feet. A model with a perfect body need not have a perfect face, especially if the plans for a client's ad campaign don't show the model's face. Stocking manufacturers, for example, sometimes use partially nude models to advertise their products. These models might be wearing only pantyhose, and their faces might be either obscured or cropped out of the ads.

Consumers are much more aware of their bodies than ever before, and this awareness has a direct effect on advertising. Muscular bodies are in great demand today for sports-oriented advertisements, as

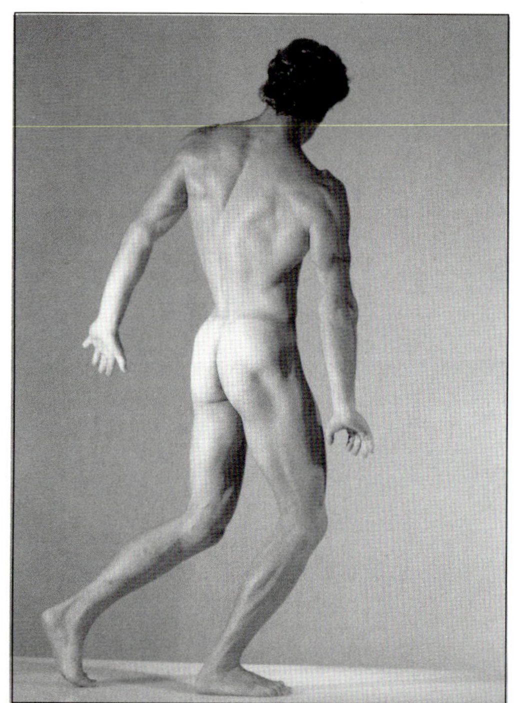

LES HOMMES MODEL MANAGEMENT
1515 BROADWAY SUITE 1132 NEW YORK, NY 10036

In addition to models who work in the nude, top professional models who have good bodies put together a composite of pictures in which one image strongly suggests a fine body. A completely nude photograph isn't necessary.

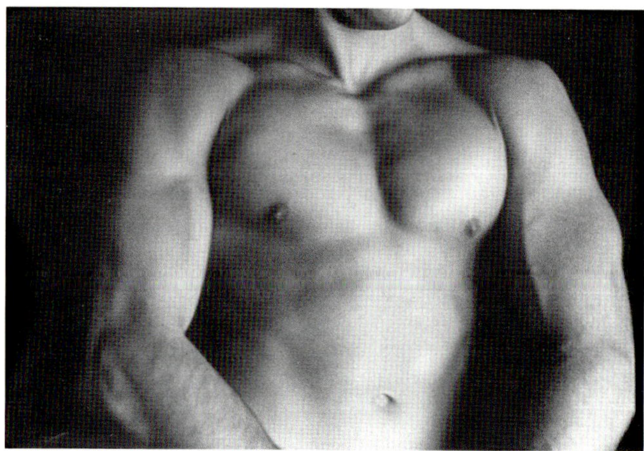

Many models are hired for specific body parts, such as hands or legs. The models' composites feature their strengths so they'll be considered for appropriate jobs. The faces of these models may never be seen.

well as for campaigns or promotions featuring body products. To fill these needs, some modeling agencies handle bodybuilders exclusively. If these types of modeling agencies exist in your city or surrounding area, contact them to see if any models need photographs for their portfolios. If so, the models may be willing to test with you in exchange for a specified number of prints. You might not find models who will disrobe completely, but you might have some luck finding a few who will pose partially nude.

If a model is willing and able, you'll put a tentative hold on his or her time for that particular day or half day. This gives you the first option on that block of the model's time. If another client requests the same model for the same date, they'll be given a secondary. This means that the other client can't use the model unless you give up your time slot; if you do, that client's secondary becomes a tentative hold.

When you're trying to coordinate a shooting day and juggling the schedules of several people, you may elect to place a hold on the model's time first. You can then proceed to find out if that time frame is agreeable to all the other parties involved. Keep in mind that once you've confirmed your model, you'll have to pay a cancellation fee should you decide to cancel or change the date. The model's time is valuable, and the model might have lost another client because you'd confirmed her time.

When you book a model through a modeling agency, it will ask you some very specific questions.

- Where and how are the photographs you'll take of the model going to be used?
- Who is to be billed? (If the client or ad agency has no credit history with the modeling agency, the agency will either run a credit check or ask that the model's fee be paid upon completion of the shoot.)
- Is there going to be a hair and makeup artist, or should the model be prepared to do his or her own?
- Should the model bring anything to the shoot? (Sometimes models will bring high-heeled shoes, pantyhose and/or stockings, sneakers, boots, G-strings, and any other garments requested by the photographer. Of course, this depends on whether the model has these at hand. If the model doesn't have access to the items you ask for, it is the agency's duty to call and inform you so that you have time to make other arrangements.)

Once all the details have been agreed upon, which may require you to make several telephone calls to the modeling agency, you can then book the model. At this point, you'll also confirm the time and place of the photo session, the model's rate, what he or she is expected to bring, and the use of the photograph. Today, many of the top agencies record the telephone booking, leaving little room for error. If a mistake occurs, the agency has proof as to where to place the blame.

When working with nudes, you must remember to tell models to wear loosely fitting garments on the way to the shoot so that no lines will mar their bodies. Tight underwear, socks, and pants can leave marks that may take at least an hour or more to disappear. It is also a good idea to check with the model or the agency to make certain that the model doesn't have any tan lines. If this is the case and your client still wants that particular model, you'll need a good makeup artist on the set to blend the model's skin tones. Otherwise, your client will have to pay high retouching costs. If you're working for yourself, you'll have to decide whether or not you mind the tan lines. Although professional models are usually aware of these problems and come prepared, it is better to repeat yourself than to assume that everyone knows exactly what to do.

Nonprofessional Models

Inexperienced models, on the other hand, often have a certain naiveté that can be very interesting to capture on film. Their awkwardness can translate into spontaneity and freshness in front of the camera, and these elements can work together to create something new and provocative. Nonprofessional models can be challenging to photograph since they have no experience to draw from. They might be comfortable immediately, or they may exhibit shyness or discomfort. You won't know until the session begins. It is imperative that you are very alert at these moments in order to shoot a potentially great photograph. I find it intriguing to work with inexperienced models, especially when doing my own shooting, because I am most creative during these sessions. I usually capture something new as I explore my psyche.

Whether you use inexperienced models for assignments or for yourself, you have much more flexibility negotiating their fee than you would that of experienced models. Nonprofessional models don't command the same high rates that professionals do because of their lack of experience in front of the camera and at the negotiating table. As mentioned earlier, you can find nude models who are just starting out and gaining experience through art schools, dance studios, and acting classes. You can hire these models at very low rates, or you can exchange photographs for their modeling time.

When you work with nonprofessionals, it is a good idea to suggest that they bring to the shoot a few personal items from around their homes that they feel might work well in the photographs. You'll be surprised at how the models' belongings might help to stimulate your imagination. For example, when Garry, a model I'd hired for a shoot, showed up with mirrored goggles and leather gloves, I visualized him on a staircase in a dark alley. And that is exactly how I photographed him.

One drawback to using inexperienced nude models is that they may change their minds about posing at the last minute and decide not to show up. I've been disappointed several times. Nonprofessionals often think twice about baring themselves in front of the camera. Since they have no prior experience, they don't know what to expect and their insecurities take over at a most inconvenient moment for you. You might have spent quite a bit of time, as well as money, setting up the shoot. At least when you work with models who have posed nude for art classes, they know what to expect and will undoubtedly show up for the shoot. However, as I've mentioned before, some of my most exciting sessions have involved models with no experience at all.

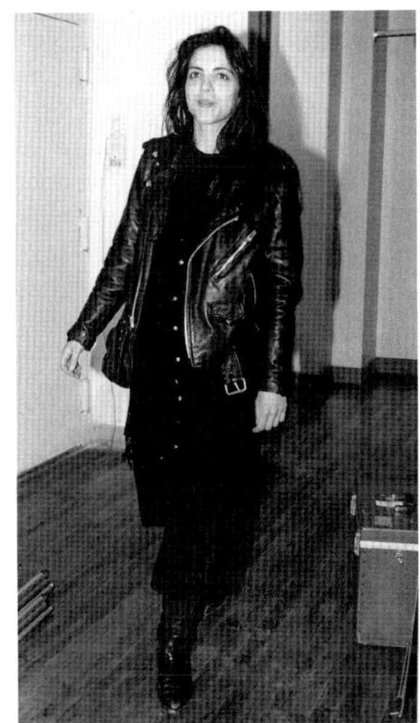

I chose Carmela for one shooting session because she has a cute, petite body. Although she'd never posed in the nude before, she'd studied dance for several years. When models have dance backgrounds, their movements are usually fluid, and they can handle a wide variety of poses. Carmela arrived at my studio with freshly washed hair and no makeup, and wore loose clothing, as I'd instructed her to. Any tight garment would have left marks on her body, and delayed the session.

HAIR AND MAKEUP ARTISTS

Hair and makeup trends change as quickly as clothing trends do, and a dated or inappropriate makeup style could ruin a shoot, especially if you're working for a client. So it is important for you to keep up with these changes from season to season. Of course, when you're shooting for yourself, you are at liberty to have your models look any way you want, however your imagination dictates.

Keep in mind that most models aren't adept at styling their own hair and applying their own makeup unless they're also involved with the fashion side of photography; here, they're exposed on a daily basis to the latest styles in hair and makeup. As a result, a hair and makeup artist is used during many sessions. Hair and makeup artistry is performed by one or sometimes two professionals. In addition to enhancing the model's appearance, hair and makeup artists build up his or her confidence. When models feel good about themselves, they perform more effectively, and the impact on the final images will be great.

Of course, you must be able to convey to hair and makeup artists precisely what type of feeling you're aiming for and how you want the model's hair and makeup to look. The makeup artist can soften and lighten dark circles under the model's eyes and emphasize facial structure. Makeup must be applied with great care so that it doesn't look too heavy or artificial. Good makeup artists are experts at evening out tan lines, as well as concealing scars, cuts, bruises, black-and-blue marks, and birthmarks. Depending on how large and how dark they are, tattoos can be a bit difficult to cover. Makeup artists often use baby oil on nude models. When applied evenly over the body, baby oil makes skin glisten. The dazzling effects in the final photographs are well worth the additional time applying the oil takes.

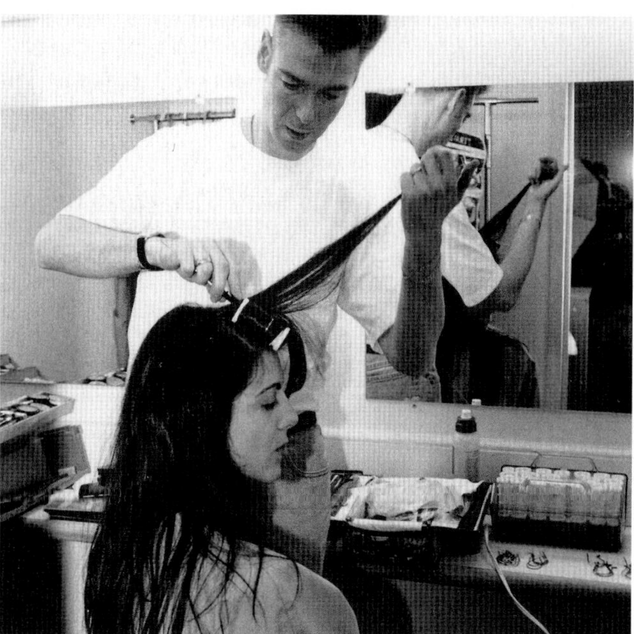

Hairdresser Timothy Downs added hot rollers to Carmela's straight hair to give it more volume and body with a soft curl. I hired Timothy because I knew that he would do exactly what I expected him to. It took Timothy about 10 minutes to set the model's hair and about another 15 minutes to brush it out and pull it up.

Although the reasons may not be immediately clear, you should consider hiring a makeup artist when you work with male subjects, too. A man can wear a light base of foundation to even out his skin tones. And for black-and-white photographs, a male model can get away with wearing more foundation than he can when posing for color shots. Many male models also use eye liner and a light coat of mascara in order to play up their eyes.

If you haven't worked with hair and makeup artists before, you should look through their portfolios to get a sense of each one's style and what each prefers to do. Some artists like to style the hair in a very structured fashion, and others prefer a soft and natural feel. This is also true of makeup applications. Some artists get carried away with showing off their talents and end up using too much makeup, while others have a light hand and need to be coaxed into using more.

When preparing for a shoot, keep in mind that makeup application can take anywhere from half an hour to an hour. The determining factors are the model and the look you are after. If major flaws have to be camouflaged, such as tan lines or bruises, the makeup artist will need a great deal of time in order to successfully blend the makeup.

My horror of tan lines stems from an underwear ad I was commissioned to shoot not too long ago. Two days before the session, I cast a male model who had all the qualities the client, the ad agency, and I were looking for. Most important, however, he had no tan lines. But when the model arrived at the studio the morning of the shoot, he had tan lines! I froze. When I asked him what had happened, he explained that since I was going to do a body shot, he thought he would look better with a slight tan. So he went to a tanning salon. Solving this major problem took up time that I hadn't anticipated losing. Although the makeup artist had some tanning gel in his kit, it was the wrong shade. I immediately sent someone out to find a darker color gel, but he returned empty-handed. At this point, the makeup artist had no choice but to make do with what was on hand and improvise.

Hairstyling also takes varying lengths of time. If a model's hair is long and curly and needs to be blown out straight, the process can take about half an hour. If hair has to be curled, the artist will wrap it in rollers before the makeup application begins.

Because of high costs and tight budgets, I find that more and more clients prefer to work with one artist who can do both hair and makeup. (Keep in mind that hair and makeup artists get top dollar for their creative abilities today. All costs related to the session should be discussed and agreed upon with the art director during meetings held before the shoot. No one likes unpleasant surprises when money is involved. Obviously, if you're shooting your own work, you are in control of your film and processing costs; you'll also be responsible for making arrangements with hair and makeup artists that will benefit everyone.)

My experiences have taught me, however, that an artist who does both hair and makeup is usually more skilled at one or the other, despite protests to the contrary. Depending on what you hope to achieve, you must consider whether the model's makeup or hairstyle is more critical in terms of the final outcome of the shoot and, even more important, the final photographs. This decision should help you choose the best hair and makeup artist(s) for the job.

If you're hard at work putting together your portfolio, you may not have access to hair and makeup artists. To remedy this situation, simply visit the makeup counters of the larger department stores near you. Most of the time, artists hired by cosmetic companies to apply makeup to potential customers (in an attempt to sell company products) are trying to build their own portfolios. Try approaching a few of these individuals to see if they would be interested in doing the makeup for your shoot in exchange for a photograph to add to their portfolio. If the artists you talk to do only makeup, contact a local beauty salon and ask if any of the hairstylists would be interested in a similar arrangement. I am sure that many of these artists will jump at the opportunity.

This is a good way both to establish contacts and to develop resources. In larger cities, hair and makeup artists are usually represented by agents you can call in

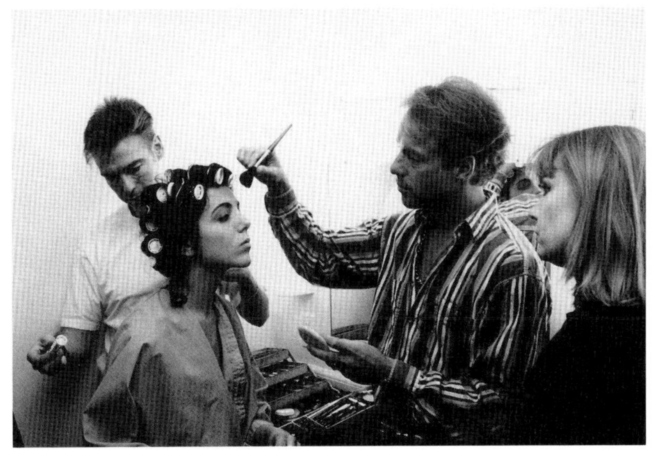

Here, makeup artist Peter Brown powdered Carmela's face to set her makeup. To save time, Timothy removed the rollers simultaneously, careful not to disturb Peter. I continually look in on the hair and makeup artists while they work. I might spot something that needs adjustment, such as lipstick applied a bit higher on one side of a model's upper lip. If a change must be made, this is the time to do it. I also keep a close watch on the time because some artists get carried away.

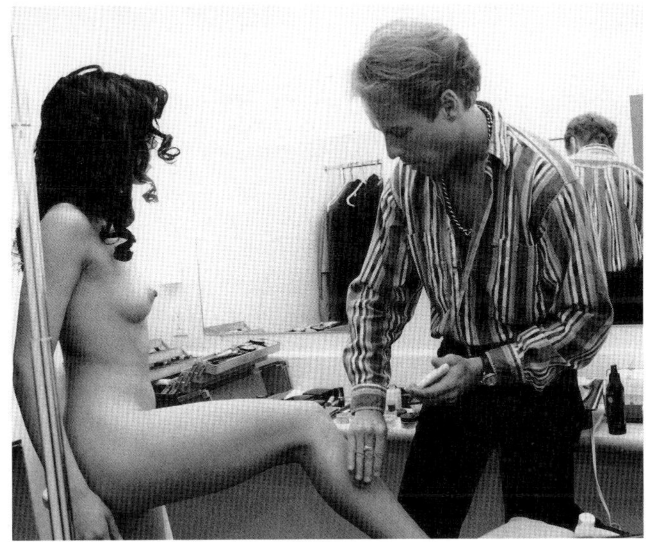

Most makeup applications, including those where a few spots on the body must be covered, take about one hour. Peter applied makeup to a bruise on Carmela's leg, blending it in so that the mark wouldn't show up in the final photograph.

order to view portfolios. You can also look for hair and makeup artists in industry books, such as *Professional Photo Source, New York Production Guide,* and *New York Theatrical Source Book.* These contain information on various aspects of the photography business, and most of them list hair and makeup specialists.

A word of caution: Don't be impressed by an artist's portfolio that contains only tearsheets from various jobs. Many of the photographs ultimately used in an ad or promotional piece have been retouched, which means that the makeup or hairstyle looks much better than it actually was.

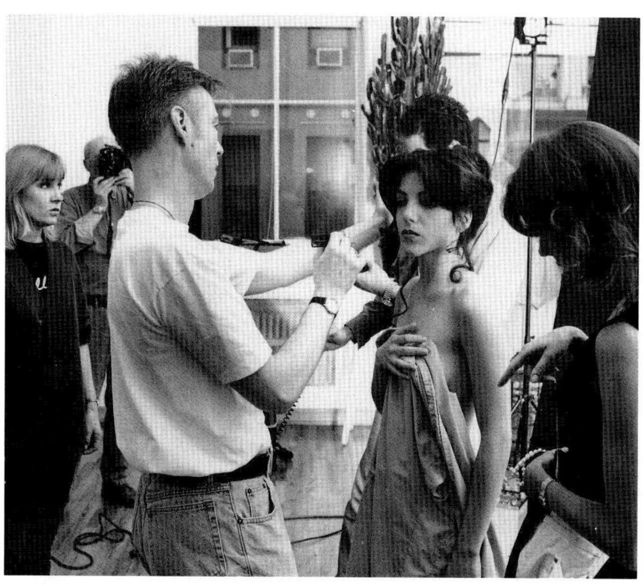

Five minutes before shooting began, everyone involved was making last-minute decisions and adjustments. While I discussed the exposure reading with one of my assistants, Timothy added the finishing touches to Carmela's hair.

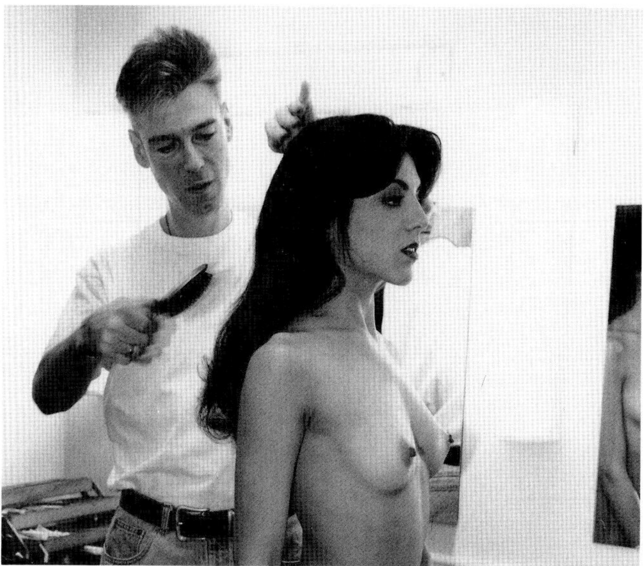

In between shots, Timothy brushed out Carmela's hair in the area sectioned off specifically for the model to change and have her hair and makeup done. For another series of shots, he gathered up the model's hair to give her a soft, romantic look.

STYLISTS

These individuals are hired to accessorize and pull together a certain look. Although most stylists are female, an increasing number of male stylists is entering the field. A talented stylist has a well-informed sense of style and is sensitive to the balance of the various forms and textures working together in an image. Stylists are responsible for providing props, garments, accessories, and, perhaps, a specific sofa or chair needed for a shoot. Photographing nudes often requires the use of props, and, on occasion, such articles of clothing as sheer scarves or elbow-length gloves. These items can help to establish the ambience you want to create or further emphasize the subject's nudity.

So it is critical for stylists to find exactly what you want. Obviously, they must know exactly where to obtain the necessary accoutrements. To this end, stylists maintain a variety of contacts who assist them in locating anything from the simplest to the most extravagant prop or accessory. Many experienced stylists, particularly those working in larger cities, spend years building their resources.

Depending on what is needed for the session, stylists can sometimes obtain clothing in exchange for a credit line if the garments will be used in an advertising layout. At other times, a rental fee is required, and you must consider this when drawing up the original budget for the shoot. For example, suppose that a layout calls for a lounge chair used against seamless paper. Before you make a final decision about what kind of lounge chair to rent, the stylist will provide you with some Polaroids of lounge chairs available for rental from a number of prop houses. It is the stylist's responsibility to show you a variety of chairs; rental fees can range significantly depending on the type of chair, its extravagance, and its rarity. You, in turn, show the Polaroids to the art director or client and together you choose the most appropriate chair.

During the shoot, stylists' primary concerns are details: How does the garment hang on the model when he or she moves? Are any pins used to tighten the garment on the model showing? Are the props working in relation to what is going on? Stylists should always stand behind you so that they're looking at the set from the same angle you are. Skilled stylists also know how to fit, fasten, and quickly pin an ill-fitting piece of lingerie, both on the set and off. Stylists must also see to it that nothing is abused during the shoot. They are responsible for returning all goods to their owners in their original condition.

Depending on the size of the assignment and what is involved, stylists need a day (and possibly more) to locate and gather the items or props necessary. This is called a preparation day, and stylists get paid for it, as well as for the day of the session. Even when only the simplest article of lingerie is required for a shoot, the art director will probably want to see an assortment of garments. The art director may tell you to shoot the same setup with two or three different garments in order to have a choice in the final photographs or to determine which garment will produce the most powerful image. The garment that works best will become obvious when all the other components are assembled on the set. In black-and-white pictures, the color of a garment is important in terms of contrast.

When a shoot calls for clothing, the stylist either sends the garments to the studio the night before the session or brings the items to the shoot before the scheduled starting time. Every situation is different. Several days prior to the actual session, you and the stylist discuss the details of the clothing delivery.

Once you've decided to hire a stylist, the next step is to choose one. This process is identical to that used for hiring a hair and makeup artist. In most large cities, stylists designate an agent to set up an appointment for you to look over their portfolios and meet with them in person. When examining a stylist's portfolio, ask the following questions.

- Exactly what did you provide for this shoot?
- Did you stay within budget?
- How much time did you need to prepare for this shoot?
- Did you get the garments for credit, or did you have to rent them?
- Who are some of your contacts?

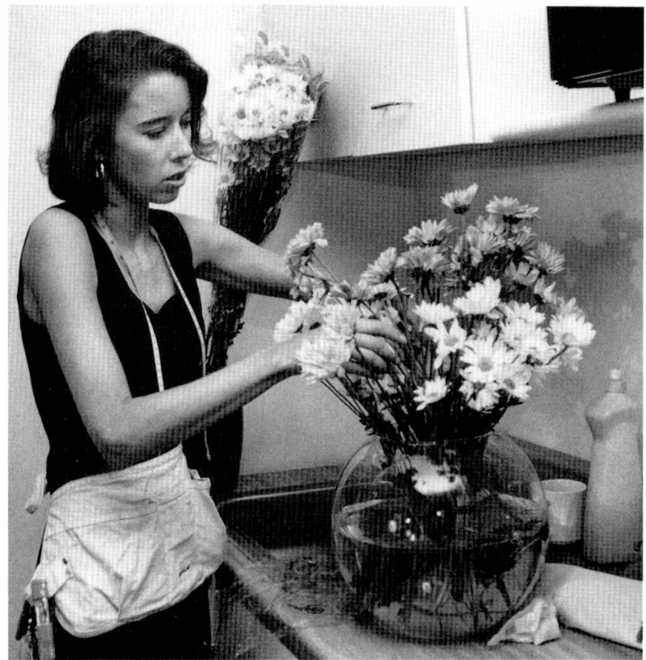

Stylists are responsible for gathering all the props and accessories required for a shoot. Here, stylist Jeanne Munson arranges the daisies in the round glass vase she and I'd chosen because of its bulbous shape. Jeanne's waist bag contains tools she might need during a shoot, such as scissors, tape, safety pins, straight pins, and a tape measure.

Don't be afraid to ask for a reference and to call another photographer for a recommendation.

During the selection process, you must also give some thought to the stylist's fee. Stylists' day rates don't include any expenses that they incurred while preparing for the shoot. Many times a stylist will ask for an advance of money to cover out-of-pocket expenses, such as necessary purchases and taxis to and from appointments. Besides payment for preparation and shoot days, the stylist will also ask to be paid for the time involved in returning rented and/or loaned items to their various sources, unless everything can be delivered by messenger the morning after the session. It is important for stylists to maintain an accurate accounting of their expenditures and to keep receipts.

If you decide not to use a stylist but want to have some props on hand, it will be up to you and/or your assistant to pull together the necessary items. The disadvantages are that it may be harder and will certainly be more time-consuming for you or your assistant to find props than it would for a stylist. In addition, the two of you may not possess as keen a sense of style as a stylist. Over the years, I've collected props that are interesting for a photo shoot: lacy gloves, pieces of beautiful fabric, antique lingerie, and ornate jewelry. As a photographer, it is a good idea for you to collect props that engage your eye and fuel your imagination; you can pick up these items inexpensively at flea markets or garage sales. This ability comes in handy when you're working with a small budget.

Moments before I was about to shoot another setup, Jeanne brought out a pair of black gloves and began discussing the impact they would have with Carmela. I then asked Carmela how she felt about wearing them, and she said that the gloves were fine with her. Sometimes a model just doesn't feel right about an accessory or prop and has a difficult time using it. This is something stylists and photographers must be sensitive to because it can have an adverse effect on the pictures.

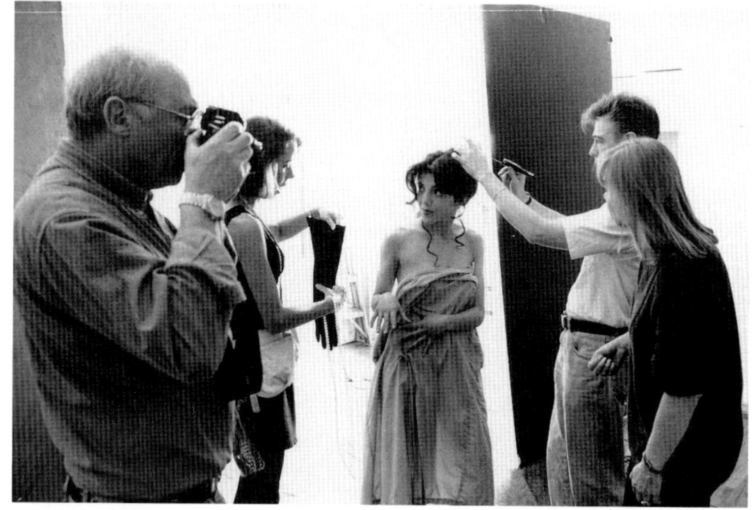

Carmela struck a different pose as I looked through my camera to see how it would read on film. I liked what I saw, so I told the model to hold that position. Just before I was about to begin shooting, Jeanne made a critical last-minute adjustment to the flower arrangement.

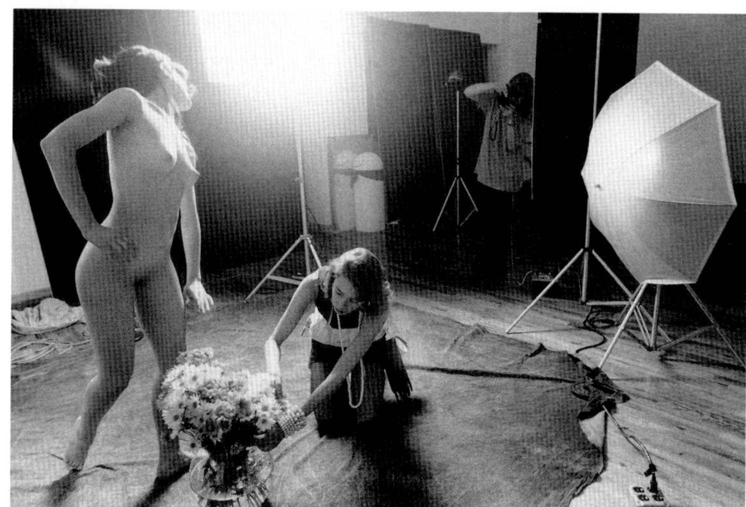

Ted Carrasco, an assistant, took a final meter reading near Carmela's face right before I started shooting. It is always a good idea to have an assistant double check the accuracy of the exposure. At the same time, Gerald Kornblau, a friend, popped the strobe because Ted hadn't attached the sync cord to the meter.

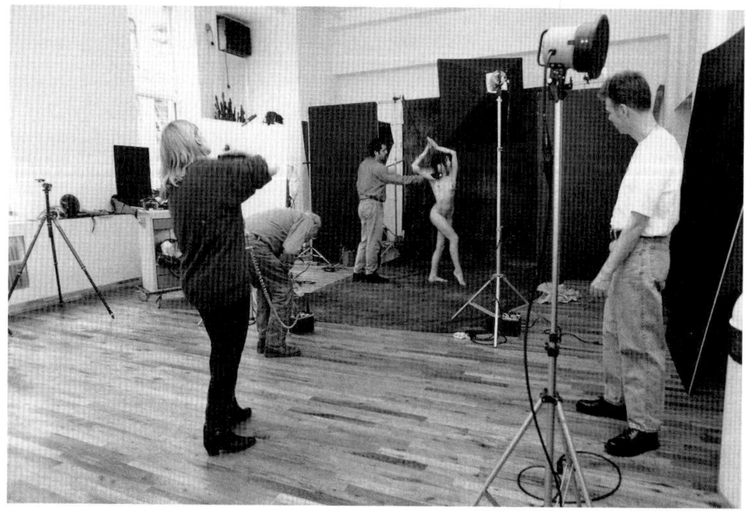

ASSISTANTS

Photographers hire one or more assistants in order to make their job easier. Good assistants understand the photographer's needs and perform their duties responsibly at all times. Once you are an established photographer, assistants will find you. They'll see your work in print as well as your advertisements in industry books. They'll send their resumés to you and call afterward to set up appointments for interviews. When meeting candidates, try to get a good feel for who they are. If a potential assistant has worked professionally with other photographers, you should ask for the names of people you can contact for recommendations.

When you hire assistants, tell them what you expect from them. Advise them that assisting isn't a nine-to-five job. You should also inform them that arriving on time is a must and that a photo shoot might not end at the time originally designated. The nature of the business is such that a host of variables comes into play and throws schedules off. Your assistants must be able to plan their day accordingly.

You should have more than a few assistants you can call on a regular basis. I have at least five, all of whom I've worked with before and feel comfortable hiring for a job. When trying out someone new, I usually like to ask the individual to assist on a small test that I'm doing for my own work. For jobs, I go with an assistant I've worked with before so that he or she already has a sense of who I am as a photographer and how I like to work. Working with a new assistant can be disconcerting. You have enough to worry about during a photo shoot for a client without having to train a new assistant and explain the proper way to do things.

When I'm doing a rush shoot, I make several telephone calls to assistants I prefer to work with. I find that most assistants will call you back as soon as they possibly can, even if they aren't available for that particular day. This is part of their professionalism. If they aren't available, you can then call other assistants on your list. Most freelance assistants are in continual contact with their answering machines and will return your call within a few hours.

Once you hire assistants, it is their responsibility to follow your instructions regarding the lighting set up, as well as to check all equipment before the shoot to make sure that everything is clean and in working order. During the shoot, assistants must keep accurate records of each roll of film you shoot, including numbering each one. They must also note any lighting changes, and watch carefully to see that all strobe lights are working continuously. They must be the photographer's extra pair of eyes. If something isn't functioning properly, they must immediately advise the photographer of the problem.

Many assistants have very strong ideas about how they would conduct the shoot. If they disagree with or have something else to say to the photographer, they should discreetly call the photographer aside and make their suggestions. Assistants can even whisper in the photographer's ear. But whichever way they make their recommendations, their method should be appropriate to the circumstances.

An assistant's behavior on the set should be low-key and professional. Most photographers welcome suggestions, but they must be delivered at the proper time and place. Assistants shouldn't voice their opinions out loud in front of all parties on the set. This sort of unprofessional behavior, which I've encountered on several occasions, is a sad ploy to attempt to convince the client that the assistant, not the photographer, is controlling the shoot. (Needless to say, I've never worked with those assistants again.)

Finally, assistants must also adhere to a code of ethics. They shouldn't socialize with clients or attempt to take a model's telephone number for their personal use. And when the session is over, I expect assistants to put away all my equipment in a neat and orderly manner. Assistants are on the set to make my life easier, not to make more work for me.

DESIGNING A STUDIO SET

How big must your studio be? Studio size doesn't matter to me; it is what I do with it that counts. I can say this with conviction because I've been working out of my apartment for 14 years. I have a very limited shooting area, but I make do and I've shot some pretty outrageous photographs there. I believe that limitations sometimes jog your unconscious mind into taking over and being more creative than you expected. However, when I need much more space for a shoot than the work area in my apartment affords, I rent a large studio for half a day, for an entire day, or for whatever length of time I need it. Short-term studio rentals are becoming commonplace because the high monthly rental charges of large studios can be prohibitive.

Some of the top photographers' most successful images were made in the controlled environment of a studio. This is partly the result of the many advantages working in the studio provides. You have more control over the number of people on a set than you have at a location. Furthermore, in the studio you and your model can be alone because you can ask everyone else to remain off the set. (Of course, if you're shooting a job, the art director will insist on seeing the Polaroids in between shots.) And if your subject has never been photographed in the nude before, the model most likely will prefer that no one else be on the set during the shoot. Sometimes, however, an assistant is allowed on the set because the model knows that an assistant functions as the photographer's right hand.

There are other benefits associated with working in the studio. Weather isn't a factor, so you can preplan and effectively control all aspects of the shoot, particularly the light. You know whether or not natural light comes through your windows and, if so, at what time of day. You can take the time to test the light, and you can readily make any necessary adjustments and manipulate lighting effects since you're creating the lighting in surroundings that you are familiar with. You know both your equipment and the capabilities of your electrical system.

When designing a studio set, you need to think about the background. If you decide to use seamless paper for your background, you must choose a color. Of course, in black and white, the tonal qualities of the color you select will be reproduced in black and white and shades of gray. If you want to provide a contrast to your nude subject, I suggest using either a very dark or very light background. You can, however, use a neutral background. And once you've made your decision, you can alter the tone of the background by adjusting the amount of light that actually hits it. You can lighten a dark background by increasing the amount of light that shines on it so that it is more brightly illuminated than the foreground. Conversely, you can darken the background by decreasing the amount of light hitting it.

You have other background options, too. Many companies sell inexpensive canvas backgrounds, which can be worthwhile investments. You can also consider the many and varied backgrounds that artists paint and rent out to photographers for assignments. These artists usually advertise in photographic publications, so you shouldn't have any difficulty finding them. Some backgrounds may depict wonderful scenes, while others are composed of mottled tonal qualities, a textural elegance that I prefer for my own work. Check the backdrop's measurements before ordering, especially if you anticipate shooting full-length images. Many backgrounds don't sweep in front, which means that they aren't long enough to cover the floor in the foreground. Shorter backdrops are ordinarily used for closeup or three-quarter-length shots.

Rental fees for painted backgrounds range from $250 to $500 for a day, depending on how extravagant the background is and how big it is. Be aware that you are also responsible for the trucking costs to and from the studio. A word of caution: You must be very careful when rolling up these backgrounds before returning them. Anything sharp that may have fallen on a background could end up tearing the canvas.

The next step requires you to envision your model on the set, plan the concept, and make it materialize. Do you want your subject to be all alone, stark naked against the background, or do you want to use your imagination and go through the process of introducing props and/or creating a set? Both approaches are valid. Because working in the studio with a specific background increases your control over the shoot, as well as over the final images, the use of abstract props can add another dimension to your work. For example, while photographing a model against a white seamless background, I decided to have her work with the "S" curve of a 3-foot-high hook. The model, inspired by the hook's form and shape, moved in new ways, and the photograph immediately took on another dimension.

A set can be extravagant, but it can also consist of a simple background with a single prop. For example, the set that I used for the step-by-step section shown on pages 110–125 consisted of a gray canvas background, a round glass vase filled with flowers, daisies that were taped to and a piece of fabric that was fan-blown against the model's body, a pair of black gloves, and some white pearls. I decided on a canvas background instead of seamless paper because bare feet get sweaty and leave footprints on the seamless. As such, I would have had to change the seamless occasionally. Obviously, I have less to worry about when working with a canvas background than with seamless.

While planning this shoot, I decided together with the stylist that I would keep the set uncluttered since I was primarily interested in capturing the body in motion. The use of too many props or a very complicated background, such as a couch or a bedroom scene, respectively, might have interfered with my vision. In keeping with this, the stylist suggested just enough props to add an interesting touch and, at the same time, to keep the focus on the model in motion. The stylist even chose a very simple vase so that nothing would detract from the model.

Unlike this basic set, designs based on fantasy can be quite elaborate. Some photographers like to shoot only what their fantasies suggest to them. And if you're executing a layout for an art director, it is your job to add spark and vitality to the session and to create a wonderful three-dimensional representation of a working concept shown in two dimensions. Although art directors provide fairly detailed layouts, they may ask photographers to suggest ways to enhance the sketches. Many photographers, then, have the opportunity to contribute their original ideas and substantial talent to new campaigns. In some cases, photographers actually help establish the image for the product that the client is advertising.

The remainder of the studio design is fairly routine from shoot to shoot. You need to provide a workstation or some other place where the hair and makeup artist can work. Appropriate makeup lights are used in the studio; this arrangement differs from on-location shooting, where makeup artists sometimes have to do the best they can in existing light.

In addition to the model's changing area, you must designate a very specific area within the shooting space as the model's domain. When I'm shooting, the subject will move only within the borders of this very small, specified area. If the model moves too far in front of or behind this space, my assistant will advise me to check the light reading. When a model moves, I must reevaluate the light levels and make any necessary adjustments to the original readings. If I don't, the resulting images might not be what I expected.

Whether you choose a stark or complicated studio set design, keep in mind that a relaxed atmosphere in any studio brings about the best of all possible outcomes. The type of music that you play in the background can contribute to the mood in the studio. If you want your model to really move, choose upbeat rock music. If you want the model to move slowly, put on a Brahms, Chopin, or Ravel piece; New Age instrumental music has the same effect. Clearly, this is something to think about when you start planning a shoot.

PREPLANNING THE SHOOT

As a photographer working on an assignment, you are responsible for planning, implementing, and directing the shoot. Effectively communicating your ideas about what you would like to do during a particular photo session and achieve through it is essential if you expect to have the complete cooperation of everyone involved. Perhaps the most important communication takes place between you and your subjects. You must guide the models by explaining what you're trying to capture on film and what they should do to help you achieve success. If you don't discuss anything with your subjects, they'll probably ask you what you want them to do. Therefore, it is a good idea for you to have some direction in mind before you begin and to converse openly with your subjects as you go along. I find that such frank exchanges pay off in great shots.

The rhythm of the session and the impact of the images you shoot are based entirely on your ability to inspire the subject to evince emotion, movement, and mood. The success of a photograph depends in part on the communication between you and your model and on your determination of the precise moment that should be recorded on film. If you decide to work with professional nude models, you'll find that they have a sense of where to start and how to move. Your interpretation of your subjects' movements must be strong and emotionally charged. Remember, professional models pose for dozens of other photographers, and certain positions and movements are part of their repertoire. The unique direction that you give to a model can produce something new and vivacious, something totally unexpected. Keep in mind that you'll realize this only when you see your contact sheets.

If you're using hair and makeup artists you've never worked with before, you should meet with them in advance. If you already know them well, you should at least speak to them over the telephone. During this preliminary conversation, inform them of what you expect from them and what type of makeup and hairstyle you visualize. You might then ask for their opinions regarding what they feel will work best with what you hope to achieve. If you plan to photograph your model with several hairstyles, you can ask the hairdresser to bring along either a wig or a couple of hairpieces.

At this point, you must get some idea of how much time the hair and makeup artists will need to create the look you want so that you can determine how many hours to book them, the model, and the studio. Remember, the hourly rate for nude models can be quite high. Once you have an approximate idea of how long the shoot will take, you must inform everyone involved of the session's schedule. It is essential to let the makeup artist know how much time you're allowing for the makeup application, as well as the time you expect to start shooting.

Consider this typical shooting schedule. If the shoot is planned to begin at 9:00 A.M., you'll probably want your assistant to arrive at 7:30 A.M. or 8:00 A.M., depending on what the actual shoot consists of and how much setup time is necessary. If you're shooting a job, I suggest arranging with your assistant to pick up breakfast for the crew; coffee, juice, and rolls or muffins will do. It is a nice gesture to welcome the art director, client, model, and other team members with a cup of hot coffee. If the scheduled start time is 9:00 A.M., the stylist should arrive earlier, perhaps at 8:15 A.M. or 8:30 A.M., in order to have enough time to check the props and/or garments that are going to be shown to the art director. Needless to say, everybody should arrive at their appointed time. Otherwise, one delay will inevitably lead to another.

Shooting on Location

Where should you photograph nude subjects? Should you shoot at the beach, by a waterfall, in the countryside, in a barn or a bedroom, or against a background of seamless paper? Very often, your subject determines your background choice. If, however, you're working on a job, these questions can be answered accurately only by you or your client.

If you decide to shoot somewhere other than at your studio, the next step is to confirm the amount of time you'll need to rent the designated space, such as a full or a half day. You must also find out what the rental fee is.

The cost of a location shoot can be substantial. If you're restricted by a fixed budget, an alternative to going to a location to shoot is bringing the location to you by renting a painted background, as discussed earlier. However, if you're shooting an assignment, the client's layout calls for a particular type of location, and the budget allows for on-location shooting, you need to find ideal settings. The easiest way to go about discovering locations, particularly in larger cities, is to use a location finder. This is an individual or agency that does exactly what the job title suggests by submitting to you portfolios of pictures of locations that are available for a rental fee.

When you are ready to consider potential settings, contact a few location finders and advise them of what you're looking for. They'll pull together a port-

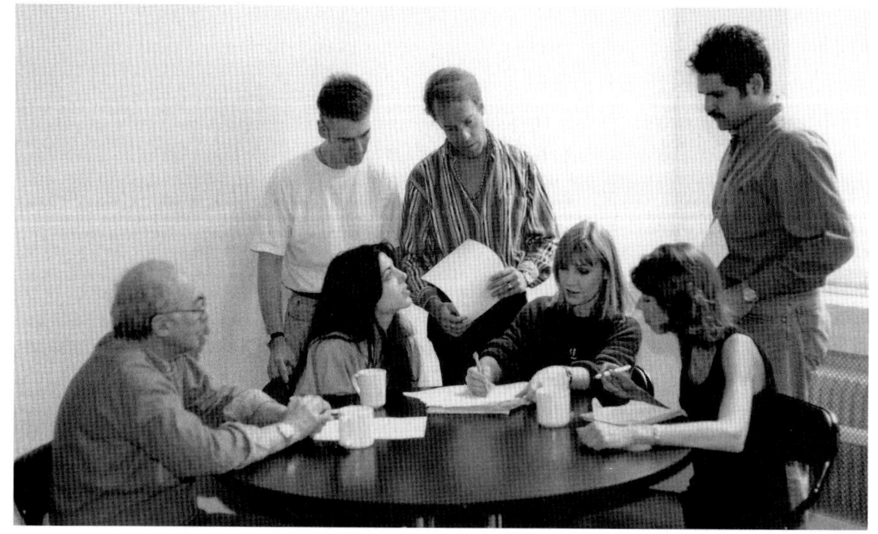

As soon as everyone has arrived at the studio, I go over the shooting plan. It is important for everyone involved to be given the same directions, and I find that a few minutes set aside before the actual shooting begins saves time and energy later. If all the team members are familiar with the day's schedule, including changes, they'll go about their duties more efficiently.

folio of various locations, such as residences, office buildings, or even specific rooms, depending on what the shoot calls for. If any of the locations interest you, you can either book the location right away or make an appointment to take a closer look at it. The location finder must determine whether the location is available for that particular day and, if you want to view it in advance, will make arrangements to have someone meet you there.

Once you've chosen a location and confirmed both the length of and the cost of the rental, you must submit a certificate of insurance to the location finder, who, in turn, assures the location's owners that the certificate exists. Unless otherwise arranged, the responsibility for getting insurance belongs to the client or advertising agency—that is, the party you're shooting the job for. This insurance assures the location's owner that should anything be damaged during the shoot, such as furniture or carpeting, your insurance will cover the owner's losses. If this insurance is inadequate, you must obtain a floater policy from your insurance company; this limited insurance covers a specific location on a specific date at a specific rate.

Renting a location for a shoot doesn't give you any special privileges. Unless you're renting out an entire house, you'll probably be confined to the area within the location that you agreed on with the owners. You should tell the owners specifically where you'll be shooting, how many people will be on the shoot, and how much time will be needed. Remember, everyone involved with the actual shoot must act responsibly or problems will undoubtedly follow.

Recently, I was assigned to do a shoot in the bathroom of a brownstone for the packaging of a new shower hose. The model would be nude from the lower back up and seated on a tub chair in the bathtub, spraying herself with water from the shower hose. I was told to photograph the subject sporting several different hairstyles, as well as with a towel wrapped around her head.

Having been in the planning stages for months, the job came about suddenly. Out of the blue, the advertising agency called to say that the shoot had to take place the very next day or that the agency would lose the client. I immediately called location finders and requested that portfolios of pictures depicting possible sites be sent to the advertising agency. Working under extreme pressure, I hired a stylist to collect the items needed for the shoot at once, quickly decided on a model, and contacted the modeling agency to book her.

Several portfolios arrived at the agency later in the day, and at about 4:30 P.M., the agency made a decision. I then called the location finder to confirm the location and time of the shoot. Before the final details were wrapped up, the location finder called the client to verify that the location was fine for the following morning. I asked for permission from the location owners to see the brownstone at about 6:30 P.M. that evening. I wanted to have an idea of what I was getting into. Only the advertising-agency representatives had seen the portfolio. At the brownstone, I was given a choice of two bathrooms. I selected the one that had been featured in the portfolio.

The next morning, the art director, my crew, and I all arrived at the location at the same time. We began to set up the shoot. Of course, when you're working near water, you must be extra careful. Anything can happen! If water were to come into contact with live electrical equipment or outlets, you could end up with a major disaster. Because the model was hosing herself with water, the potential for danger was great. Needless to say, everyone on the set exercised extreme caution. All of a sudden as the session proceeded, there was a loud bang. The model jumped out of the tub; I jumped up in horror, not knowing what had happened; and everyone else looked stunned. For a moment, I thought that water had hit the electrical contact on the powerpacks. Fortunately, the problem was only a short in one of the plugs connected to a socket and ended up being more noise than anything else. That scare and the resulting trauma put everyone on the alert for any future disasters.

Although the photographs from this shoot turned out well, I must caution you to beware of what might, and often does, happen on a shoot. If the electrical outlets aren't powerful enough, you might continually blow circuits. This will not only interrupt your rhythm but also cause you to lose precious time. And if you're paying a model a high hourly rate, lost time is definitely something to be concerned about.

Try to see the designated location if at all possible before you go on assignment. If this can't be arranged, find out as much as you can about your shooting capabilities there. Know what the electrical-power situation is like if you're planning to use strobes. It is a good idea to split the cords up so that you aren't

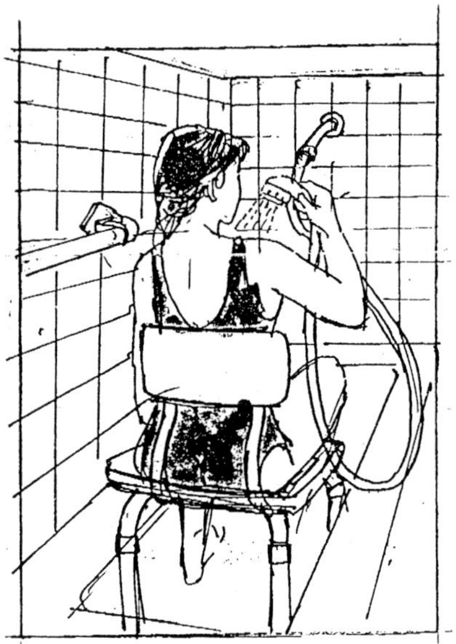

The art director gave me a layout sketch for this job (above). While shooting, I tried variations of the model holding the hose and tilting her head. As I guided her, the art director made sure that I got what he needed. The final image differed from the sketch in that the model had a towel wrapped around her head and wore only the bottom of a bathing suit (right). The model was booked through a modeling agency and the bathroom found by a location finder during the planning stages of the shoot.

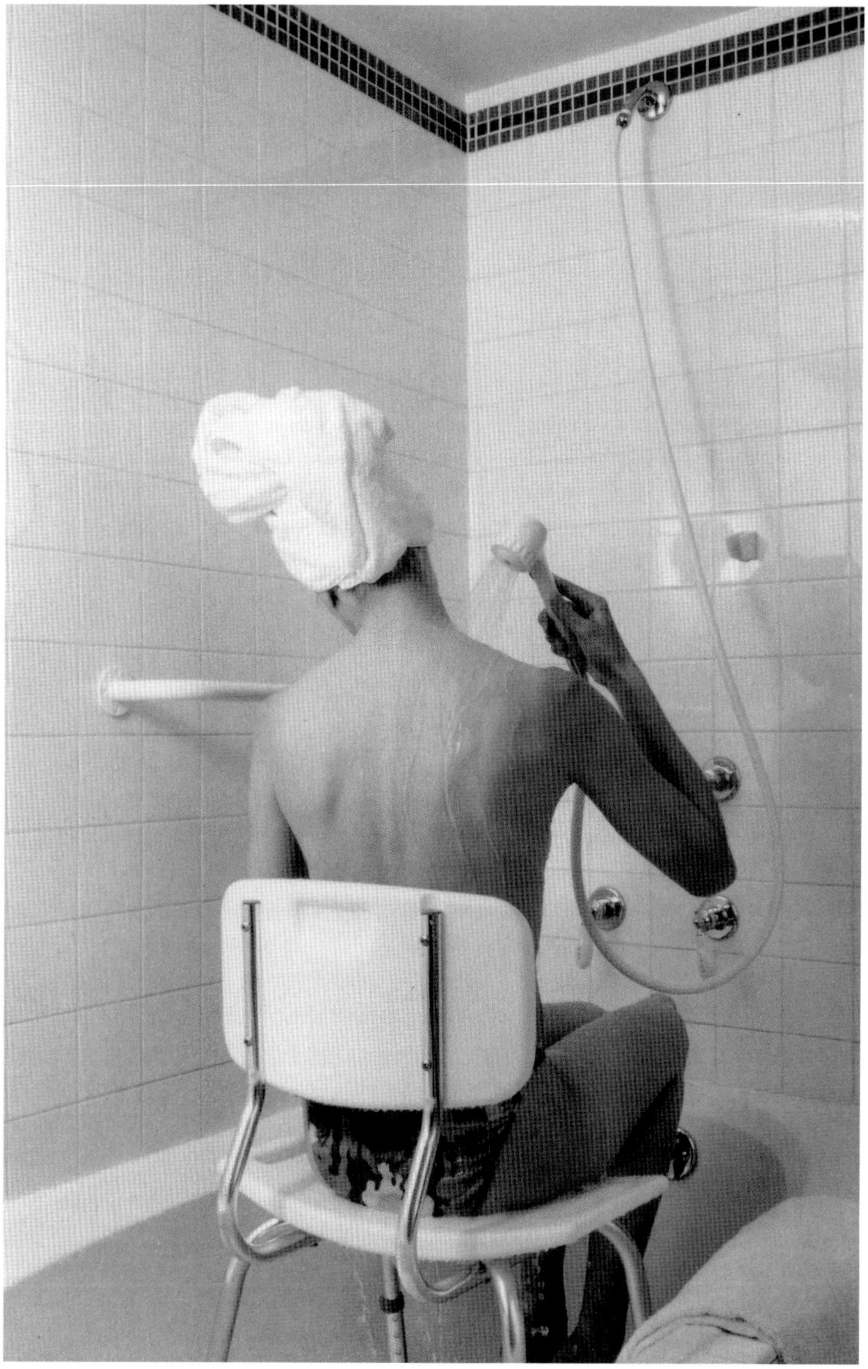

drawing power from one single circuit. Otherwise, circuit breakers will blow. Backup equipment is a must, especially on a location shoot. I had a supplemental powerpack with me while shooting in the brownstone bathroom, but I immediately called a rental place to deliver another powerpack in case something else went wrong. By doing this, I wouldn't lose any time if another problem were to have occurred.

Based on my experiences, some crisis will inevitably arise during a shoot. It can be major, such as mechanical failure, or relatively minor, such as the late delivery of accessories. If you're always prepared for emergencies, you'll never be caught off guard if something goes seriously wrong. I can't stress this enough.

If you plan to use available light as your primary light source while shooting in an interior location, check to see what time of day the light filters through the windows. You should bring along several reflectors or a strobe to provide fill light just in case. You may want them to reflect the light or bounce the light back onto the model or, if the day of the shoot turns out to be hazy, you might need more overall light. I like to be prepared for any type of lighting condition. Sometimes using artificial light sources may be necessary in order to enhance the natural light or to create special effects. This is when your imagination comes into play. Whenever you use supplemental light, though, you must make sure that it doesn't overpower your main light source.

On-location shooting can be challenging in other ways as well. My own experiences have shown me that there is bound to be a significant difference between the preconceived idea photographers might have about a location and what they actually record on film. When you arrive at a site, you may be so excited by the ambience that you ultimately decide to capture this on film. You may even wish to distort the mood to achieve dramatic results. If you're working on an assignment, you might have to alter your thinking in order to shoot exactly what your client is looking for. In this situation, you might suggest to the client that you shoot a roll of film your way at the end of the session, time permitting of course. I've found that clients very often prefer the results of my approach more than their own.

Shooting on location can also be fun for every member of the team. A new environment can stimulate you and your subject because it offers fresh opportunities and adds to the excitement and creative energy of the session. For example, a bedroom setting is ideal for photographing a nude model. It lends itself to intimate shots that readily convey a variety of moods. A bedroom decorated with white lace and bursting with daylight can imbue your final photograph with a soft, dreamlike quality. A dark bedroom, on the other hand, can enhance the drama and mystery in an image, by evoking a sense of what is going on or, perhaps, what is about to happen.

While shooting on location outdoors can be fun and exciting, too, keep in mind that you have less control over many factors, such as the weather and privacy. You'll have to look for a secluded beach or forest because, I guarantee, your model won't want to disrobe in front of an audience of strangers. A distinct advantage to outdoor location shooting is that you have many sites to choose from. Furthermore, if you find these places on your own and they're secluded, you can save yourself money. You must, however, provide transportation to the location and back for your model and crew.

If you decide to use a beach or a swimming pool for a shoot, you must work extra carefully so that neither sand nor water ends up in your camera. Both can cause a great deal of costly damage. When working near sand, I protect my cameras by placing them in plastic bags with holes cut out for the lens. This way, the main parts of the camera are covered when a strong wind comes by. And as mentioned earlier, you must be particularly cautious when using electrical power near water. Just one drop of water can produce an explosion.

Experiment. Photograph nude models on location, at both interior and exterior sites, as well as in the studio, in order to determine which environment you're drawn to. Perhaps, like me, you'll enjoy working in both. I've discovered that on-location photography offers many new challenges. It also adds another dimension to my work, suggesting a specific moment and a place like no other.

THE NUDE, STEP BY STEP

The day of an actual shoot is the culmination of all your planning and preparatory work. It is now time for you to reveal a part of who you are, as well as for your assistants to combine efforts and act like a team. How you see and what you have to say are about to be documented on film. Keep in mind that anything can happen during a shoot, even when you think you've prepared fully and taken every precaution. Some problem inevitably arises during most shoots. Each shooting session is different and has its own rhythm. The pressure can be overwhelming, especially when you're working on an assignment. Some people aren't able to cope with the stress and high-pressured situations. As a professional you must be flexible enough to handle all types of problems and emergencies without losing your cool for even a moment.

One of the most important aspects of a nude photo session is coordinating a team effort. As the photographer, this is your responsibility. You must also keep in mind that team spirit contributes significantly to the success of your final photographs. Your ability to communicate effectively has a tremendous impact on the way your team members come together in support of your efforts. You must be capable of getting the most from all members concerned. After all, you are the director of the shoot and the leader of the team, so you must have absolute control over the session.

When your hair and makeup artists arrive, walk them over to the area set aside for them. When the stylist arrives, she may be carrying bags containing clothes and accessories needed for the shoot, or she may need you to direct her to the packages already delivered by messenger. You must also show the stylist her designated work area where she can spread out the items she is responsible for in full view of the art director and client. A sturdy clothing rack should be available, as well as a table on which the stylist can arrange jewelry, accessories, and small props.

As soon as everyone involved with the shoot has arrived (on time), eaten the breakfast you've supplied as a courtesy, and taken his or her position, either go over any last-minute details with the art director or, if you're working with only an assistant, discuss what you intend to shoot and any lighting changes that might take place. Advise your assistant to maintain careful records of each roll of film. After the subject is ready on the set and you've taken a few Polaroids to judge more clearly whether you need to make any last-minute adjustments, let your creative drive take over.

During the shoot, your assistant should be fully aware of what you expect and should proceed with one objective in mind: making your job easier. The

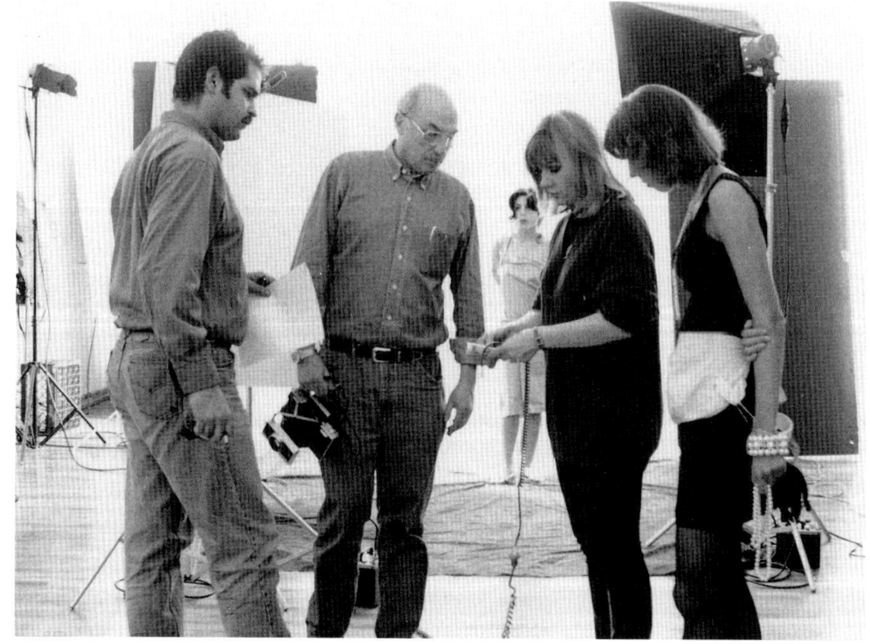

During this all-day shoot, I planned to photograph two female models in various poses and with a number of lighting setups. After taking a test Polaroid of Carmela, the first model, and studying the shot, I discussed necessary changes and adjustments with Ted Carrasco, my assistant; and Gerald Kornblau, my friend; and Jeanne Munson, the stylist. Carmela covered herself and waited patiently during this brief delay. A successful picture is truly a team effort.

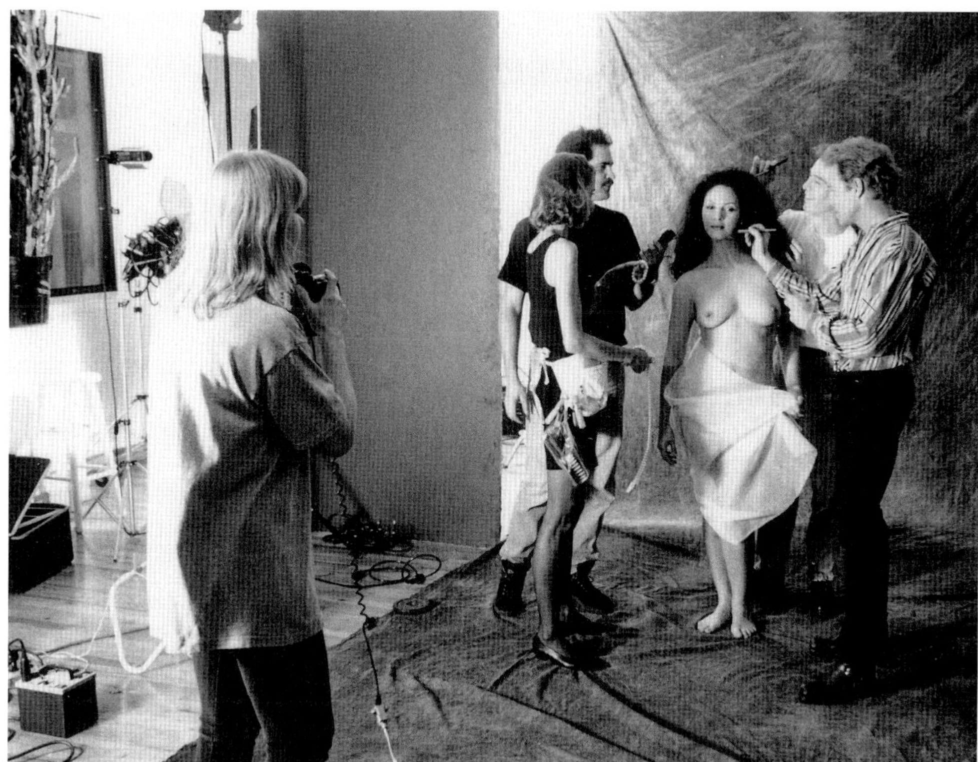

Here, Regina Hawkins, the second model, photographed later that day, waited on the set. Every member of the team was busy: I was going over the shot in my head; stylist Jeanne Munson, hairdresser Timothy Downs, and makeup artist Peter Brown were doing some last-minute touch ups; and Ted Carrasco, one of my assistants, was taking a final exposure reading. Throughout the session, Peter paid careful attention to Regina's mouth; he wanted to make sure that the billowing fabric didn't accidentally smear her lipstick.

hair and makeup artists and the stylist should stand behind you and concentrate on the set. You wouldn't want a stylist standing 5 feet to your left telling you that she can see a pin holding a garment in place when you can't see it from the camera's angle. If a model's makeup is smudged, however, the makeup artist should alert you to stop the session in order to correct the problem. Similarly, if a model's hair needs to be completely restyled or is falling in his or her face, the hairdresser should interrupt you. Your team should function as one unit with everyone working toward the same goal: the best possible photograph.

As you shoot, you have a sense of how all the components of the shoot are coming together. You somehow know when you've captured exactly what you're looking for on film. I simply allow the situation to develop. What I record depends on the energy of the people involved and their environment. I continually explore my psyche, as well as my perceptions as a photographer and a person. My curiosity might take me farther than I expected to go, or I might change direction suddenly and explore avenues that I didn't even consider earlier.

Your rapport with your subject largely determines what you capture on film. That decisive moment, which is the split second you click the shutter, distinguishes your work from that of other photographers. Occasionally, the perfect chemistry between the team members at one particular moment in time develops purely by accident. When you function on a high energy level, the model and other team members pick up on your enthusiasm and contribute accordingly. And when this happens, you have the ideal opportunity to capture something spectacular. Move around and shoot from a different camera position. Change your angle. You might just see something even more fabulous from another perspective. Take chances. Exceed your self-imposed limits.

The images that you record will be part of your growing process as a photographer. I am instinctual: When I see something I like, I get very excited and go for it. By this I mean that I shoot, shoot, shoot, and direct, direct, direct. I feel the energy and take off. Obviously, if you are on location shooting a specific job, you must be concerned with executing the layout and following the art director's guidelines. I suggest that you first execute the layout the way it is presented to you and then, if time permits, shoot at least one roll (if not several more rolls) of your interpretations. You may eventually find that the other team members prefer your own renditions over the original layout.

LIGHTING THE NUDE

Light is the main element in any photograph. Light establishes mood and provides the essential ingredient for the making of photographs. Light casts shadows and creates textures and forms. It can also add contrast or define the lines of the human body. How you work with light depends on how you see. You can use it, for example, to produce a mysterious or daring effect, or to create an ambience of seduction or playfulness. You can leave the interpretation of your photograph to the viewers, or you can tell all. You can be a story writer, an image maker, or a reporter documenting a specific time and place. The impact of the final image comes from you and your unlimited imagination.

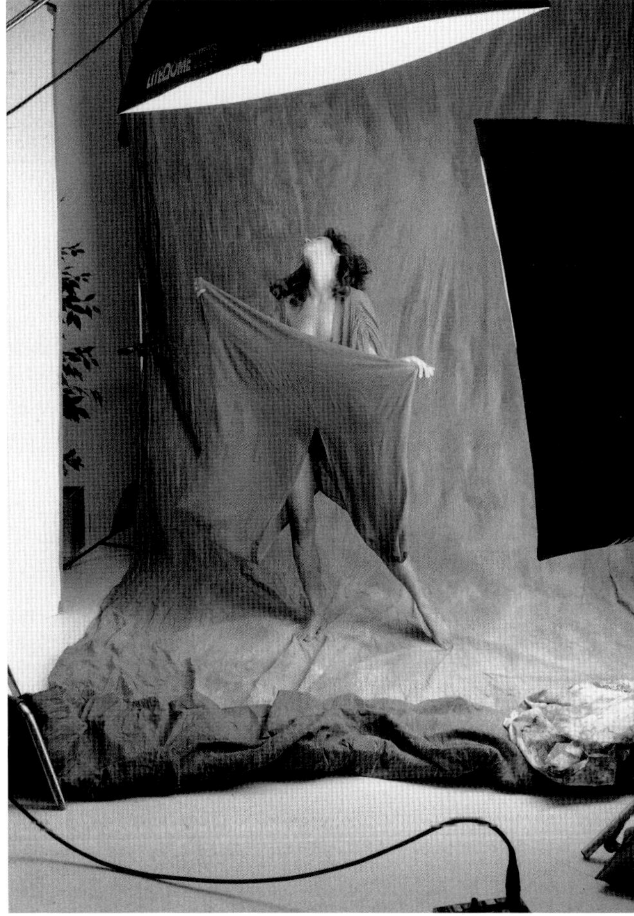

For this picture of professional model Holly Moyes, I decided on diffused illumination in order to achieve a soft look. I shot this nearly nude model's dramatic poses and fluid movements against a canvas backdrop. The main light source was an overhead Litedome XTC softbox; another softbox off to my right provided fill. The lighting setup also included a large white reflector to my left.

You can illuminate your subjects in one of three ways: with available or natural light, with artificial light (strobe or tungsten), or with a combination of available and artificial light. Some photographers, such as David Hamilton and Lucien Clergue, prefer to work with only available light. Others opt for the studio, where they can be in total control of the lighting. Still other photographers enjoy location work. Eventually, you'll gather enough experience with the various lighting options available to find what is right for you.

Light varies from the extreme of direct light that produces a harsh effect with strong shadows, to indirect light that is diffused before it reaches the subject. Diffused light can bounce off something, such as a ceiling or wall. This type of light can also pass through something, including a fabric, such as silk; a piece of translucent plastic placed in front of the light source; a softbox; or an umbrella. Light that is diffused by passing through a translucent white umbrella is softer than light that is reflected or bounced into one.

Another type of light, fill light, softens the shadow areas produced by the main light source. Whether it takes the form of strobe or reflected available light, direct or diffused fill light should always be less powerful than the main light. The intensity of this additional light depends on how much fill you're seeking. You can use a reflector to bounce the light into shadows or into any area that needs more illumination in order to show detail. Fill flash is an artificial but very convenient way to fill, for example, harsh shadows created by bright sunlight. Like fill light, fill flash helps to soften shadows as well as to improve the rendering of details, and should never be stronger than the primary source of light.

Backlight is a source of illumination behind your subject. When this is the main source of light and no frontlight is used, your subject will be silhouetted in the final image. You can also have your backlights read as your main light and use a slight fill on your subject to introduce detail. Backlight enables you to emphasize and create highlights on certain parts of the subject; however, this highlight must read higher than the frontlight.

Of course, the quality of available light varies according to the time of day and the season. In addition, the number and type of clouds in the sky affect the softness or harshness of the illumination, and the sun's intensity and the resulting glare may continue to change with the passing clouds. This, too, will influence your exposures. Shooting with artificial light eliminates the problems associated with unpredictable lighting conditions. By using tungsten or strobe illumination to control the quality of light in your images, you aren't bound by the sun or the time of day or year. You can create your own shadows and highlights when you work with artificial light. When you illuminate a nude, the subject, the situation, and the way you see the model's body all determine your lighting choices. For me, each shooting situation is different because I respond to what I see within the subject and the setting, as well as to the inspiration guiding me at the time.

Available Light

Available light is natural light that exists at the moment you choose to photograph, whether you're shooting outdoors or indoors, or it is sunny, cloudy, or even raining. Once you bring in or add other sources of light, the illumination is no longer considered to be available light; it is a combination of natural and artificial light.

The following exercise can help you better appreciate how the quality of light changes during the course of the day. Take the same picture with the same lens from the same angle at different times of the day, from early morning to nightfall. Then study the variations that you achieve. If there is very little light, you may need to mount your camera on a tripod to minimize camera shake, especially if you're using a slow film. As you examine the results of this exercise, keep in mind that the light that is right for one photographer might not be appropriate for another. The type of illumination you prefer becomes a matter of personal taste and what you choose to capture on film. Discovering which lighting effects you like and finding a method that works for you take time and patience—and a great deal of film.

Early-morning light has an unusual warmth that many photographers favor. As the sun rises at an angle, it casts side shadows that illuminate subjects in a pleasing way. Morning light is usually yellower than other kinds of daylight, so it enhances skin tones. This light doesn't last very long, but it certainly is worth capturing.

The midday sun casts overhead shadows because it is located directly above the earth. These shadows can produce unappealing effects, especially on people. However, some photographers take advantage of overhead shadows, creating graphic designs with them in compositions. If these shadows are too strong, you can open them up by using a reflector to reflect some light back into the shadow area. You can also use an electronic flash unit at a setting lower than that of your main light to fill in and modify the strength of an overhead shadow. Some photographers use diffusion material directly above their subjects in order to soften the harsh midday light. Shadows coming from above can also emphasize muscles; this effect can be quite alluring.

Late-afternoon light is also a good choice for nude photography because it is warm and creates a sense of depth and drama around the body. When this light wraps around a figure, it adds a glow to the form. Later on, when the sun is setting, you can add fill light with a strobe to achieve some interesting results. You'll also find that cloudy days are ideal for nude portraiture because the flat, seemingly boring light is diffused and flatters the face and anatomy. If you're looking for more drama, you'll have to introduce artificial light in order to accentuate certain areas of the body.

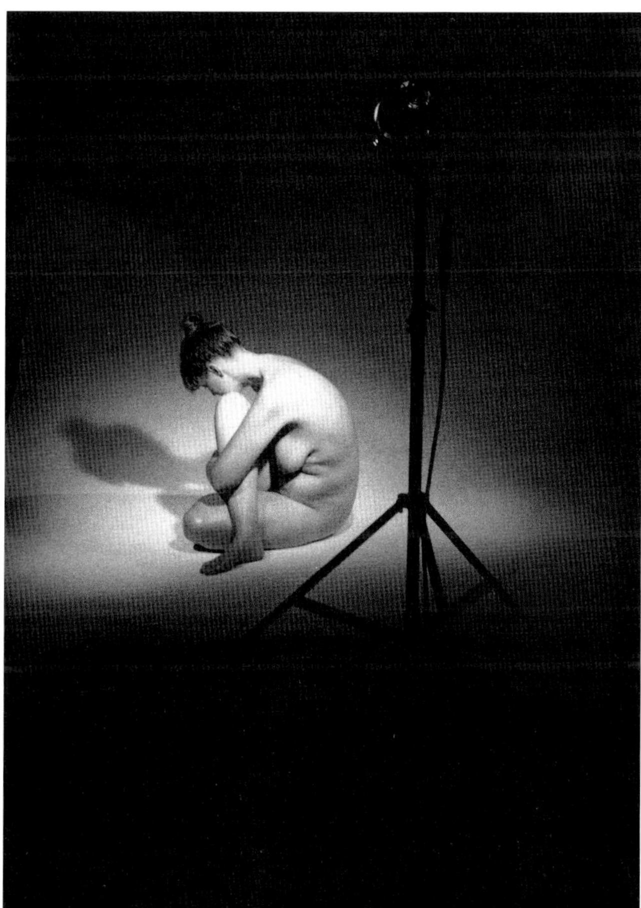

I used a single Dyna-Lite strobe head to directly light model Alice Amos. I liked the effect of the shadows that formed on the simple white seamless backdrop in this subdued image.

Artificial Light

Artificial light sources, such as electronic strobes, can be used on their own or mixed with natural light sources. Furthermore, you can use one light or multiple light sources. You can use these lights directly; for example, you can illuminate a subject with a bare bulb. Another option is to soften the light through the use of a photographer's umbrella, a softbox, or a diffusion material, such as a piece of translucent plastic or a white bed sheet. When you work with one or more lights, one of them serves as your main light, one might be used to highlight a part of the scene or the body, and the others provide fill. You can use background lights to separate the background from the model.

A bare flash tube used as a primary light source produces harsh, intense shadows. You can place a grid, which is a round accessory with small openings, in front of the strobe to focus the light directly on the subject. Grids are available with a variety of size openings so that you can control the spotlight on your subject. You may also elect to use a snoot, either alone or in conjunction with a grid. A snoot is a tube, usually black, that you place around a light source in order to control the light; you can direct it to fall only on your subject or wherever else you choose.

I enjoy playing with the shadows that direct strobes aimed at the model cast across seamless backdrops. As I look at the shadows produced by my modeling light, I simply move the light if I don't like the way they fall. Shadows are more intense when the light comes from the side. During the shoot, I move slightly from one place to another to change my angle, which increases or decreases the shadows. I experiment with the light as well as the forms and shapes it casts on the body, searching for new angles or new ways to interpret a scenario.

If you place a piece of fabric in front of a bare bulb, the light will be somewhat diffused. This softens both the illumination and the shadows cast on the subject. When shooting, you must be very careful to block the strobe light; otherwise, it will bounce back into the camera and cause flare.

Softboxes provide even more subdued results than umbrellas do, and can be small or quite large. Some softboxes accommodate only one flash head, while others can be used with several flash units. This is how softboxes work: A strobe head is placed in the box and bounces the light inside the box before the light filters through the translucent material. I often use a softbox as my main light and add fill via a strobe attached to a shoot-through umbrella.

Many photographers prefer to work with tungsten light rather than strobe because tungsten light lets you see the details and subtleties in highlight and shadow areas more readily. You can experiment with different quantities of light, from a 50-watt to a 1000-watt bulb. If you can see the highlights and shadows, you can record them on film. The disadvantage of

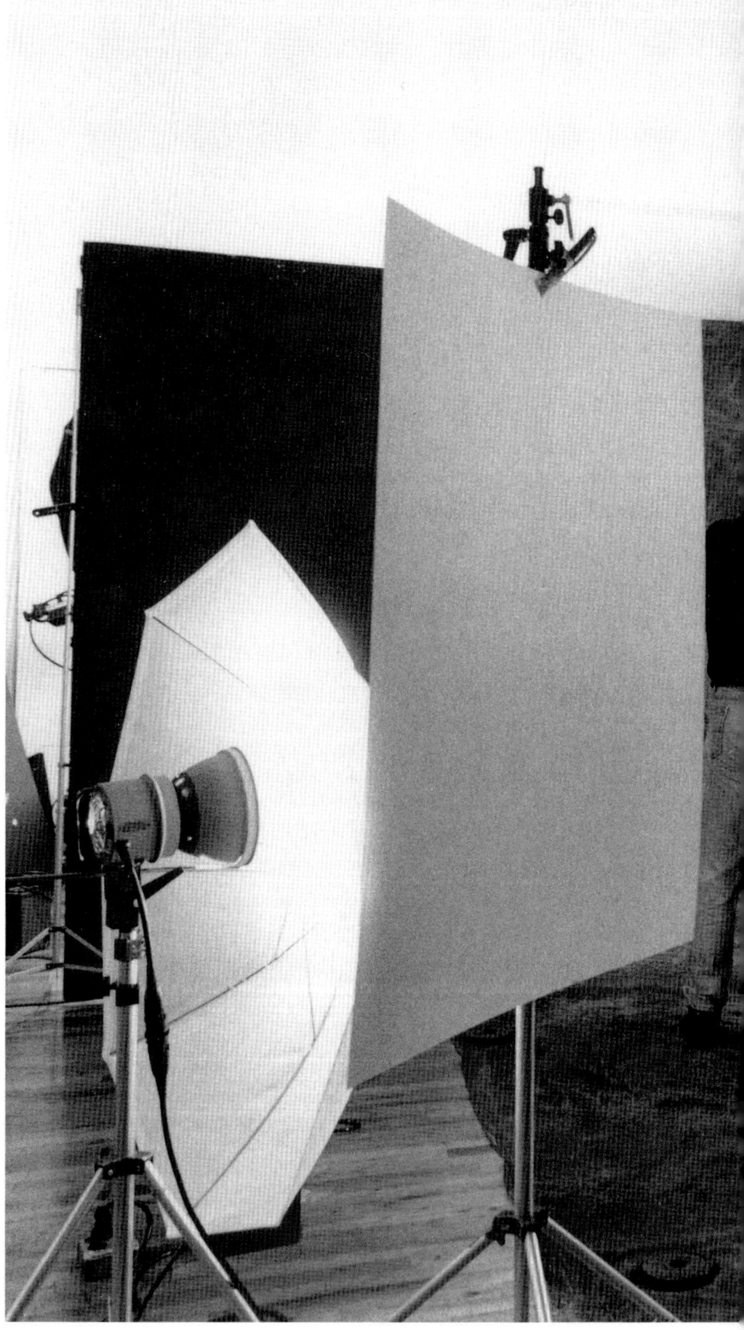

tungsten light is that it generates a great deal of heat, making the shooting conditions very uncomfortable for your subject. Some photographers use tungsten light because they want to recapture the dramatic mood of the 1930s and 1940s. Still other photographers work with HMI, a new style of "hot light" currently used in fashion photography. It is more intense than a 500-watt bulb and has the quality of daylight. The advantage of HMI is that you can use it to create daylight at any time of the day or night.

Today, countless manufacturers are coming out with new strobe equipment. Photographers must decide what is appropriate for them. One reason why I use Dyna-Lite equipment is that the powerpacks are compact and lightweight, and have the same power as heavier units. If you travel to numerous locations, it is obviously a good idea to keep the weight of your equipment to a minimum. The lighting variations that you can achieve are staggering. Remember, you are the director, and this is your shot.

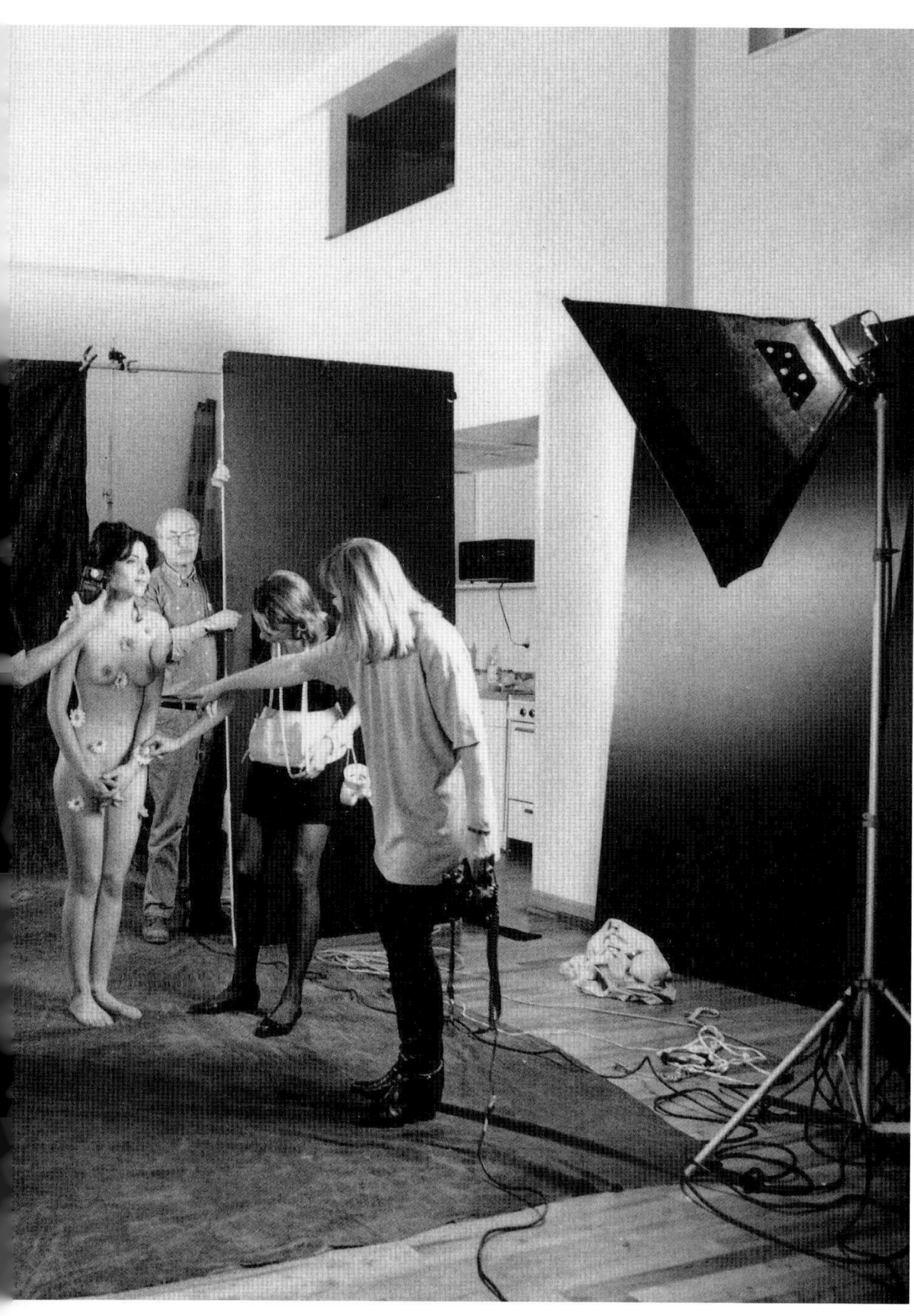

Between shots, Ted took yet another exposure reading. This is essential because the model may have moved off her designated spot; you also need to make sure that the lights are reading consistently and shooting off as they should. Jeanne used double-sided tape to attach fresh daisies to Carmela, checking to see if the tape was visible. The stylist then gently pushed the flowers down so that they angled toward the camera. Notice all of the lighting equipment needed for this series of pictures: an electronic strobe head attached to a shoot-through umbrella to add some fill light to the shadows on the model's left side, a softbox to provide diffused light, and a few reflectors to prevent the background lights from hitting the model and causing flare. A gobo is used to block the light from bouncing back into the camera, which can produce flare.

Composing with Light

How you decide to illuminate the body's curves, shapes, and contours ultimately creates your vision of the human figure. This is the essence of composition. You can emphasize various parts of the body by controlling the amount and quality of light that hit each one. Suppose, for example, that you want to emphasize a model's derrière. You need to concentrate more light on it in order to highlight the roundness of the form. Here, then, the backlight producing the highlight effect must be stronger, or hotter, than the frontlight, which is the main light. If you use artificial light, you can control the illumination via the ratio of frontlight to backlight. The backlight can be anywhere from half a stop to a full stop hotter than the frontlight, depending on how you position the lights. Check the illumination by shooting test Polaroids before you actually begin photographing. Make sure that the backlight doesn't wash out the lines of the model's derrière.

When working with nude subjects, you should also look for abstractions within the figures. The body's many curves and shapes lend themselves to graphic compositions. This is what you want to extract from shooting situations and capture on film. You can go about this two ways.

Some photographers arrive at a shoot with a very clear, concise idea of what they're going to photograph, especially when they're doing work for themselves. Some of these individuals even sketch out their ideas, including their lighting designs. Another approach is to follow your instincts as you shoot. Feel free to take chances. Be creative. For example, as you compose an image you might decide to produce shallow depth of field by opening your lens to a large aperture; alternatively, you might use a smaller aperture for greater depth of field and sharpness. These decisions will add to or detract from the quality of your images.

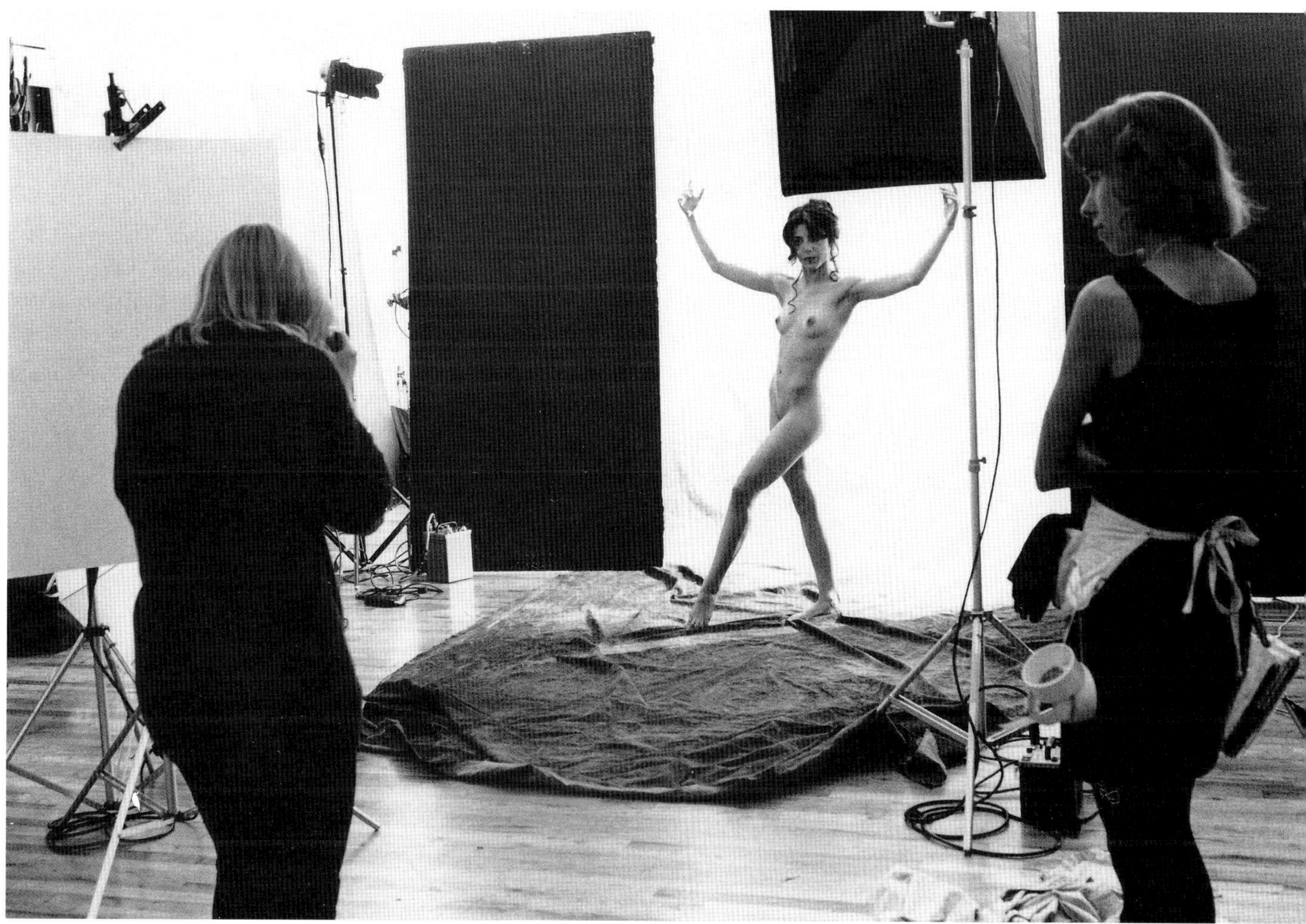

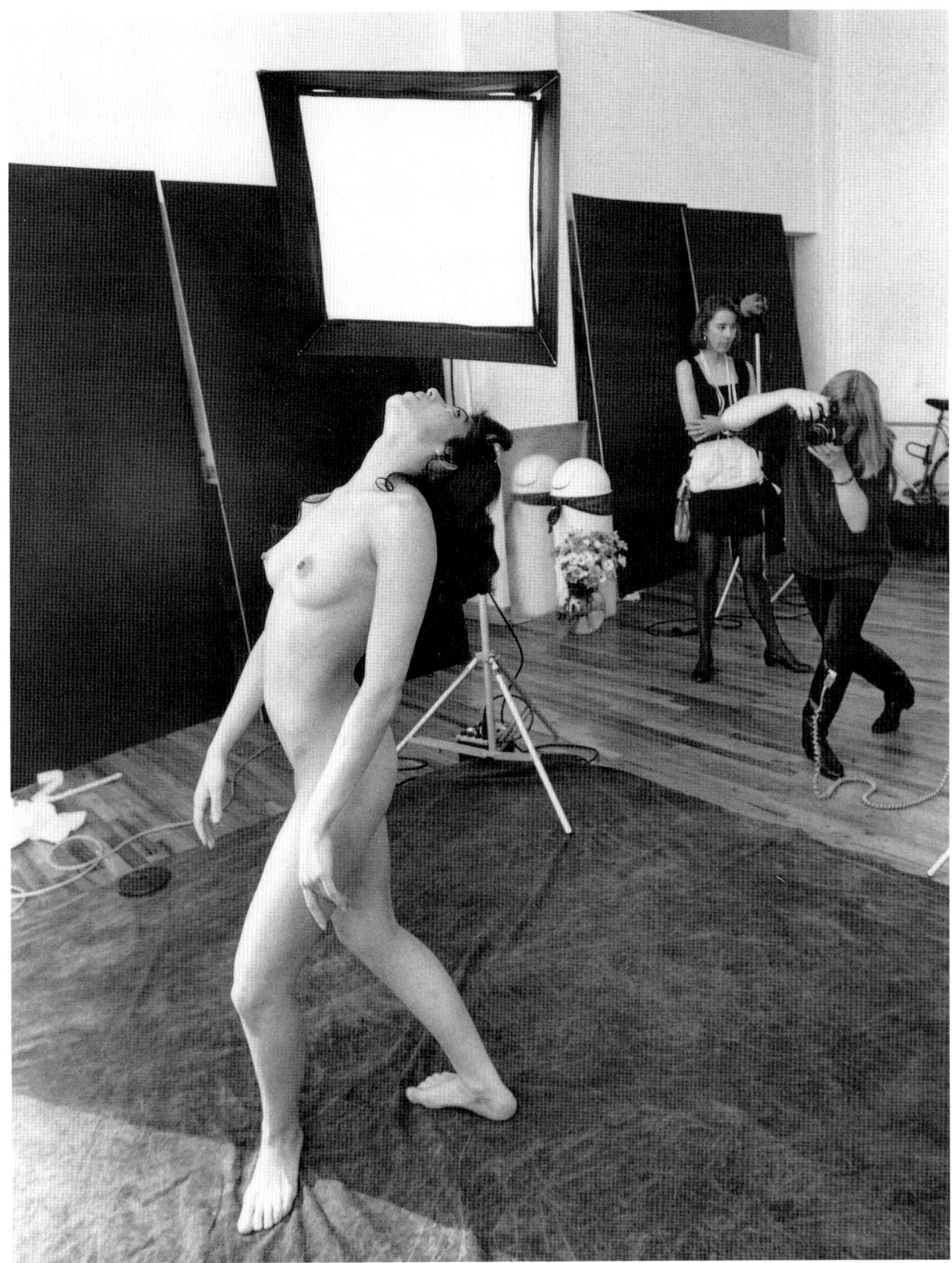

For a shot of Carmela striking a mock body-builder pose, I decided to use a softbox on the right and a strobe shot through an umbrella to provide fill (opposite page). The background lights illuminating the canvas backdrop were blocked off by two 4 x 8-foot boards, thereby preventing light from reflecting back onto the model. This created a diffused effect. Using the same lighting setup, I directed Carmela to give me a nice back view as a variation (above).

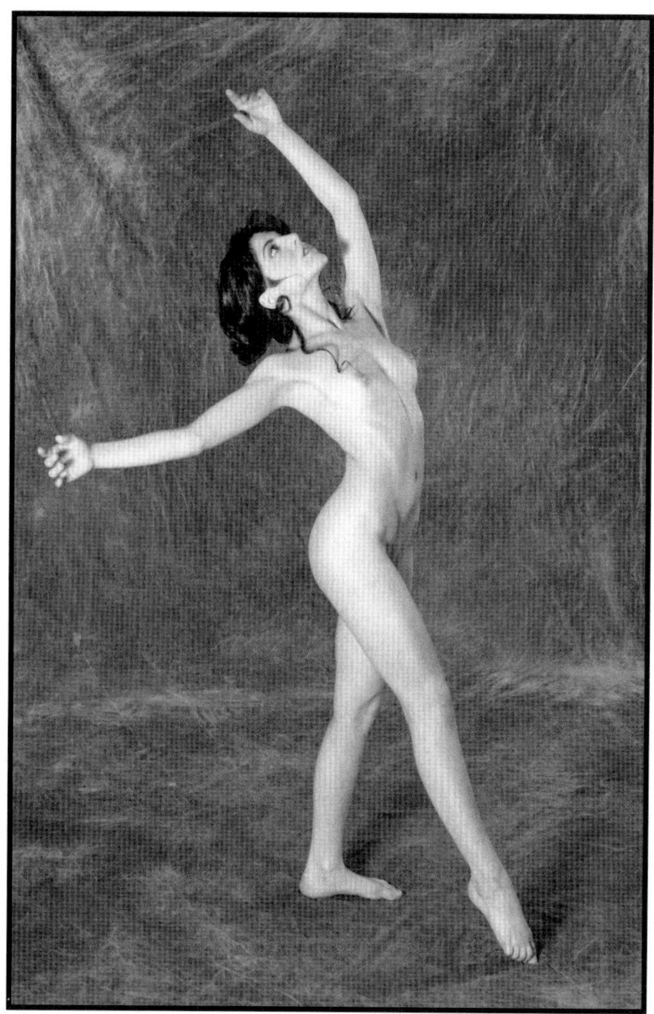

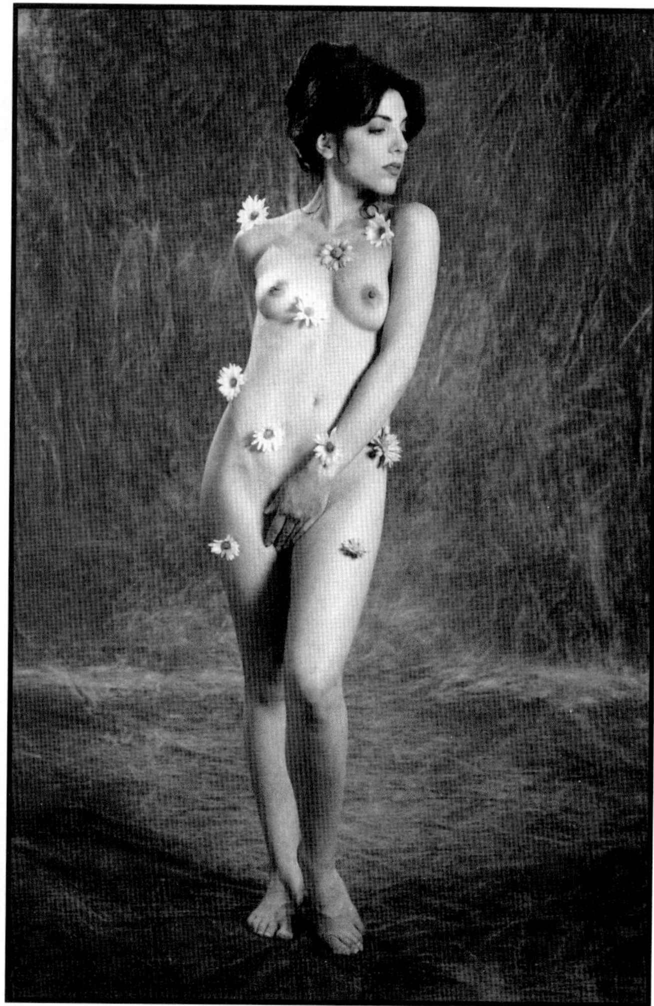

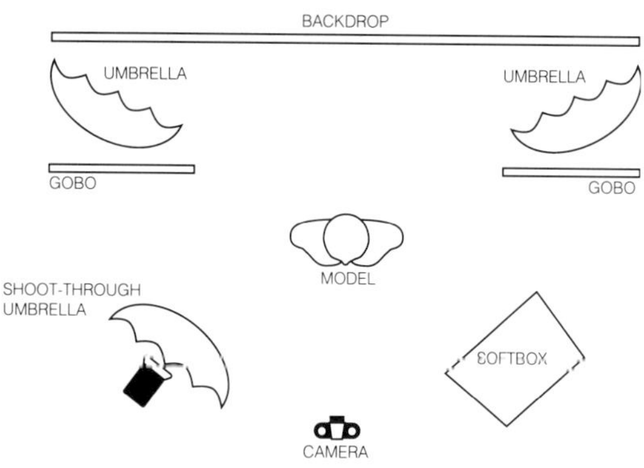

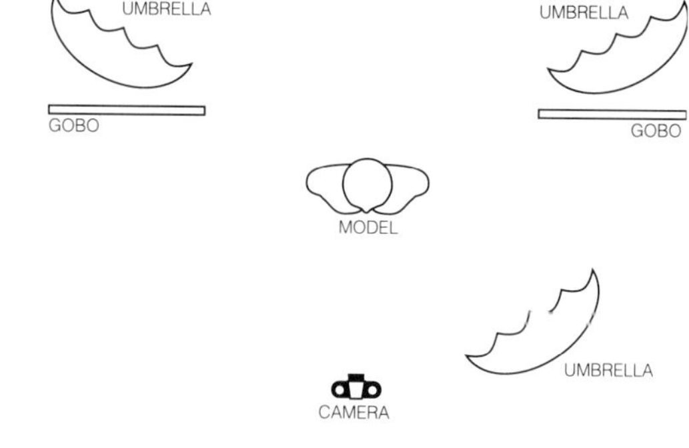

Here, Carmela struck a very graceful pose. I shot this image with a softbox to my right and a shoot-through umbrella to my left for fill. I also used two strobe lights, one on either side of the background; each reflected into an umbrella and was aimed so that it illuminated the background.

For this picture of Carmela wearing daisies and looking demurely off to the side, I had one umbrella placed high and to my right; I decided against using any fill light. Once again, I used two strobe lights, one on either side of the backdrop, reflecting into an umbrella and positioned to light the background.

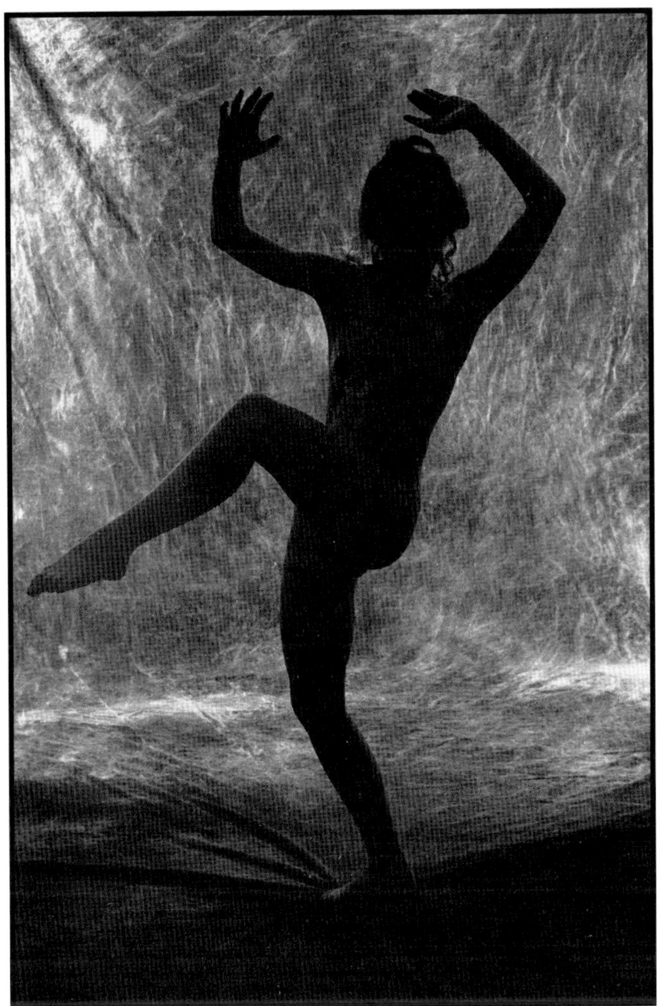

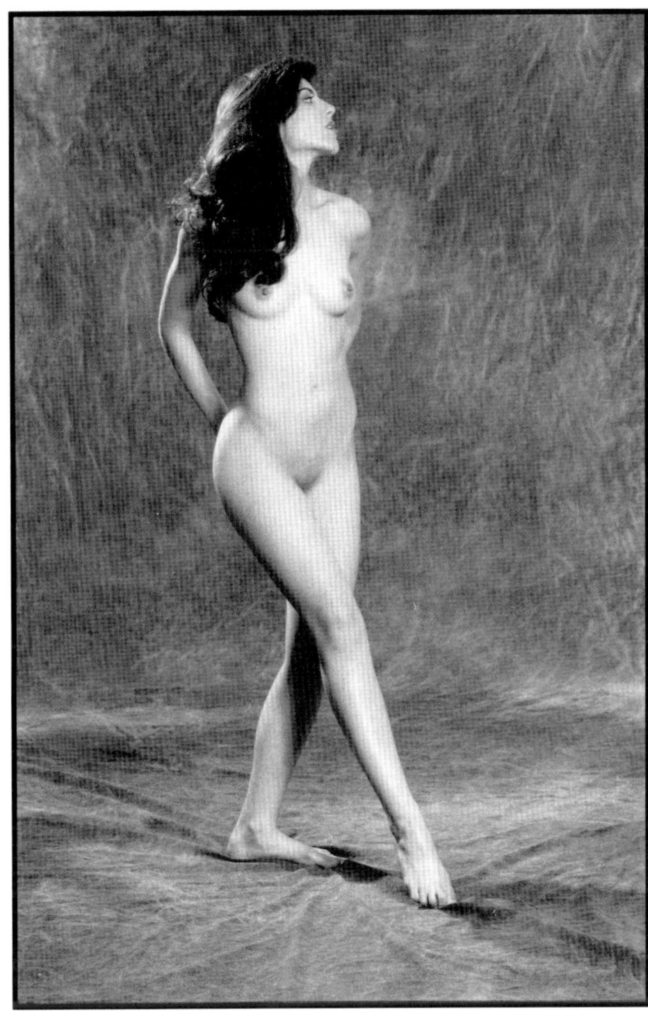

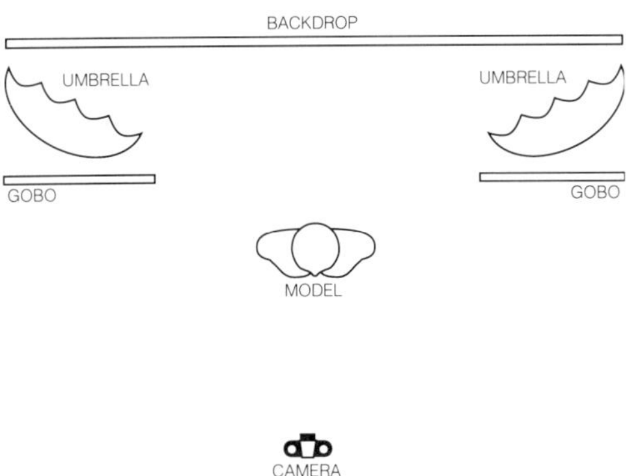

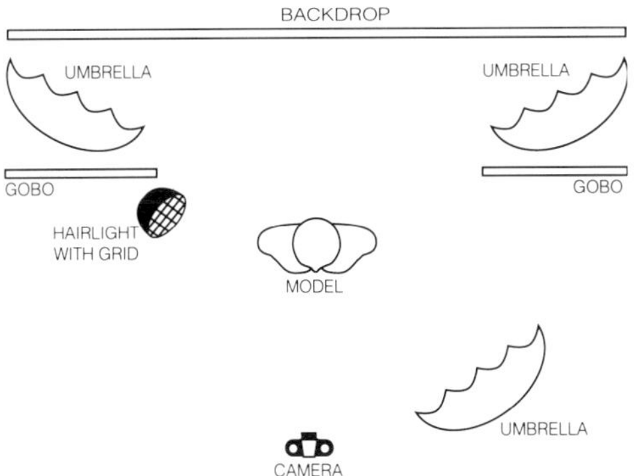

During this session, I wanted to shoot a silhouette. I had the perfect opportunity when Carmela struck this dramatic pose, raising her arms and kicking out one leg with a slight bend at the knee. I used only two Dyna-Lite strobes, placing one on either side of the backdrop and shooting it into an umbrella to illuminate the background. The result: a silhouette with strong graphic impact.

Toward the end of the session, Timothy changed Carmela's hairstyle, letting her long dark hair fall on one shoulder. To enhance the effect, a hairlight was added to the lighting setup, behind and to the right of the model. Two strobes reflecting into umbrellas illuminated the background. The foreground main light was provided by a strobe aimed into an umbrella positioned to my right.

DIRECTING MODELS

When inexperienced models first walk on the set, blank or uncertain expressions often spread across their faces. The first words out of their mouths might be, "What do you want me to do?" You should be prepared to say something reassuring to help make your subjects feel comfortable and to ease them into the work. Next, suggest that they strike a certain pose. For example, you might ask them to stretch out on the floor. For a much livelier shot, have your models act like a leopard by crouching, leaping, pouncing, and jumping.

If you've never worked with nude models before, you may also be a bit nervous. You may not know what to say or how to direct them. A first-time or novice photographer of the nude might cut out pages from a fashion magazine and use the poses as examples. Don't show your models poses from *Penthouse* or *Playgirl* magazines; these pictures might scare them. Be considerate with all of your models, whether they are professional, amateur, experienced, inexperienced, male, female. You're asking your subjects to expose their feelings to you and your camera, so never use harsh language or speak abruptly.

At the beginning of shooting sessions, the energy level is either very high or very low. This is determined by the degree of the subjects' comfort. I often strike up a conversation about a completely different topic right before I start shooting. This relaxes the models; they stop focusing on what they're expected to do and pose naturally. If models seem apprehensive, I assure them that they'll feel better after the first five minutes or so of the shoot. I explain that I regard the human body as a work of art and that I get involved in the form, not the particulars. In this way, I see the models within the context of a photograph. In other situations, I might start off by photographing the subjects wearing some clothing to gently lead them into the session. Most models tell me that my methods enable them to feel comfortable almost immediately.

Music helps to relax models and establishes a mood. Choose the kind of music that you feel is right for each session, remembering that the music will help to establish the ambience you'll capture on film. Play rock music if you want a charged session full of vitality, and play classical music if you want to create a low-key environment.

As the session continues, work with the energy being generated between you and your model. Don't be concerned if there doesn't appear to be much going on. Shoot the exact moment when nothing seems to be happening. You'll be surprised at what this can lead to in terms of your creativity. Change lenses. Move around and shoot from a position you ordinarily wouldn't shoot from. Stretch your imagination.

Tell your models to look directly into the camera or off to its side. As you direct them, notice the flow of their bodies; the subjects' hands should have a natural, fluid movement, and their feet should be

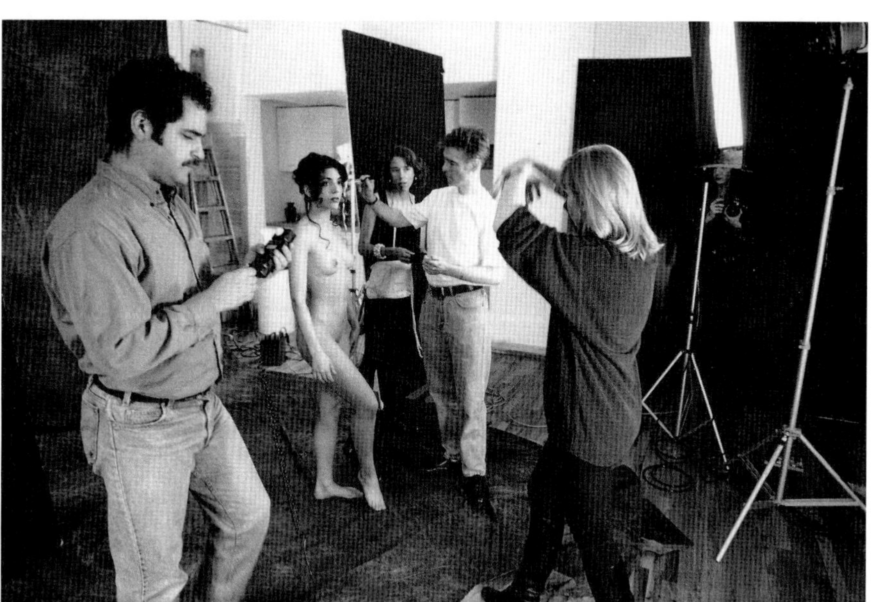

At the beginning of the shoot, I gave Carmela some direction regarding her poses. In fact, I actually showed her how to move her arms and took her through a series of motions. Her natural grace, her willingness to listen, and her dance background all combined to make directing her a pleasure.

posed in a flattering manner. There are, of course, countless ways to pose models. One perennial favorite is the crossed-legs position. This pose results in a fluid look whether your models are sitting or standing. With practice, you'll be able to determine almost immediately which variation of this classic pose works best for a particular model. Crossing the legs also covers the pubic area, which might be preferable for some shots.

You might also want to direct your models to strike a dance pose. Instruct them to pretend that they're tap dancing or doing the mambo or the tango. As you shoot, make sure that the models' hands aren't covering their faces. When I photograph subjects dancing, I sometimes try to silhouette their faces through their hands. To do this, I simply have the models extend their fingers and hold them apart to make them resemble fans.

If you decide to experiment with dance positions, keep in mind that ballet poses are always a good starting point. Have your models do a plié, in which they bend their knees outward while holding their backs straight. You might also want to ask them to try an arabesque. In this position, your models stand on one leg, bend their bodies forward, extend one arm forward, and extend the other arm and leg backward. These poses lead to graphic and graceful images, respectively.

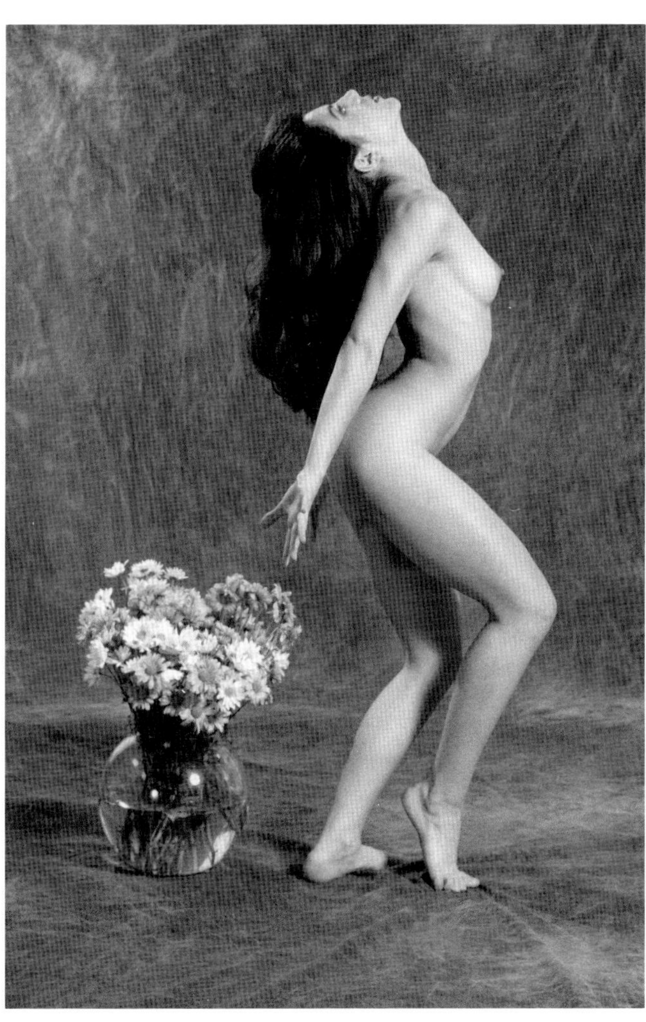

Here, I directed Carmela to bend her right leg and rest its weight on the ball of her foot. Next, I told her to stretch her arms straight back and to throw her head back, keeping her eyes open and gazing up at the ceiling. The flower-filled vase played a central role in this image; it provided a graphic element and a point of interest.

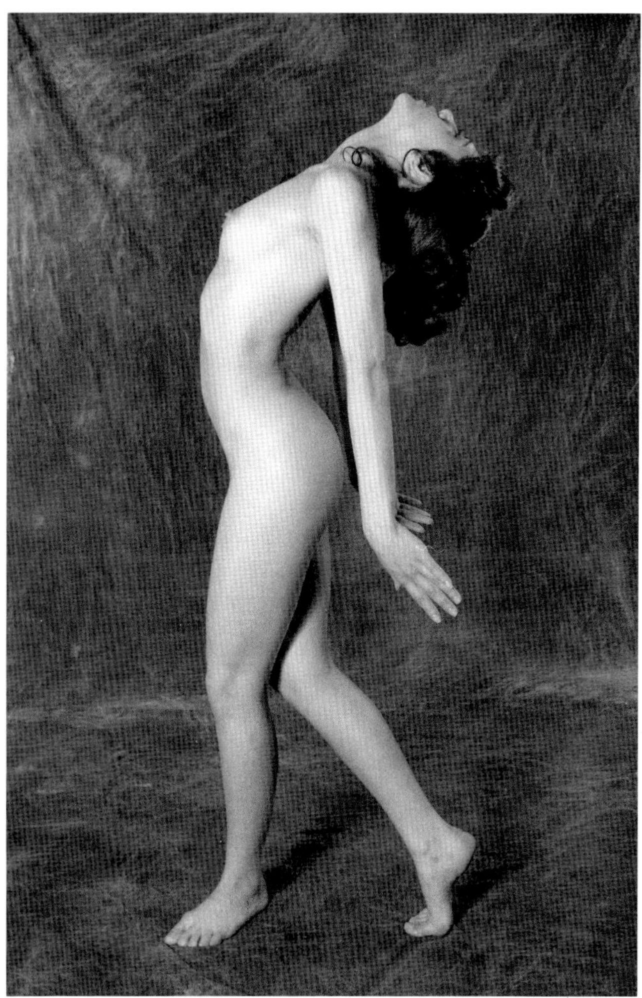

For this shot, I asked Carmela to arch her back, throw back her head and arms, and angle her hands. I then had her put her left leg forward and step on the ball of her right foot. Carmela followed my direction perfectly. As I looked through my camera, my last instruction to her was to move her arms farther back in order not to cover the roundness of her derrière.

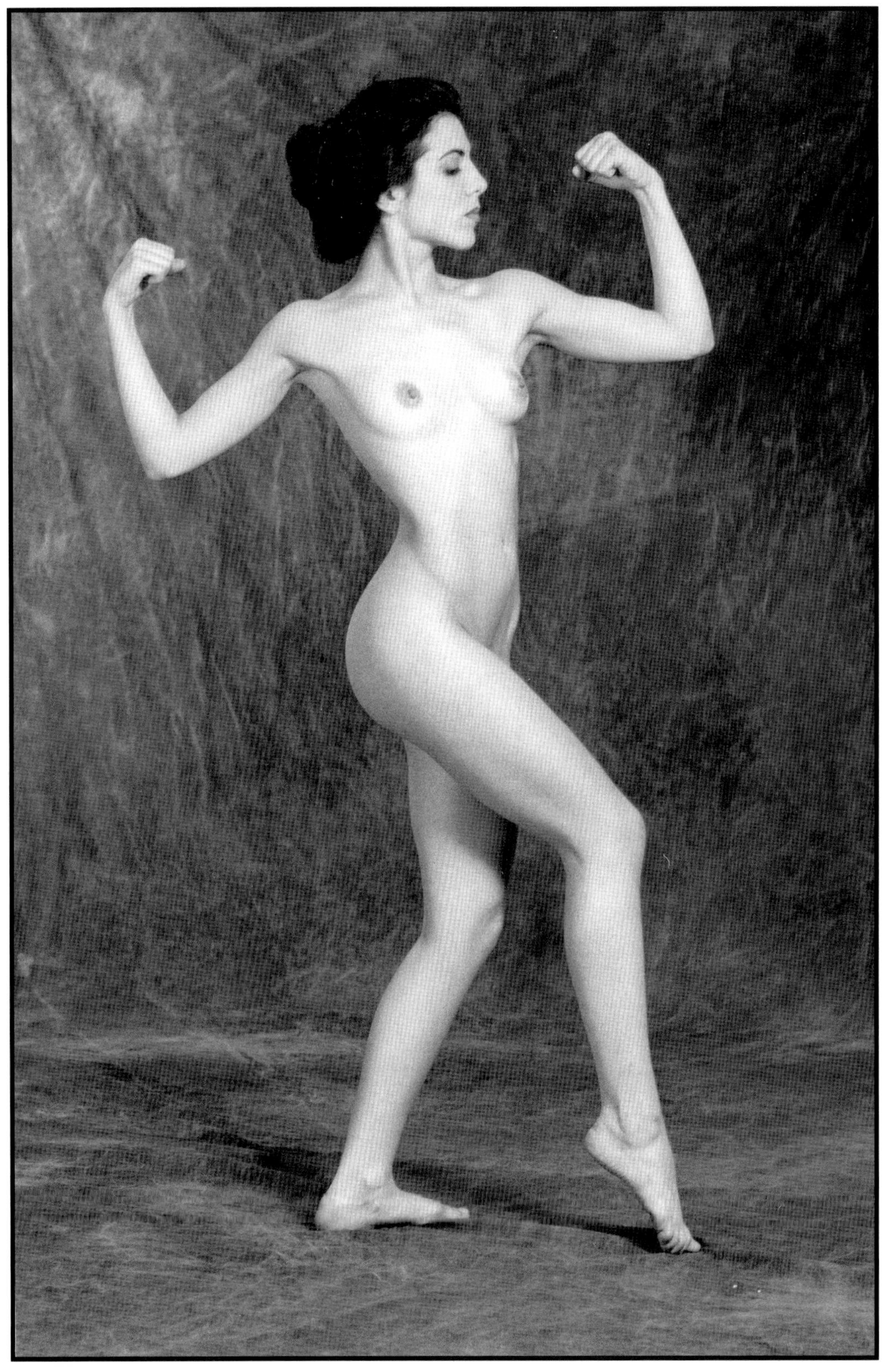

Sports also offer some great ideas for nude-photography poses. Ask your models to imagine that they are about to dive into a swimming pool, first from the side of the pool and then from a very high diving board. You can also direct them to pretend that they're fencing, playing basketball, surfing, flexing their muscles the way body builders do, or moving to music the way members of an aerobic dance class do. Obviously, the range of sports-oriented poses is extensive.

You might find art to be yet another source of inspiration for model positions. Picture Rodin's magnificent sculptures, *The Kiss* and *The Thinker*. Even garden statuary, with their nymphs, gods, and goddesses stretching, prancing, and laughing, might help you come up with unusual but compelling positions for your models. Painting also offers a variety of striking poses: Think about Degas's ballerinas, Matisse and Ingres's reclining odalisques, Renoir's bathers, and David Hockney's many paintings and drawings of the male figure.

In addition to helping your subjects relax in front of the camera by giving them specific posing directions, you can use props. These give your models something to hold on to, touch, or play with, and can get them moving freely. A net, a fur boa, a slinky nightshirt, and a pair of gloves are examples of props that can ease models into feeling more comfortable on the set, as well as reinforce the illusion that the models are completely nude. Sometimes the inclusion of even the sheerest of garments or a small prop can enhance an image.

As the session proceeds, continue to give your subjects some direction and encouragement, such as, "Try standing up and dancing in slow motion. I bet you'll look great." Always keep in mind that models move differently according to their interpretation of the music they hear. After a series of shots of the body in motion, you might want to ask your models to sit or lie down on the floor. Explain that these positions will provide you with some graphic forms, including the body as a sphere, and the juxtaposition of lines and curves.

You should also have your subjects vary the pose. Direct the models to move a leg forward or backward and/or to change the position of an arm. Take a few shots in between changes even if the resulting image isn't perfect. This continuity gives subjects more confidence. They feel that they're doing something right and, in turn, they'll feel more secure about revealing themselves. The models' attention is now on studying the pose, not on their own nudity.

These are a just a few ideas to get you started. In time and with practice and patience, you yourself will feel confident, and directing models will be second nature to you. Remember, there are no rules. So take risks and follow new directions. In return for your efforts, your images will reveal sensitive moments. More important, perhaps, they'll make a statement, whether it be social or political, erotic or sensual, or simply artistic. Eventually, you'll find what works best for you, and you'll be able to define your own approach.

When I asked Carmela to show me her biceps, she instinctively assumed this stance. She placed one leg forward with her foot lifted to give a nice definition to her leg muscles. It is a good idea to start a session with several poses that you've thought about in advance. From there, you can tell the model to move freely. Some models need more direction than others, so you must be prepared.

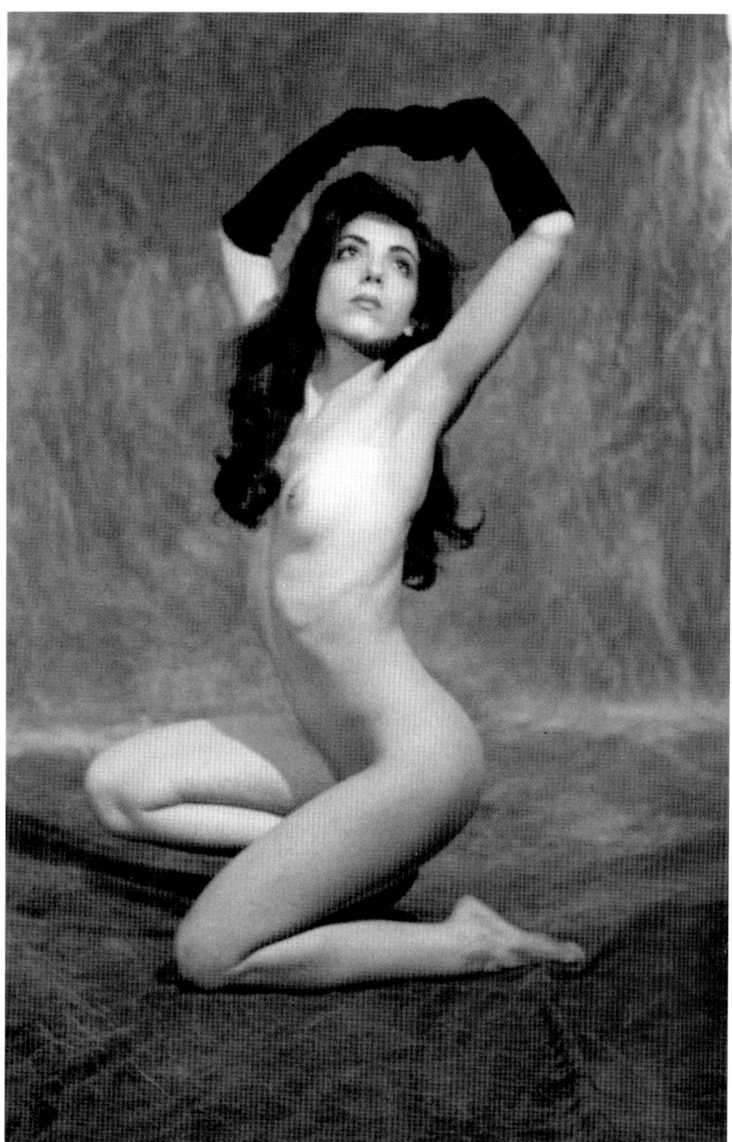

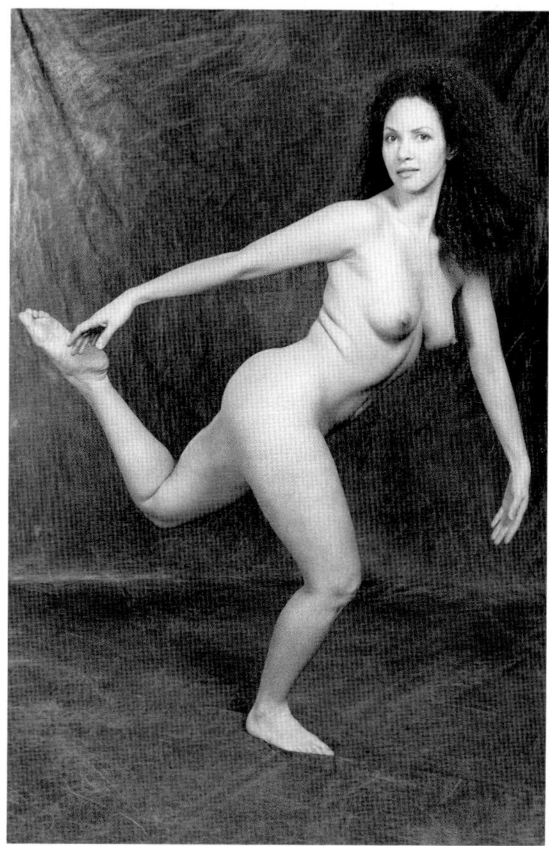

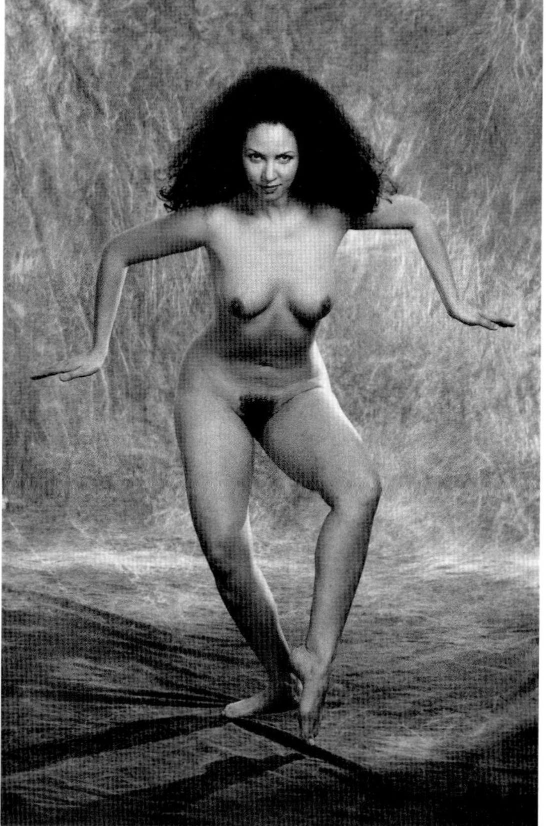

While photographing Carmela and Regina, I asked them to pose in a variety of ways. For a seductive "pinup" shot of Carmela, I had her twist her torso toward the camera, raise her arms above her head, and kneel down, leaving her left leg on the floor and raising her right leg slightly. She held her hands together over her head, which she then tilted slightly upward. This created a nice zigzag effect (above). For the softer shot of Regina, I instructed her to look directly at the camera and to bend and lift her left leg and extend her right arm to reach her raised foot (top right). Her weight rested on her right leg, and her left arm dropped forward, with her hand gently rounded. I wanted to achieve a sense of circular motion here. In another shot, I asked Regina to hold her arms and legs in the angular, very graphic position of modern dance (bottom right). While I photographed Regina, my eye kept wandering over to a large window in the studio, so I decided to have her pose in the frame (opposite page). She moved very well in this small space. I placed a strobe with a shoot-through umbrella several feet to my right and had to be careful that hot spots of the light didn't reflect in the window.

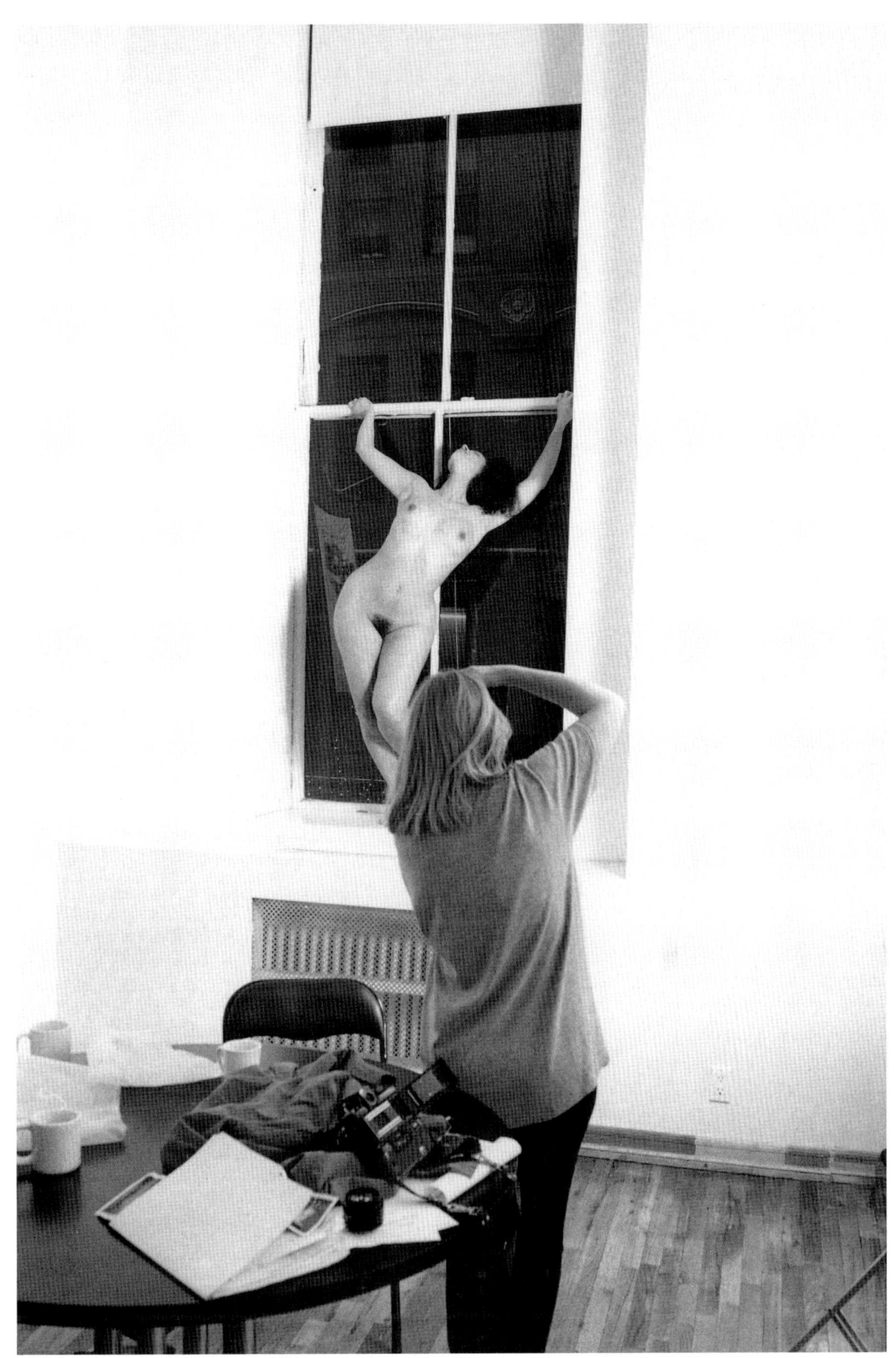

ACHIEVING THE FINAL PRINT

Once you've successfully completed the shooting session, the question asked without fail by the art director and client alike is, "How soon can I see the film?" The answer depends on whether you process the film yourself or use a commercial lab. Time is of the essence to these professionals. So be as accurate as possible when answering their question. Arrange to have the contact sheets delivered to the art director, and set up a time to meet and discuss them. After the shoot is over, art directors often take a few of the Polaroids that you shot during the session. This enables them to begin visualizing the final layouts even before the film is processed and the contact sheets are ready for viewing.

If the shoot went well and you and your model feel great about what happened on the set, you'll both be very anxious to get the film processed and see the contact sheets. The process of selecting an outstanding photograph can be painstaking. But sometimes an image is so good and so unique that it cries out, "Print me." The impact of such an image is simply that great. All of the elements in the photograph work together beautifully. A powerful image can't be overlooked or ignored.

Because photography is expensive, you must carefully decide which pictures you'll enlarge for presentation. If you're considering a photograph for your portfolio, choose the image that is a strong indicator of who you are as a photographer. You must also think about what kind of statement you want to make. Do you want to give the impression that you shoot hardcore sexual images, or sensual images based on fantasy? Obviously, selecting images to include in your portfolio is an important decision that has far-reaching ramifications.

If, however, you're working on a job and executing an art director's layout, use a grease pencil to mark the images on the contact sheets that you are particularly fond of with an "X." I keep the art director's goal in mind, and I look for the best picture overall. Art directors will sometimes be influenced by your preference and select an image based on your opinion. I find that indicating which shots I like most helps art directors, but it doesn't always dictate their choices. So don't be disappointed if they select an image you didn't mark as one of your favorites.

When schedules permit, I like to set contact sheets aside for some time, perhaps a week or even a month after my initial examination of them. Of course, this is more practical when I'm doing personal work than when I'm working for a client. By putting the contact sheets away for a while, I can separate my involvement in the actual shooting from the images I see on the contact sheets. This, in turn, permits me to be much more objective when I decide which prints to blow up. (Keep in mind that it can be difficult to adequately assess 35mm images, with or without a loupe.)

Once a photograph is enlarged, its impact on viewers might be entirely different from what you thought it would be. For example, I recently saw a ten-year-old image of mine blown up to a 4 × 6-foot print. I was so impressed with the results that I had to go back and look at the original image. All modesty aside, it was strong enough to warrant such an enlargement. Naturally, the exact opposite can happen when you decide to blow up an image. You might think that an image on a contact sheet will be quite powerful when enlarged, but in actuality, something vital gets lost in the translation.

While photographing Alice Amos, a professional nude model, I wanted a sense of drama in the shots. To achieve this effect via shadows, I used a direct light. I then guided Alice through a variety of poses, both standing up and sitting down. As I look through my camera lens and see what is working during a session, I direct the models to move or fine tune a pose by asking them, for example, to stretch out one leg for more definition or to bend one leg more. Later, I have contact sheets made in order to examine the model's poses and to choose which images I want to have made into prints.

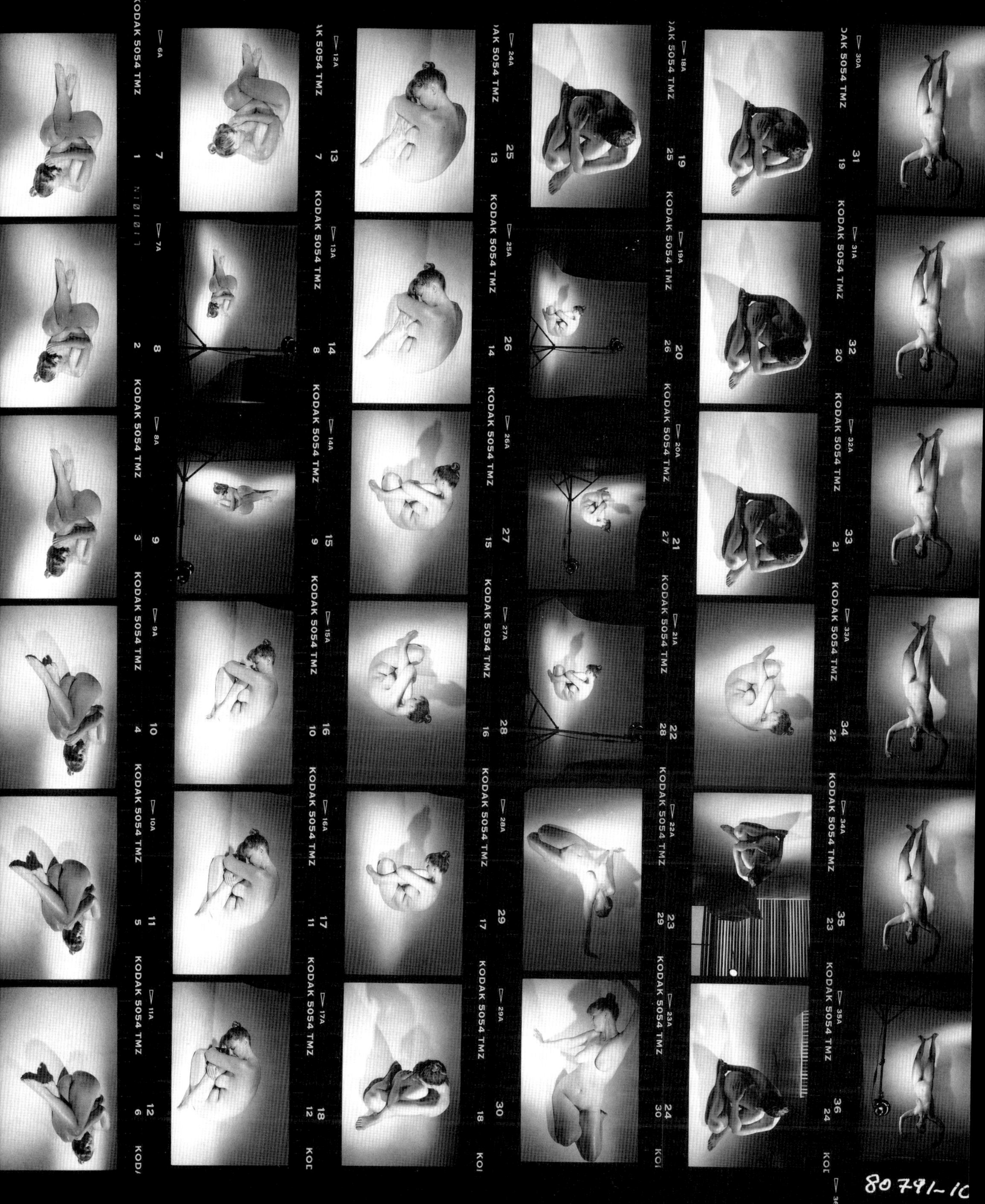

DEVELOPING AND PRINTING YOUR OWN IMAGES

Processing and printing your work has both advantages and disadvantages. The advantage of developing your own film is that you have much more creative control over the results. If you're looking for consistency, this is the way to go. The disadvantage is that you need to spend a lot of time on the film developing and printing. If you're shooting every day, you may have very little time to devote to this.

To achieve great results in the darkroom, you must become a fine technician. You can't print only occasionally and expect to be good at it. In order to hone your skills, you must continually print all the time, just like anything else. The more you do it, the better you'll become. If you don't have the time needed to develop and print your film on a regular basis, you may want to train an assistant to do the work for you.

If you or your assistant develops the film in your own studio, you can determine your own time schedules. You should, however, start with the recommended developing methods listed inside each pack of film. Once the standard process is mastered, you or your assistant can enhance your images through further experimentation with exposure ranges and various developers; each of these strategies will give you a different result.

Whether you develop your film yourself or have an assistant do it for you, you must first establish your own formula, from the length of time to the temperature. This comes with practice. Your own formula is affected by such variables as the type of developer you're using, the water available in your area, and the accuracy of your dilutions. In order to determine which developer to use, try a few with different films and compare the results. Experimentation enables you to find the formula that works best for you.

You can, of course, alter your developing process. For example, if you're shooting a high-contrast scene where the difference between the highlight and shadow areas is four stops or less, you can achieve more shadow detail by overexposing and underdeveloping the film. To compensate for the overexposure in the highlight areas, you can simply dilute the developer, which has the same effect as underdeveloping the film. This will give you a softer negative with details in both the highlight and shadow areas, which you can then manipulate further during the printing process. Conversely, when you underexpose and overdevelop film, you create more contrast but you sacrifice shadow detail. If you are seriously interested in these techniques, consult a technical manual for more specifics.

This photograph of Regina posing with a sheer drape was developed normal, or according to the film's specifications, and shows a range of contrasts (left). Notice the difference between this picture and the overdeveloped image (right), which lacks detail in the dark background.

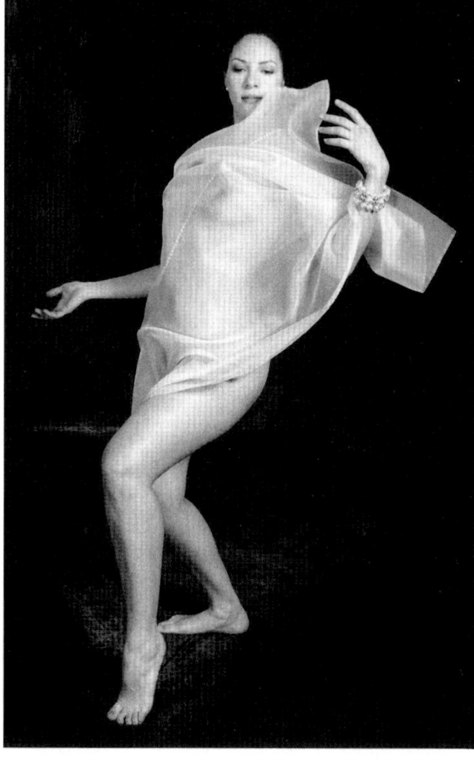

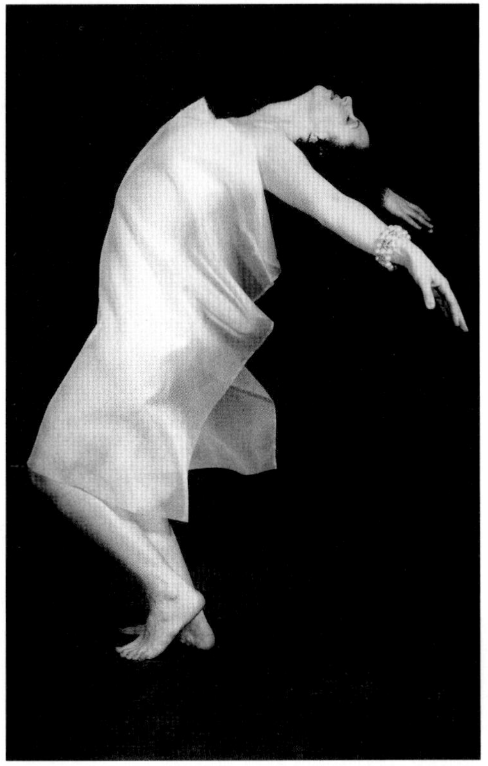

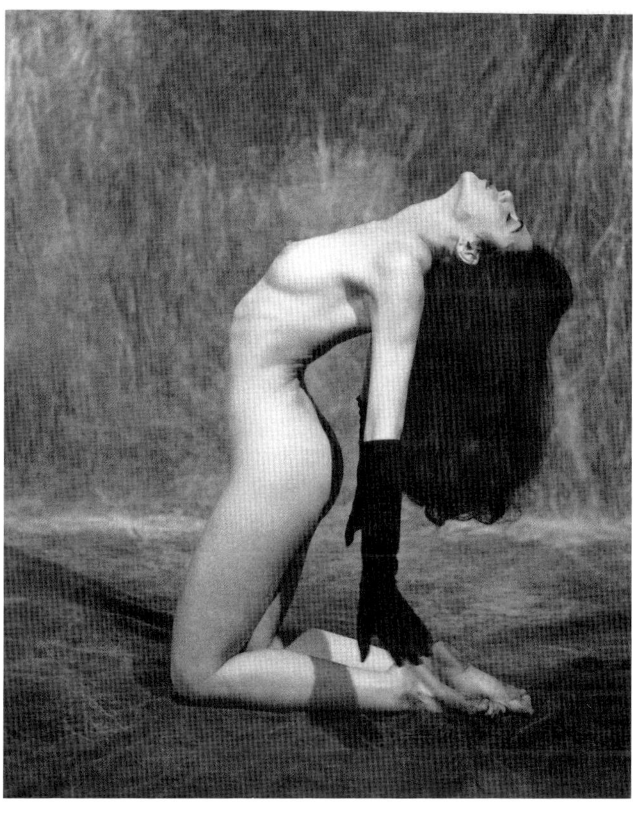

A work print of Carmela arching her back was made quickly in order to determine how this flat print needed to be altered (left). I decided to increase the contrast, burn in the highlights and the background, keep the detail in shadow areas and hair, and crop in on each side. All of these changes were made, and the final print is quite effective, focusing attention on Carmela (right).

When the time comes to print your photographs, you must make many decisions. What do you want your print to convey? What type of paper will provide the results you are after? Prints can range from a normal print to a high-key print with lots of whites, to a low-key print with many shadows and dark areas. And additional cropping of the image in the darkroom can enhance something you may not have been able to control in the camera or, perhaps, your client wants to crop a particular picture a certain way for the final advertisement. I find that most art directors prefer to do their own cropping rather than ask the photographers to crop for them. The layout will give you an initial cropping guide, but final cropping, if any, will be the art director's prerogative.

Darkroom techniques can change the impact of your images. Burning and dodging, for example, can add drama and intrigue to an otherwise ordinary photograph, just as unusual cropping or an unusual paper texture can. If you have the time and prefer to print your own work, you can experiment in the darkroom and can create many versions of the same negative. Select your paper and exposure and decide whether you should burn, dodge, bleach, tone, or crop. Do it all, and by all means, strive to do it better.

Working in black and white is an exciting creative process that continually moves forward. Keep shooting and experimenting to achieve the image quality you envision. Start a new venture today, organize a session, capture compelling images on film, and then alter and enhance them during the printing process. Remember, the human figure will always intrigue viewers.

AFTERWORD

If your desire to photograph nudes in black and white is strong, the rest will follow once you master the basics. As a fashion and beauty photographer, I've worked with some of the most beautiful subjects in the world, and I've been surrounded by "perfect" people. For years, this was my world exclusively, and my vision was defined by what I encountered day in and day out within this world. I greatly enjoyed, and actually still do enjoy, the challenge of making people far more attractive than even they could imagine.

Then suddenly, my life changed. My mother suffered a paralyzing stroke. The first year following her stroke, I was devastated. I spent that year in and out of hospitals and daycare centers. I could barely bring myself to shoot. It took me almost two years to accept the situation and realize that anyone can be struck down at anytime, regardless of age or beauty.

After that, I found myself slowly starting to photograph my parents, my mother in her wheelchair and my father, who had suffered a stroke many years earlier, with a newly broken hip using a walker and wheelchair. The more I photographed my parents, the more my worked changed. I began to shoot the reality around me, just as it was, without adding any beautifying touches. I came to see beauty in "less than perfect" subjects. I no longer photographed only models with great bodies. I wanted to explore new territory, to photograph an obese person and an 89-year-old grandfather—real people, real subjects, not idealized ones. My work was evolving, taking on a new dimension, venturing into the unknown.

You can approach nude photography in one of two ways. You can use a myriad of special effects and a variety of equipment to create and then document your efforts, or you can use the simplest form of lighting and work on creating an image. Both methods are valid and can produce powerful results. How you feel, what you see, who you are—these are the essence of photographing nudes successfully.

Some practical considerations help to determine the success of your images, too, but in a different way. Once you've taken a substantial number of compelling shots, you must decide how and where you want your work to potentially be seen. If you want to exhibit your nude photography in galleries, keep in mind that it takes time to pull together a strong portfolio. Furthermore, large, archivally printed and framed photographs are required for exhibition unless your work calls for something unusual, such as very small prints framed in excessively large mats. When you are ready to present your photographs to a gallery, call the gallery to find out the details of its dropoff policy. Most galleries permit portfolios to be dropped off either by appointment or on a specific day of the week. Others require that you shoot slides of your photographs and mail them in for review.

You can also submit your nude photography to poster, postcard, and greeting-card companies. You can find the names and addresses of these companies on the products themselves. Get in touch with the companies directly, and find out their submission policies and review schedules. If they show interest, send them copies of your nude images in either slide or rough-print form. It is better to contact a company directly first rather than to send in your work blindly. Otherwise, your work might sit on someone's desk for months. And never send in your original prints because you can't be sure of what might happen to them in the mail or while being handled at the companies. (Save your original prints for gallery shows.) If, for example, a postcard company expresses interest in your work, the staff will select the images the company wants to publish and will ask you to provide reproduction-quality prints.

If your goal is to enter the advertising field, you must develop a striking portfolio of images with a definite style. The first step is to find out the names of the art directors at the various advertising agencies you plan to contact and/or the names of the people in the advertising departments of the companies whose products you would like to shoot. Next, submit a sample of your work, and follow up with a telephone call to see if the individual has any interest in looking through your portfolio. Like galleries, some companies have strict dropoff policies.

Although it will take you some time to identify, research, and target these resources, you'll discover that it is time well spent. The number of companies and advertising agencies is huge, as is the range of products for which nude photography is appropriate. Bath products, men and women's fragrances, pantyhose, lingerie, and underwear are just a few examples. In addition, advertising companies and their clients are always looking for new ideas to sell their products and services. You might have exactly what they want.

Whatever your specialty, whatever your goals, photographing the nude in black and white should be pleasurable. It should also be a learning experience that enables you to explore your creative side and develop a distinctive style.

The Nude in Black and White is an expression of who I am and who I was. All of the images in this book are, in one way or another, reflections of Lucille Khornak, photographer, woman. Photography intrigues me because it doesn't require me to stay the same. In fact, it encourages me to keep on changing, growing, and exploring, all in the name of creativity. Pursue your vision, cross boundaries, and experiment with texture, form, and abstraction. New adventures and exciting images are in store for you.

Finally, to help you understand the many decisions that photographing the nude in black and white entails, I've listed the technical information for each of the pictures in the Gallery section. I photographed the majority of the images with my Nikon F3 35mm camera. The only exceptions are Plates 37, 48, 49, 50, 51, and 59, which I made with my Nikon F4 35mm camera. All directionals are in relation to my shooting position.

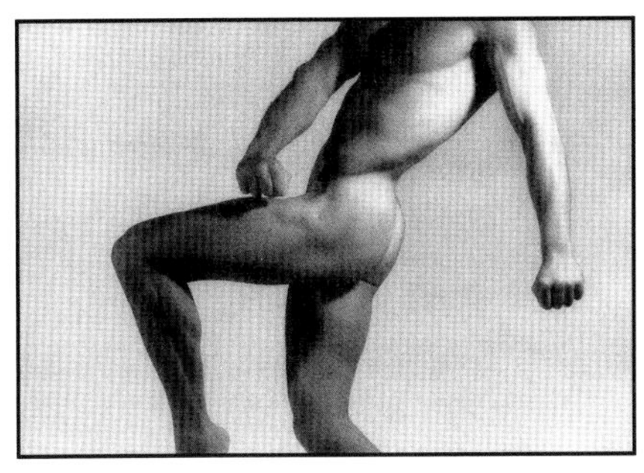

COVER
Film: Kodak High Speed Infrared. Lens: 35mm F2 with red filter. Lighting: One direct strobe from high above; and two direct strobes aimed into umbrellas, one on either side of background.

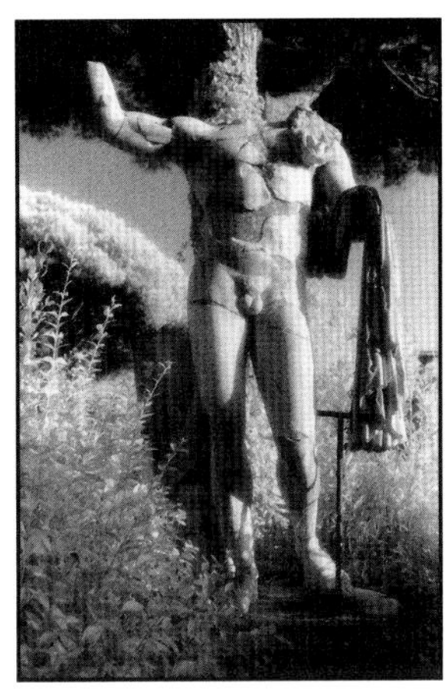

PLATE 1
Film: Kodak High Speed Infrared. Lens: 35mm F2 with red filter. Lighting: Natural light.

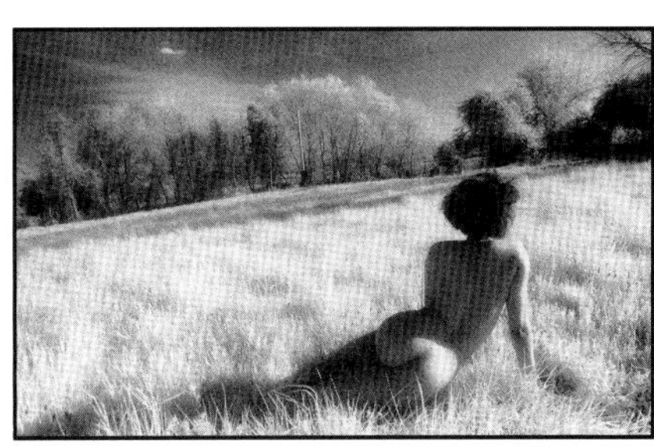

PLATE 2
Film: Kodak High Speed Infrared. Lens: 35mm F2 with red filter. Lighting: Natural light.

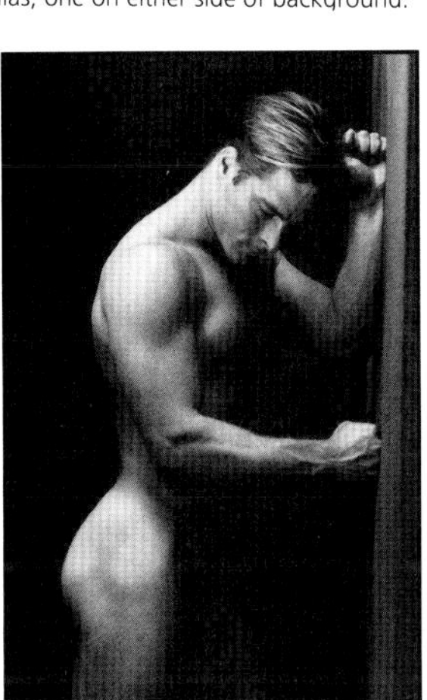

PLATE 3
Film: Kodak Plus-X Pan. Lens: 35mm F2. Lighting: Strobe aimed into umbrella from above left.

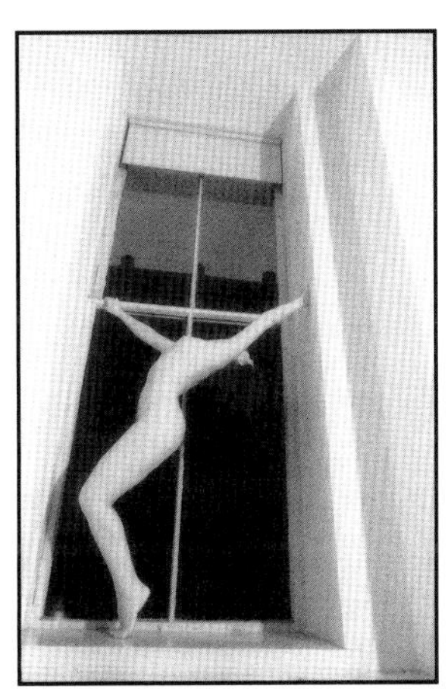

PLATE 4
Film: Kodak High Speed Infrared. Lens: 35mm F2 with red filter. Lighting: Strobe aimed into shoot-through umbrella positioned on right at an angle to prevent it from reflecting into window.

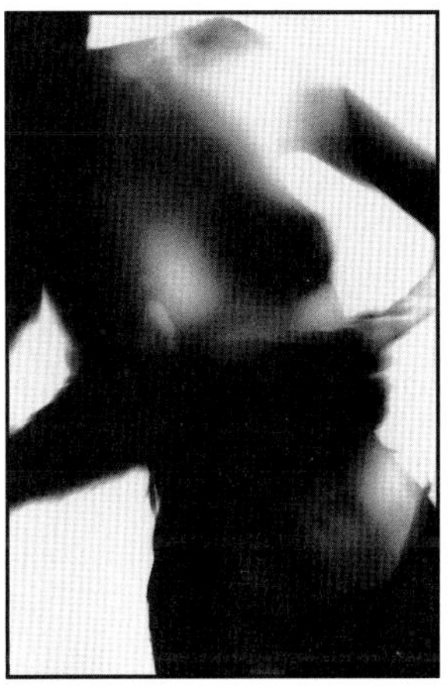

PLATE 5
Film: Experimental. Lens: 35mm F2. Lighting: Experimental.

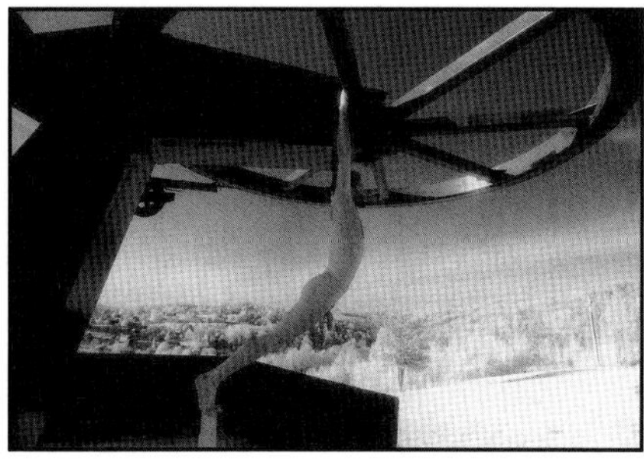

PLATE 6

Film: Kodak High Speed Infrared. Lens: 35mm F2 with red filter. Lighting: Natural light.

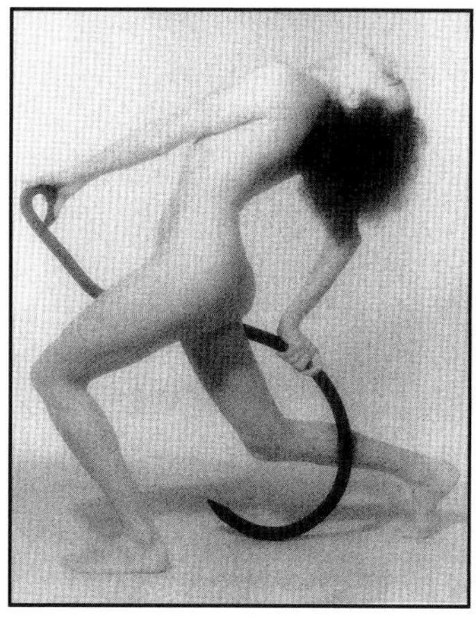

PLATE 7

Film: Kodak High Speed Infrared. Lens: 35mm F2 with red filter. Lighting: Direct strobe from right, and strobe aimed into shoot-through umbrella as fill from left.

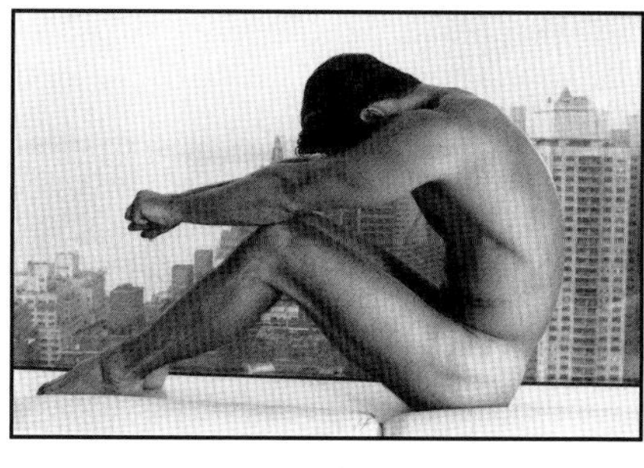

PLATE 8

Film: Kodak Plus-X Pan. Lens: 35mm F2. Lighting: Softbox from right.

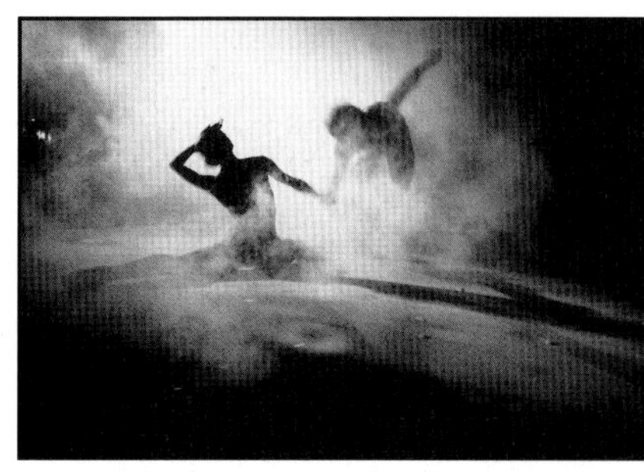

PLATE 9

Film: Kodak Tri-X Pan Professional. Lens: 35mm F2. Lighting: Stage lights.

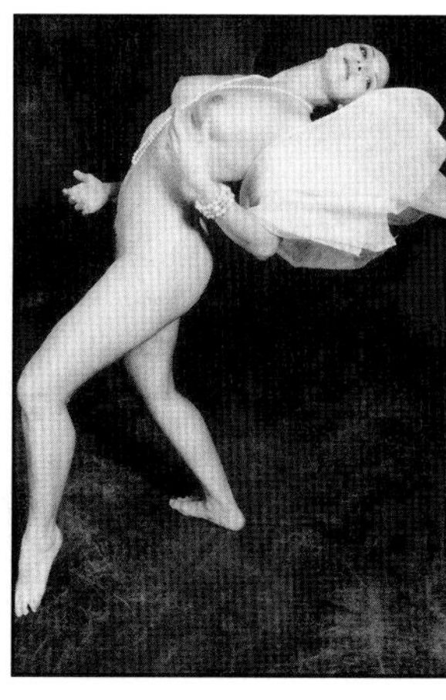

PLATE 10

Film: Polapan. Lens: 35mm F2. Lighting: Two tungsten lights as main lights, one on either side of photographer.

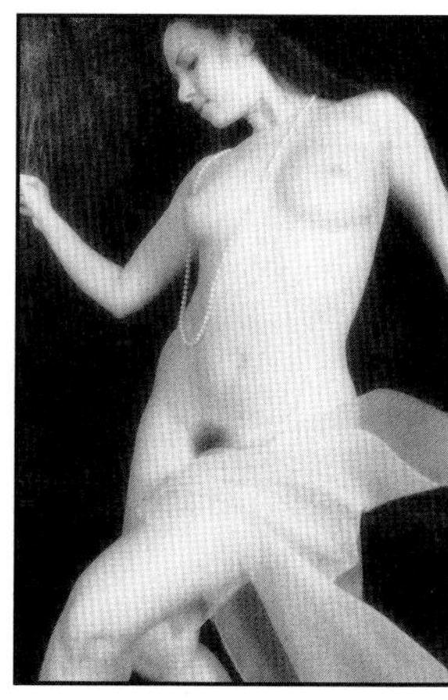

PLATE 11

Film: Kodak High Speed Infrared. Lens: 35mm F2 with red filter. Lighting: Softbox from right, and strobe aimed into shoot-through umbrella as fill from left.

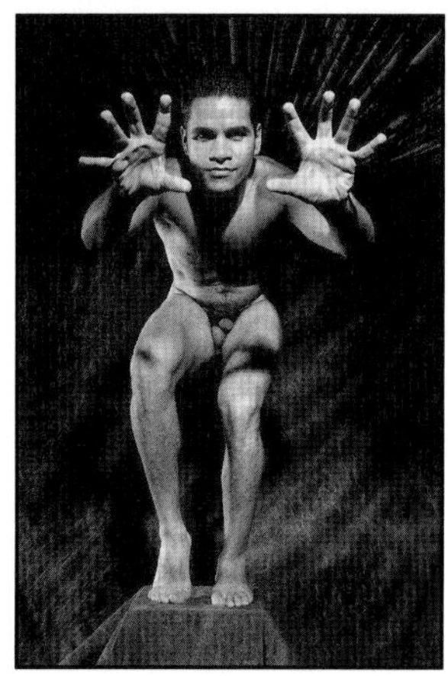

PLATE 12

Film: Kodak Plus-X Pan. Lens: 24mm F2.8. Lighting: Direct strobe with grid from above in front of model, and softbox from left behind model.

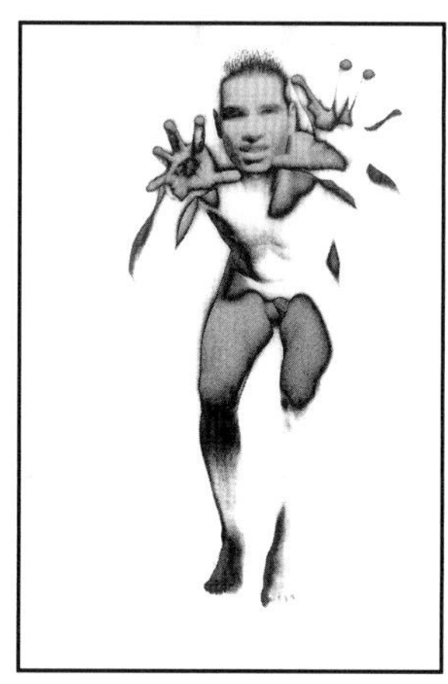

PLATE 13

Film: Kodak High Speed Infrared. Lens: 24mm F2.8 with red filter. Lighting: Direct strobe with grid from above in front of model, and softbox from left behind model. Copy negative was made from print, and then negative was solarized and printed.

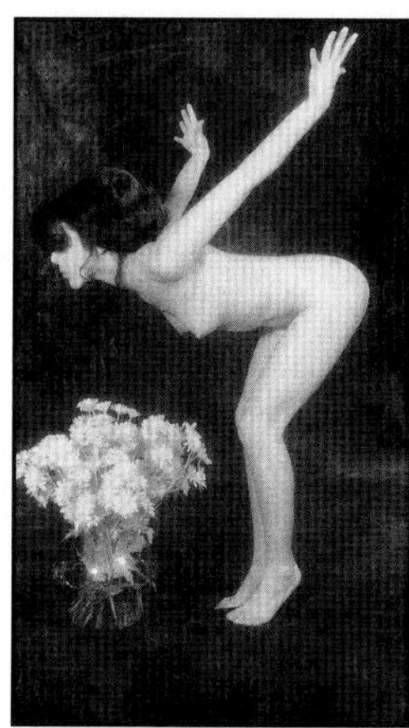

PLATE 14

Film: Kodak High Speed Infrared. Lens: 35mm F2 with red filter. Lighting: Strobe aimed into shoot-through umbrella from above right.

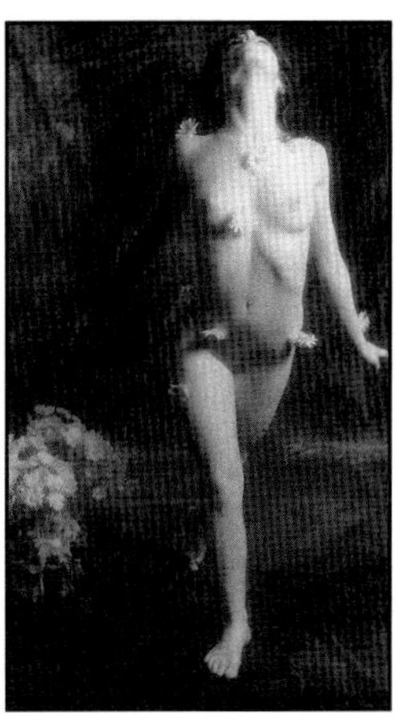

PLATE 15

Film: Kodak High Speed Infrared. Lens: 35mm F2 with red filter. Lighting: Strobe aimed into umbrella from above right.

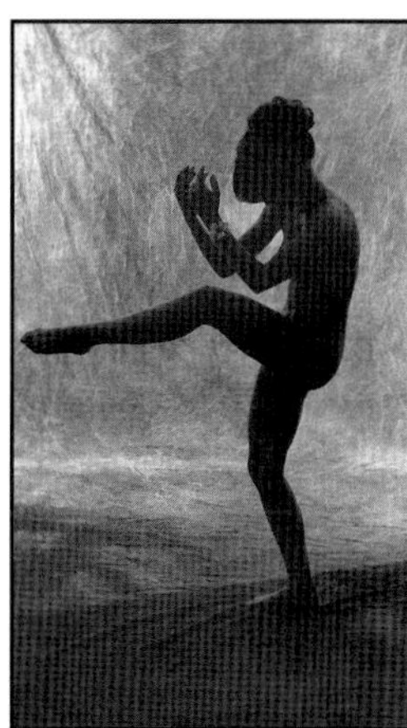

PLATE 16

Film: Kodak Plus-X Pan. Lens: 35mm F2. Lighting: Two strobes aimed into umbrellas, one on either side of background. No frontlights.

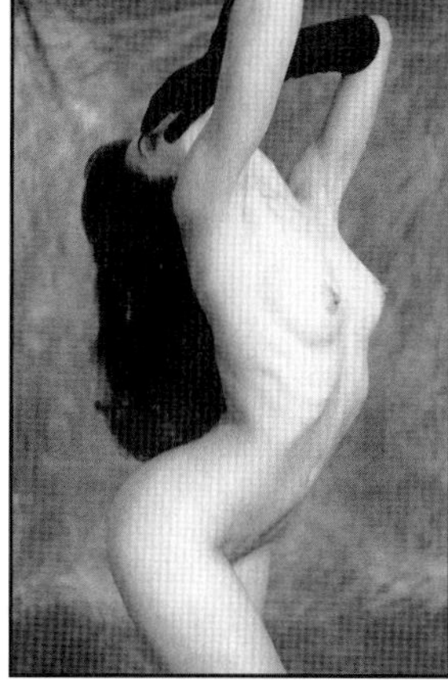

PLATE 17

Film: Kodak Plus-X Pan. Lens: 35mm F2. Lighting: Strobe aimed into umbrella from above right; strobe aimed into shoot-through umbrella as fill from low left; two strobes aimed into umbrellas on either side of background.

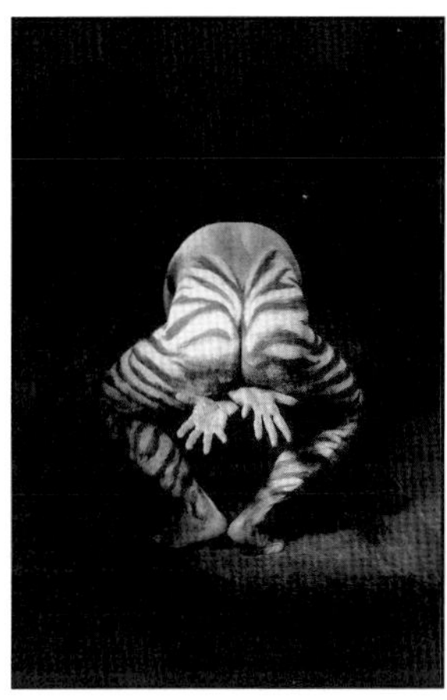

PLATE 18

Film: Kodak Plus-X Pan. Lens: 35mm F2. Lighting: Two direct strobes in front of model, and direct strobe with large grid from left behind model.

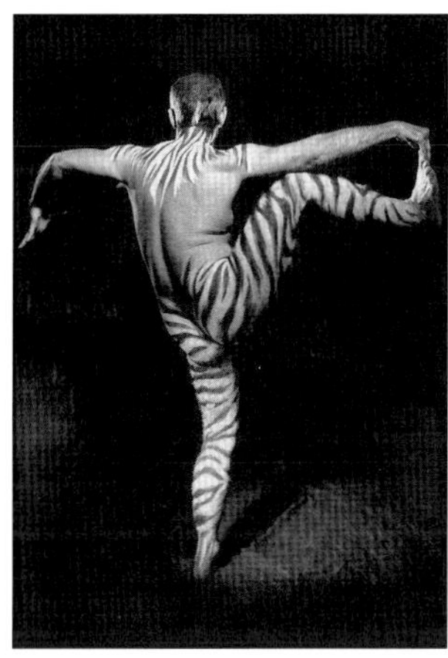

PLATE 19

Film: Kodak Plus-X Pan. Lens: 35mm F2. Lighting: Two direct strobes in front of model, and direct strobe with large grid from left behind model.

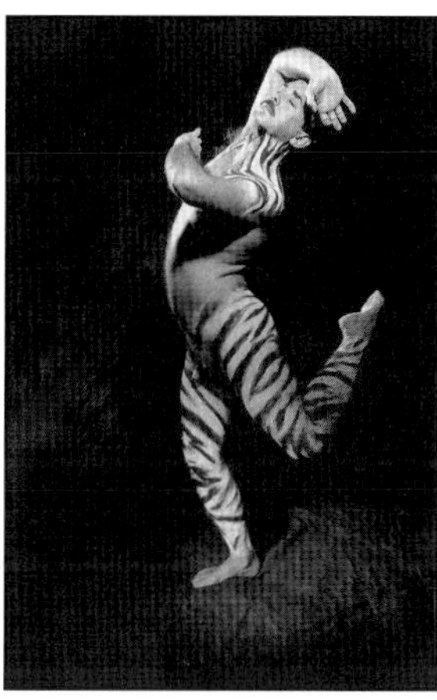

PLATE 20

Film: Kodak Plus-X Pan. Lens: 35mm F2. Lighting: Two direct strobes in front of model, and direct strobe with large grid from left behind model.

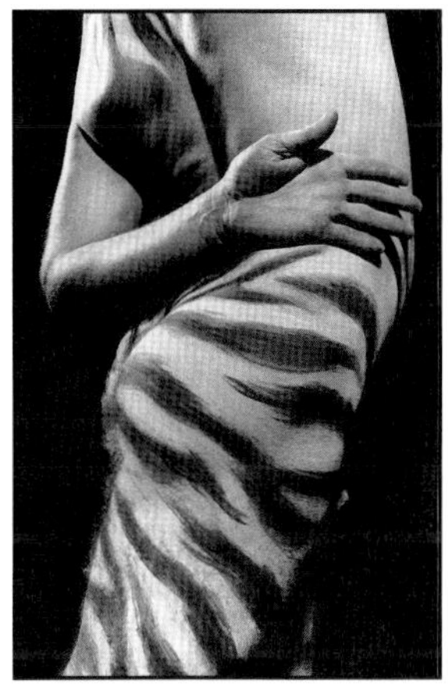

PLATE 21

Film: Kodak Plus-X Pan. Lens: 60mm F2.8 micro. Lighting: Two direct strobes in front of model, and direct strobe with large grid from left behind model.

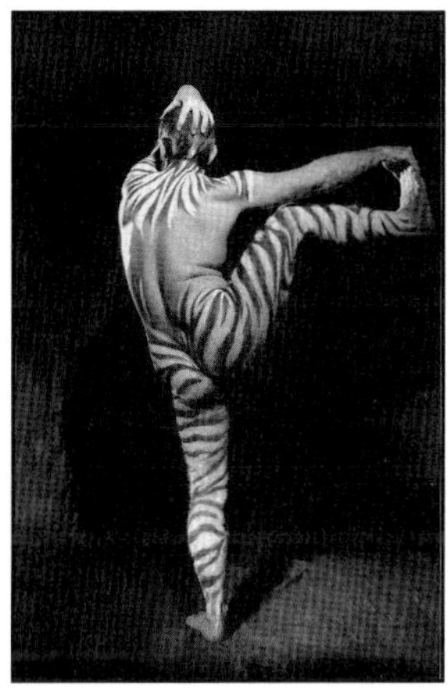

PLATE 22

Film: Kodak Plus-X Pan. Lens: 35mm F2. Lighting: Two direct strobes in front of model, and direct strobe with large grid from left behind model.

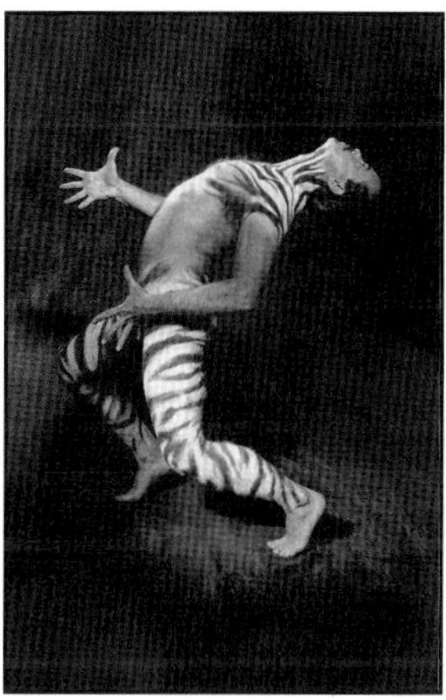

PLATE 23

Film: Kodak Plus-X Pan. Lens: 35mm F2. Lighting: Two direct strobes in front of model, and direct strobe with large grid from left behind model.

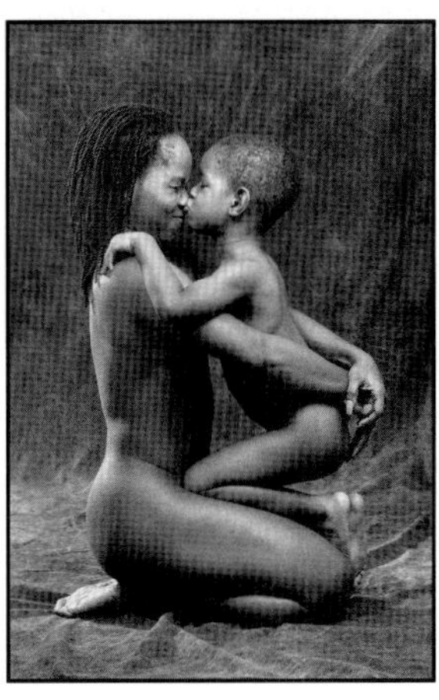

PLATE 24

Film: Kodak Plus-X Pan. Lens: 35mm F2. Lighting: Softbox from above right, strobe aimed into shoot-through umbrella as fill from below left, and direct strobe from left behind models.

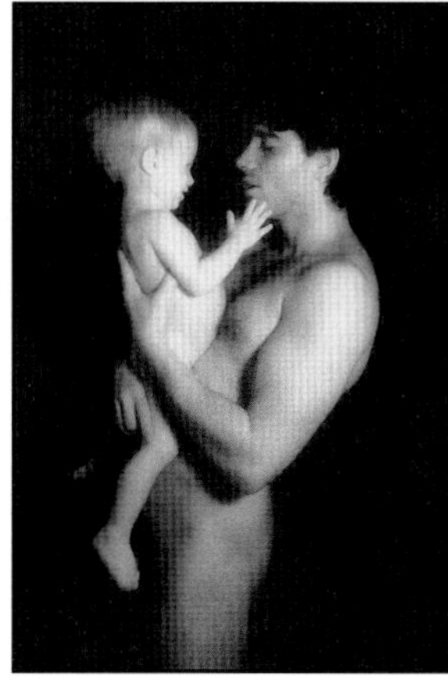

PLATE 25

Film: Kodak High Speed Infrared. Lens: 105mm F2.5 with red filter. Lighting: Direct strobe from above right.

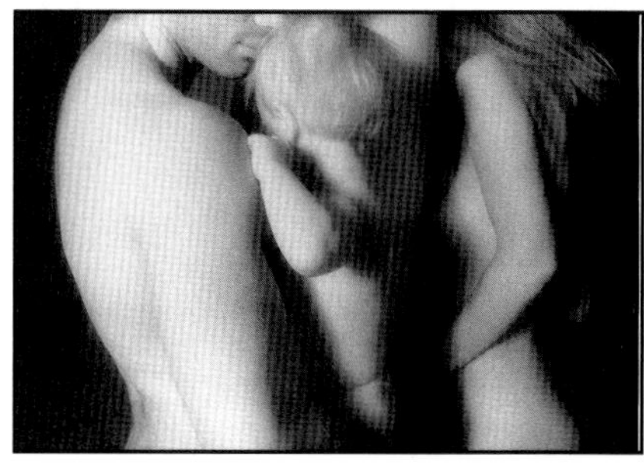

PLATE 26

Film: Kodak High Speed Infrared. Lens: 35mm F2 with red filter. Lighting: Direct strobe from left.

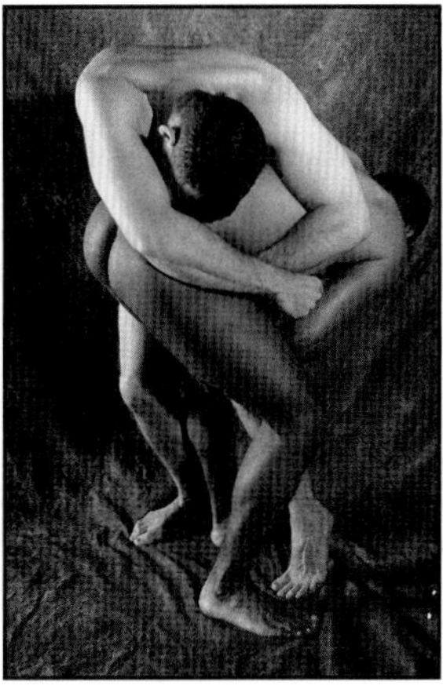

PLATE 27

Film: Kodak Tri-X Pan Professional. Lens: 35mm F2. Lighting: Two direct strobes with grids from right, and softbox angled low and flat from left behind models.

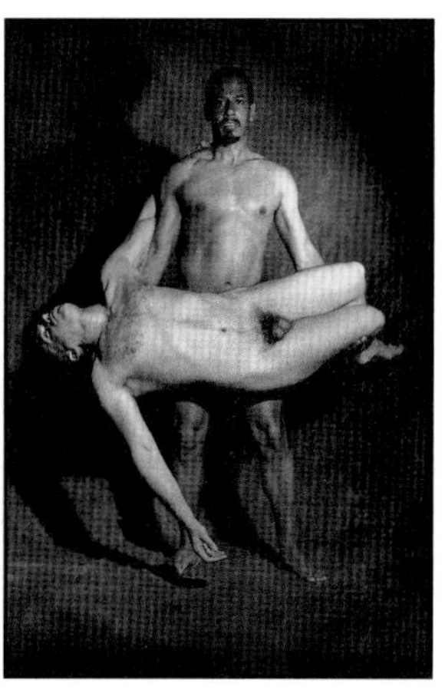

PLATE 28

Film: Kodak Plus-X Pan. Lens: 35mm F2. Lighting: Two direct strobes with grids from right.

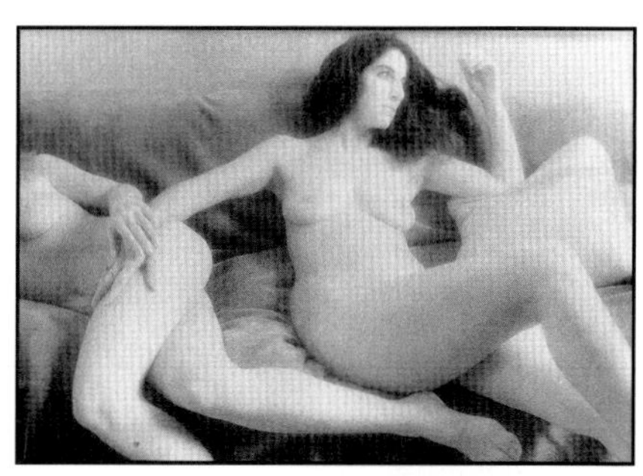

PLATE 29

Film: Kodak High Speed Infrared. Lens: 35mm F2 with red filter. Lighting: Softbox from above right, and strobe aimed into shoot-through umbrella as fill from left.

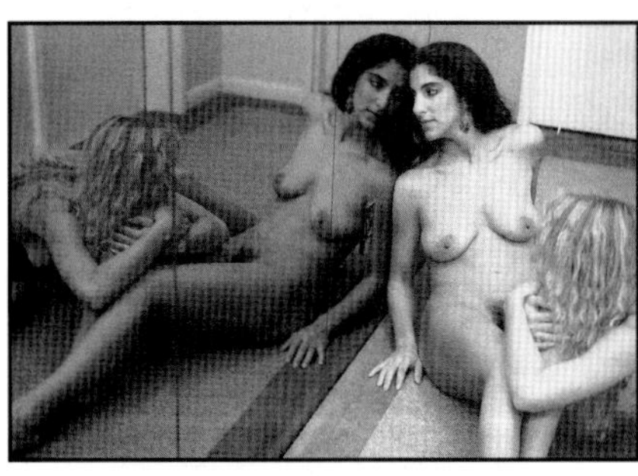

PLATE 30

Film: Kodak T-Max P3200 Professional. Lens: 60mm F2.8 micro. Lighting: Modeling light only, aimed into shoot-through umbrella from above.

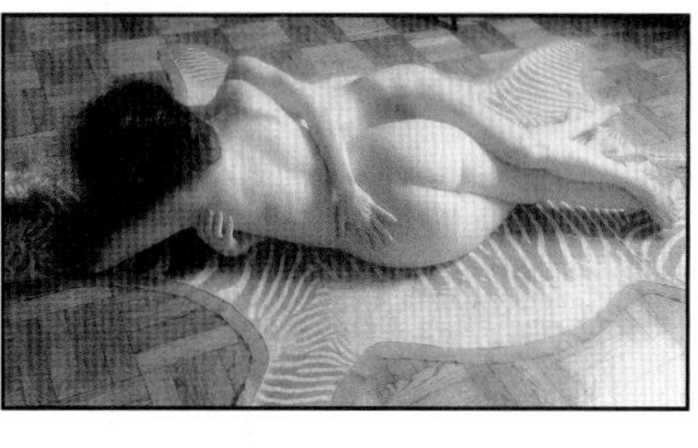

PLATE 31

Film: Kodak High Speed Infrared. Lens: 35mm F2 with red filter. Lighting: Softbox from above right, and strobe aimed into shoot-through umbrella as fill from above left.

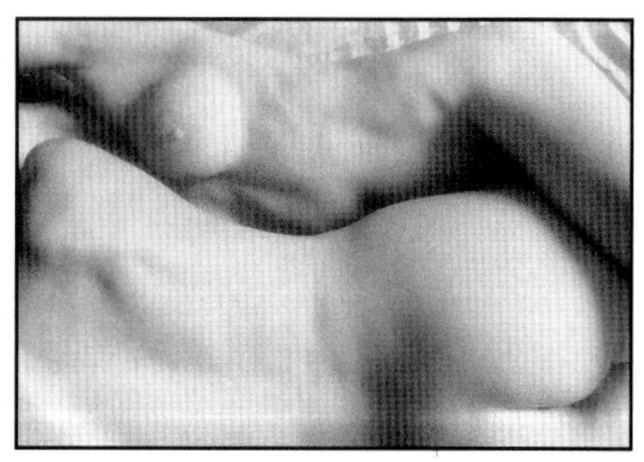

PLATE 32

Film: Kodak High Speed Infrared. Lens: 35mm F2 with red filter. Lighting: Softbox from above right, and strobe aimed into shoot-through umbrella as fill from above left.

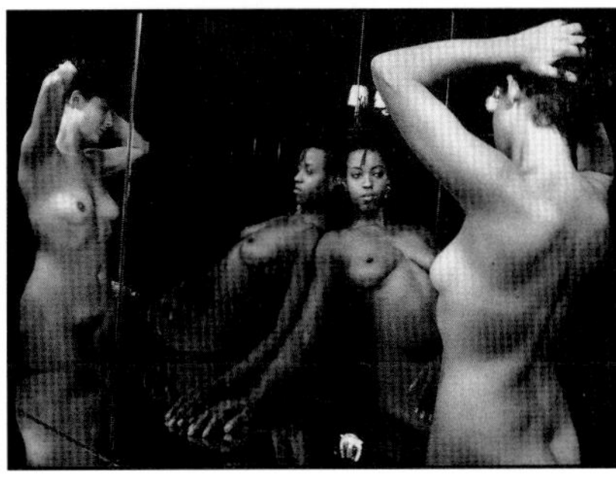

PLATE 33
Film: Kodak Tri-X Pan. Lens: 35mm F2. Lighting: Strobe aimed into shoot-through umbrella and bounced onto ceiling.

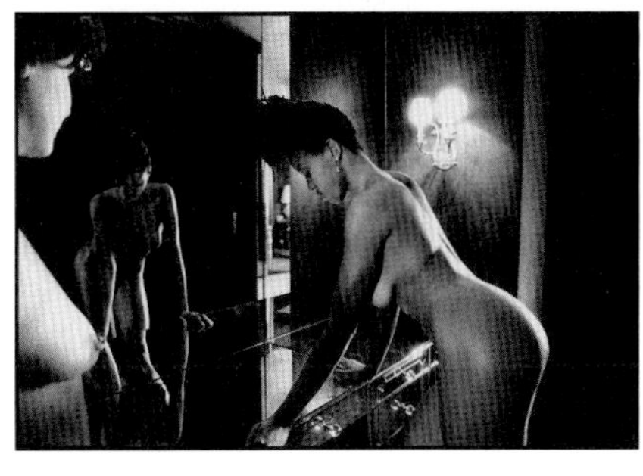

PLATE 34
Film: Kodak Recording, pushed to ISO 1600. Lens: 35mm F2. Lighting: Ambient light.

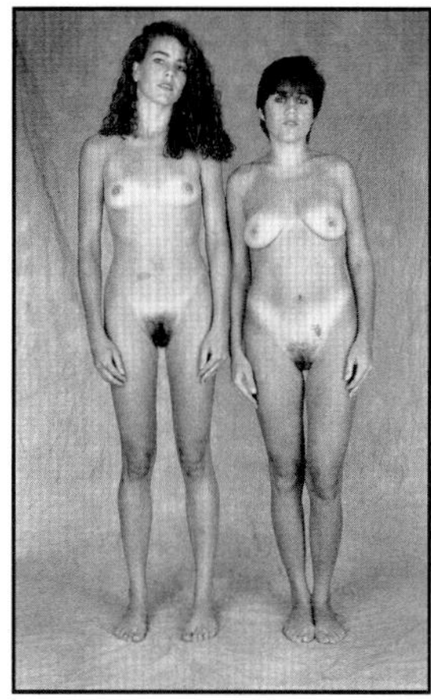

PLATE 35
Film: Kodak T-Max 100 Professional. Lens: 35mm F2. Lighting: Two softboxes, one on right of photographer as main light, one on left of photographer; and two strobes aimed into umbrellas, one on either side of background.

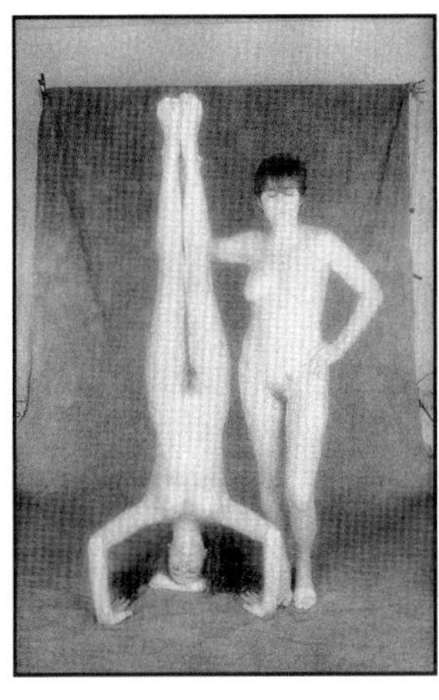

PLATE 36
Film: Kodak High Speed Infrared. Lens: 35mm F2 with red filter. Lighting: Two softboxes, one on right of photographer as main light, one on left of photographer; and two strobes aimed into umbrellas, one on either side of background.

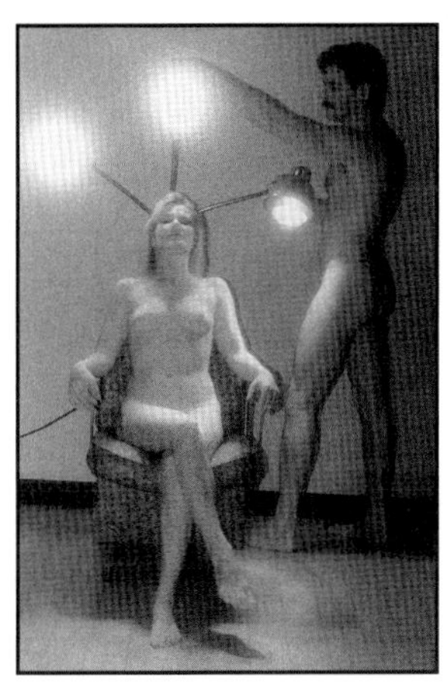

PLATE 37
Film: Kodak High Speed Infrared. Lens: 60mm F2.8 micro with red filter. Lighting: Bounced Nikon SB-24 Flash on camera.

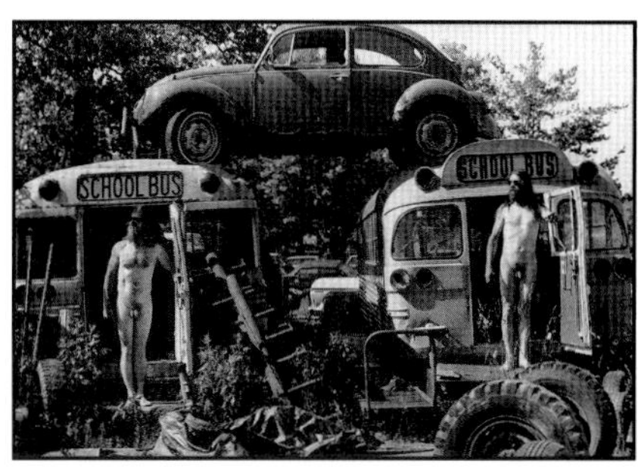

PLATE 38
Film: Kodak Plus-X Pan. Lens: 35mm F2. Lighting: Natural light.

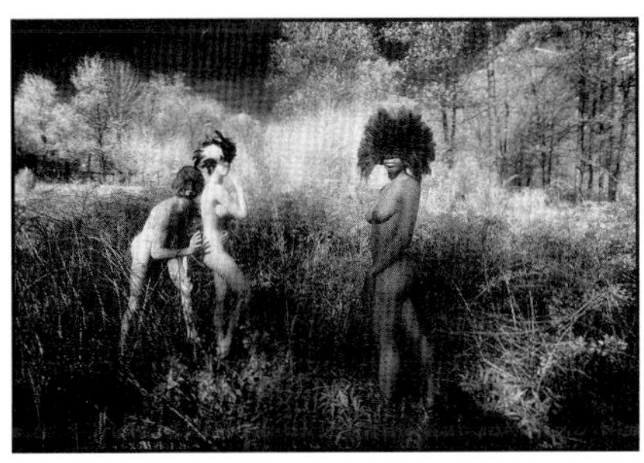

PLATE 39
Film: Kodak High Speed Infrared. Lens: 35mm F2 with red filter. Lighting: Natural light.

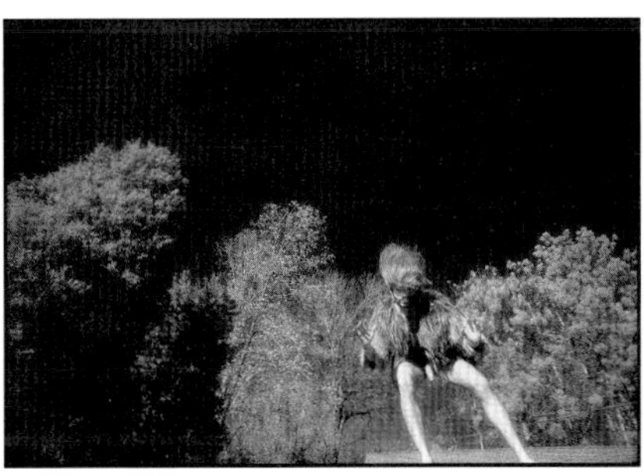

PLATE 40
Film: Kodak High Speed Infrared. Lens: 35mm F2 with red filter. Lighting: Natural light.

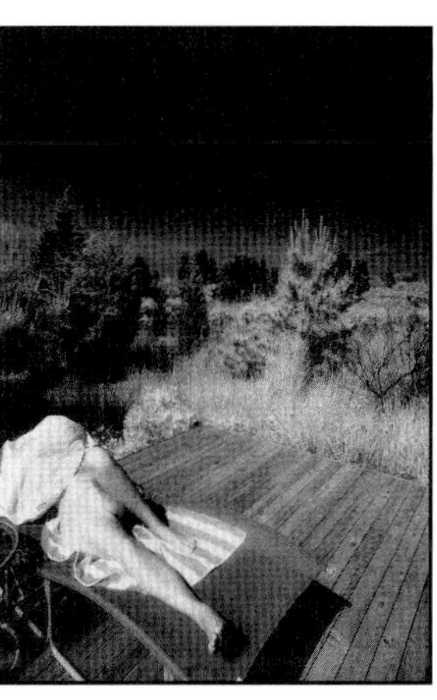

PLATE 41
Film: Kodak High Speed Infrared. Lens: 35mm F2 with red filter. Lighting: Natural light.

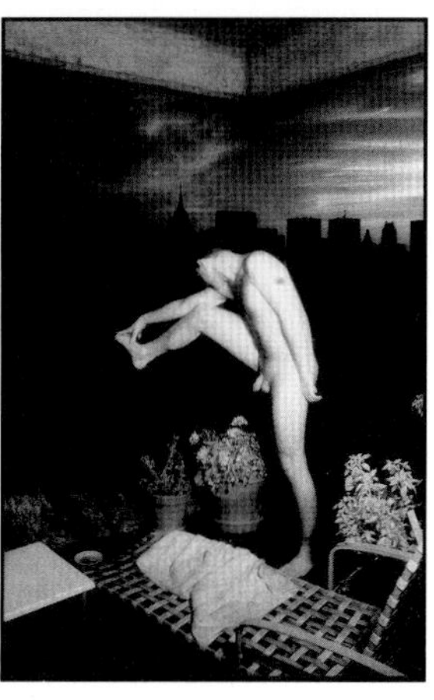

PLATE 42

Film: Kodak High Speed Infrared. Lens: 35mm F2 with red filter. Lighting: Direct strobe.

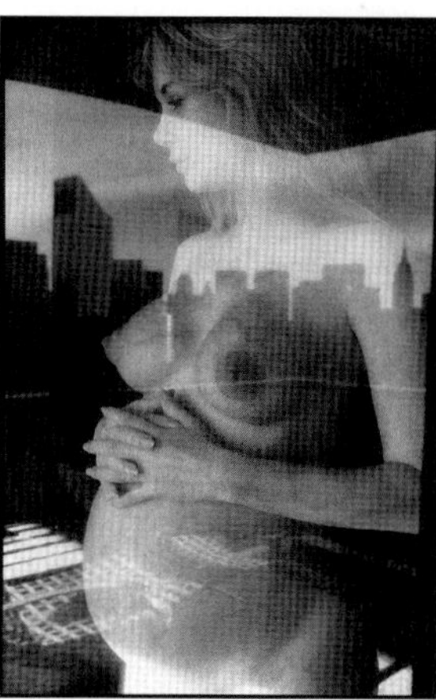

PLATE 43

Film: Kodak High Speed Infrared. Lens: 35mm F2 with red filter. Lighting: Natural light.

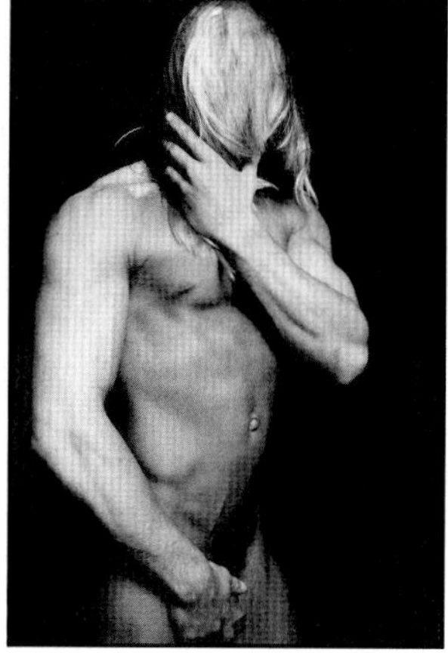

PLATE 44

Film: Polapan. Lens: 35mm F2. Lighting: Softbox.

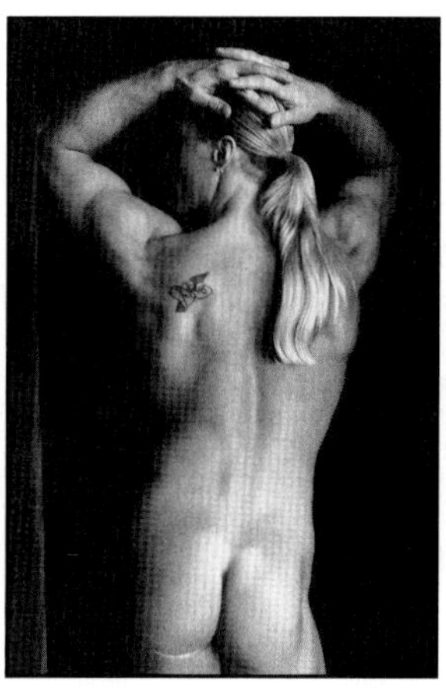

PLATE 45

Film: Kodak T-Max P3200 Professional. Lens: 35mm F2. Lighting: Modeling light only, with softbox.

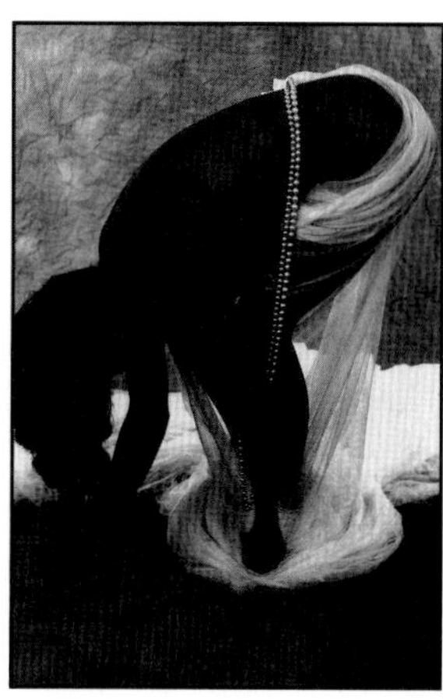

PLATE 46

Film: Experimental. Lens: 35mm F2. Lighting: Experimental.

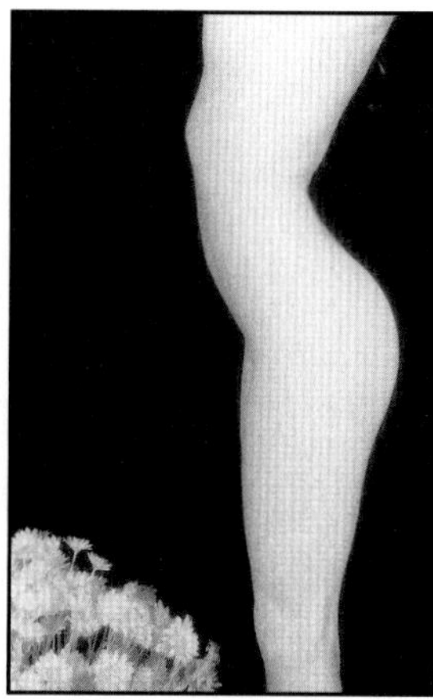

PLATE 47

Film: Kodak High Speed Infrared. Lens: 35mm F2 with red filter. Lighting: Strobe aimed into umbrella from above right.

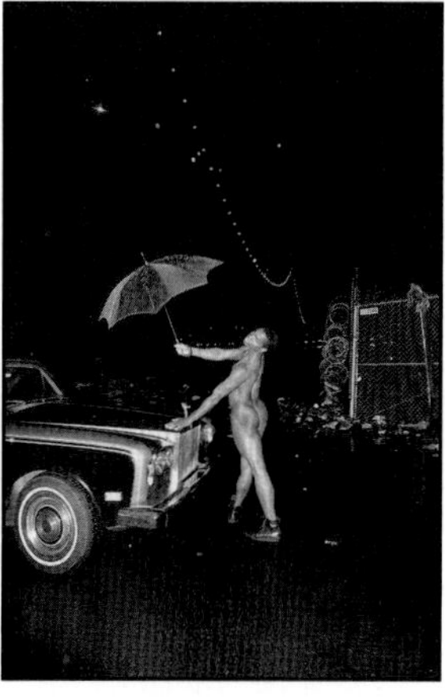

PLATE 48

Film: Kodak T-Max P3200 Professional. Lens: 24mm F2.8. Lighting: Nikon SB-24 Flash on camera.

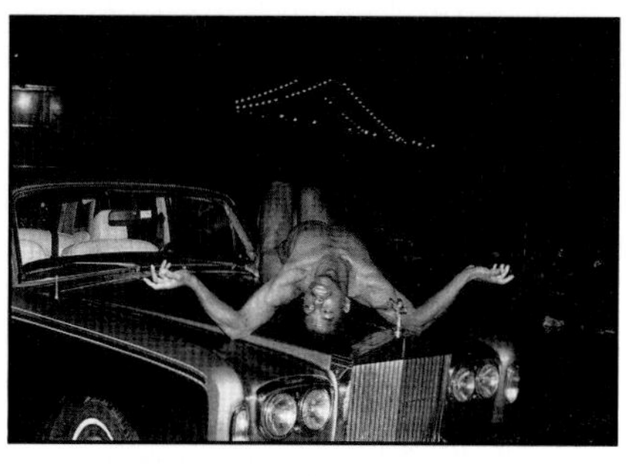

PLATE 49

Film: Kodak T-Max P3200 Professional. Lens: 60mm F2.8 micro. Lighting: Nikon SB-24 Flash on camera.

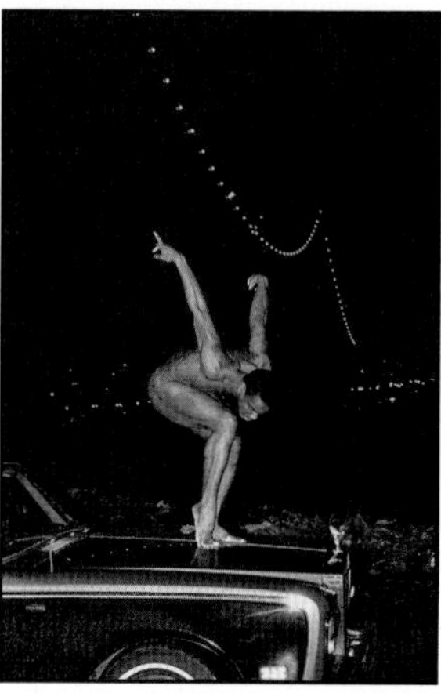

PLATE 50

Film: Kodak T-Max P3200 Professional. Lens: 60mm F2.8 micro. Lighting: Nikon SB-24 Flash on camera.

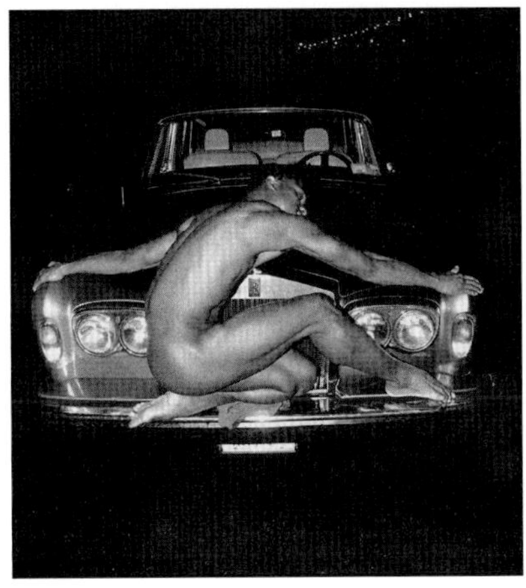

PLATE 51
Film: Kodak T-Max P3200 Professional. Lens: 24mm F2. Lighting: Nikon SB-24 Flash on camera.

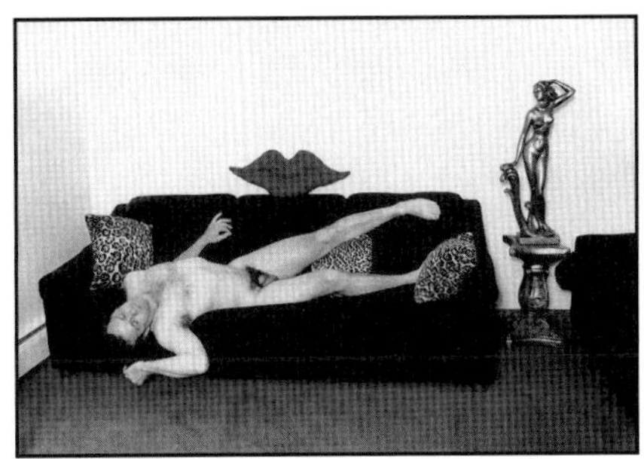

PLATE 52
Film: Kodak Plus-X Pan. Lens: 35mm F2. Lighting: Bounced strobe into umbrella.

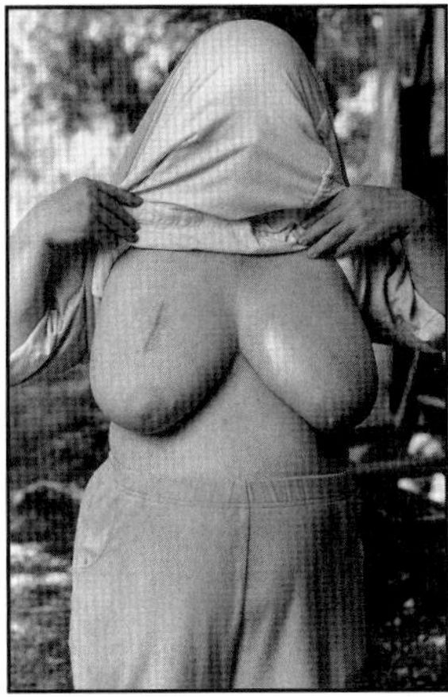

PLATE 53
Film: Kodak Plus-X Pan. Lens: 60mm F2.8 micro. Lighting: Natural light.

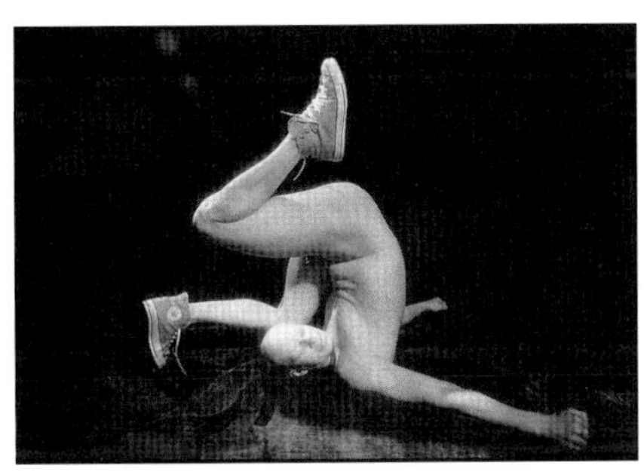

PLATE 54
Film: Kodak High Speed Infrared. Lens: 35mm F2. Lighting: Direct strobe from above, and direct strobe with grid from left behind model.

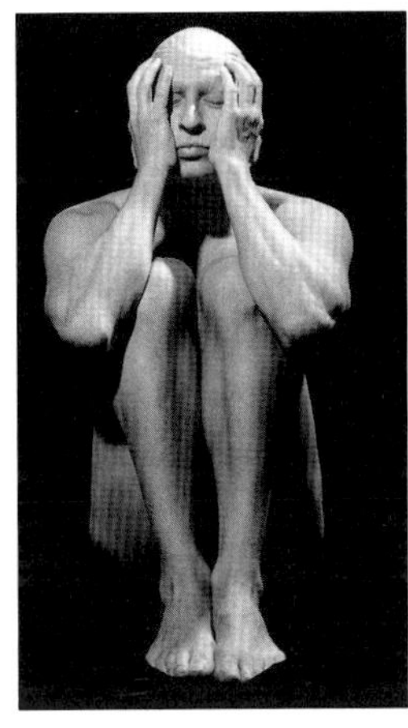

PLATE 55
Film: Kodak Plus-X Pan. Lens: 60mm F2.8 micro. Lighting: Direct strobe from above, and direct strobe with grid from left behind model.

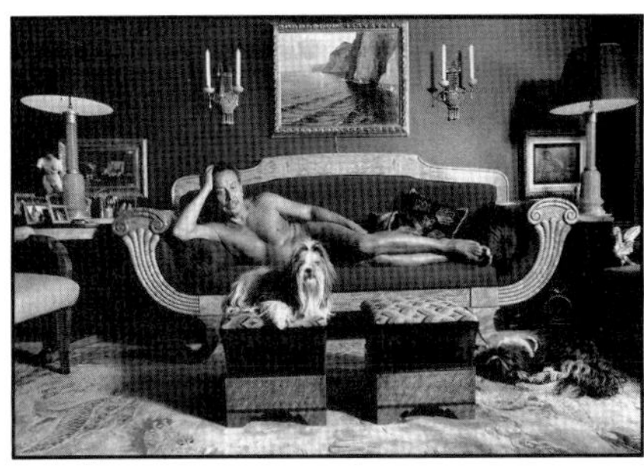

PLATE 56
Film: Kodak Tri-X Pan. Lens: 24mm F2.8. Lighting: Strobe aimed into umbrella.

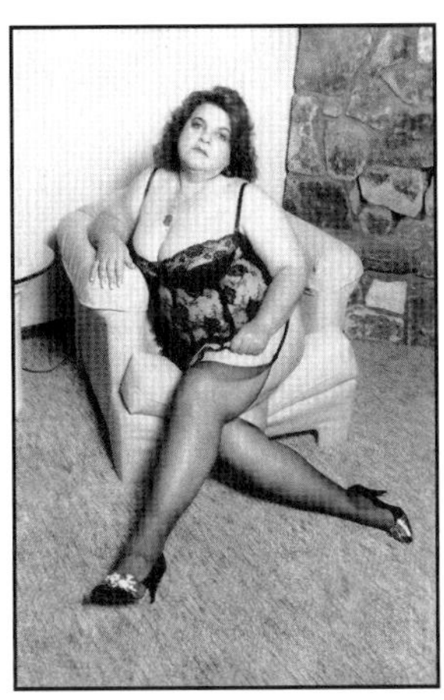

PLATE 57
Film: Kodak Plus-X Pan. Lens: 35mm F2. Lighting: Strobe aimed into umbrella.

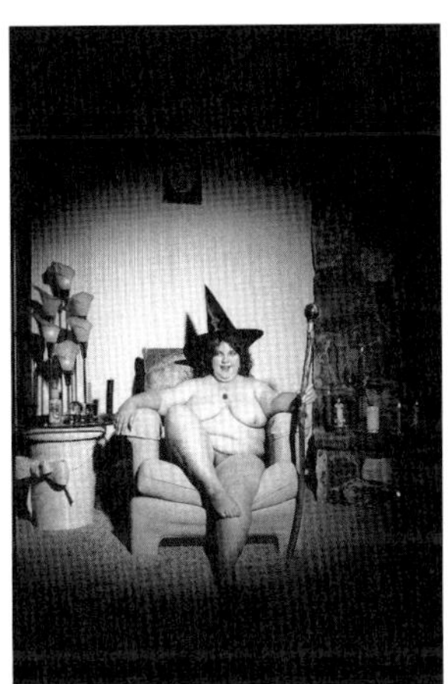

PLATE 58
Film: Kodak Plus-X Pan. Lens: 35mm F2. Lighting: Direct strobe with grid.

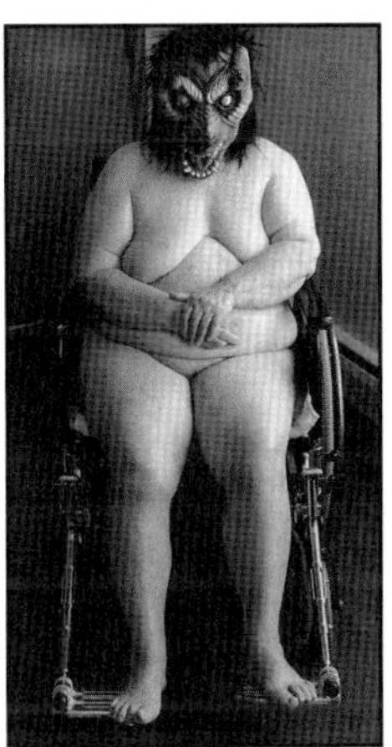

PLATE 59
Film: Kodak Tri-X Pan. Lens: 60mm F2.8 micro. Lighting: Natural light.

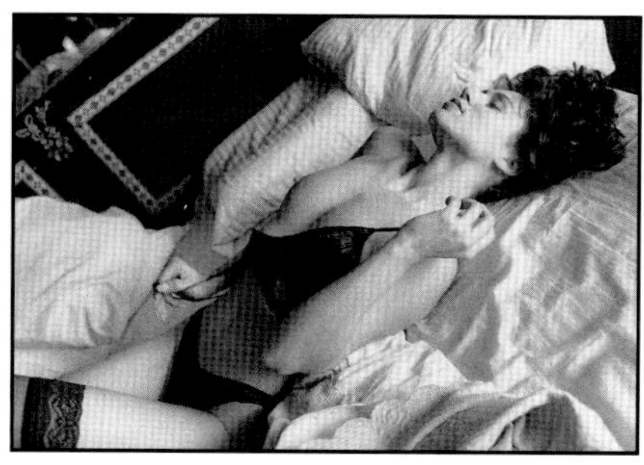

PLATE 60
Film: Kodak Tri-X Pan. Lens: 35mm F2. Lighting: Natural light.

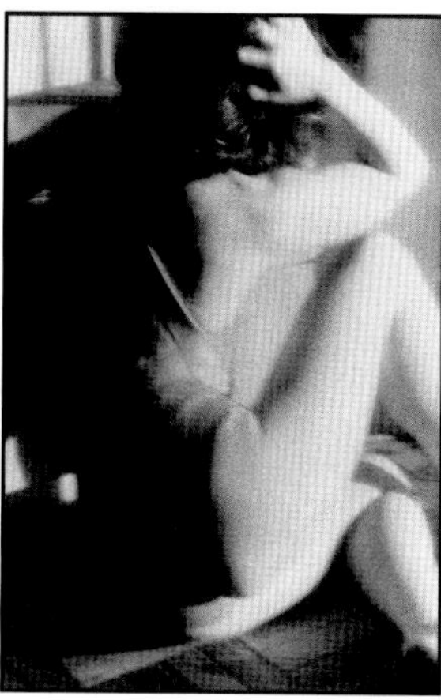

PLATE 61
Film: Kodak High Speed Infrared. Lens: 105mm F2.5. Lighting: Natural light.

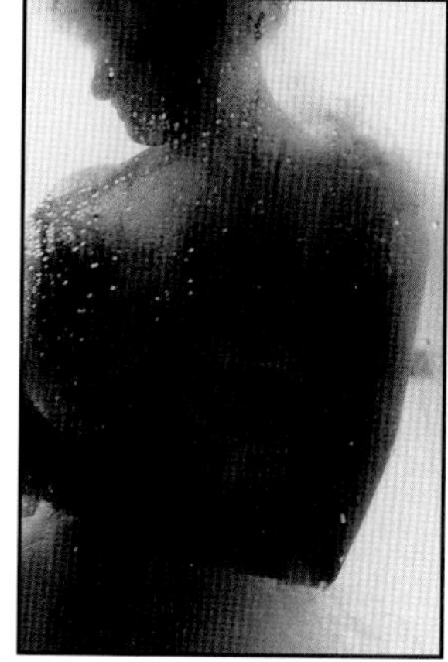

PLATE 62
Film: Kodak Tri-X Pan Professional. Lens: 105mm F2.5. Lighting: Natural light.

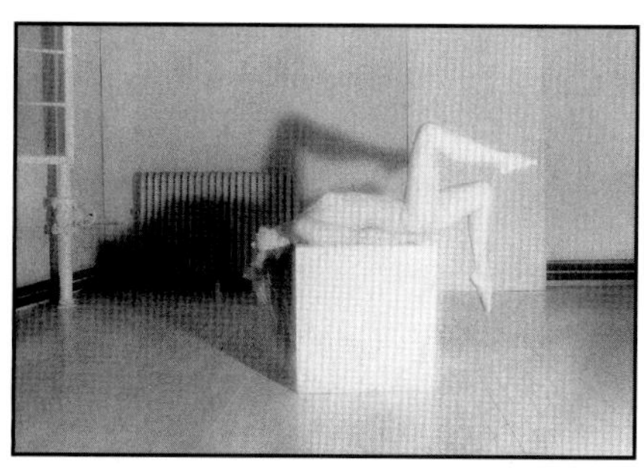

PLATE 63
Film: Kodak High Speed Infrared. Lens: 35mm F2. Lighting: Direct strobe from right.

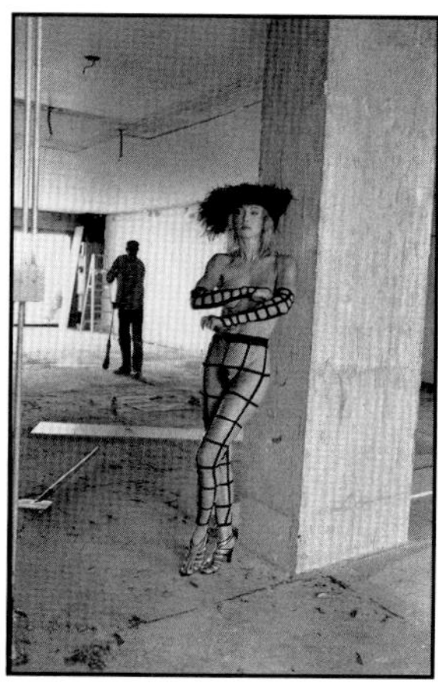

PLATE 64
Film: Kodak T-Max P3200 Professional. Lens: 35mm F2. Lighting: Natural light.

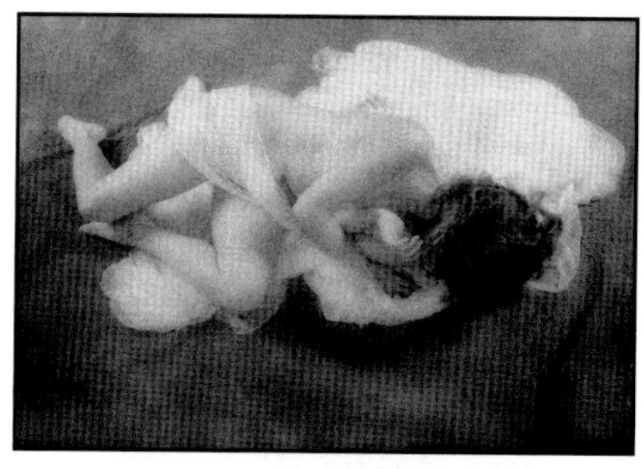

PLATE 65
Film: Kodak High Speed Infrared. Lens: 35mm F2 with red filter. Lighting: Softbox from above.

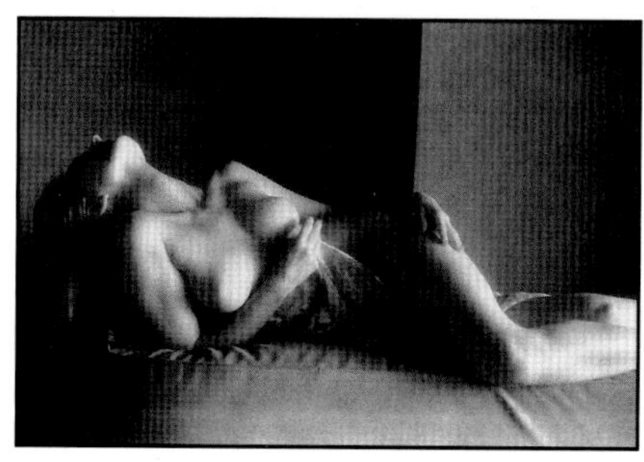

PLATE 66
Film: Kodak High Speed Infrared. Lens: 35mm F2 with red filter. Lighting: Natural light.

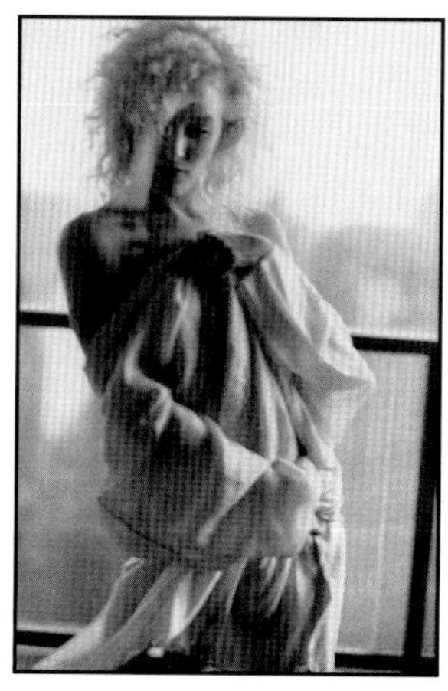

PLATE 67
Film: Kodak Plus-X Pan. Lens: 105mm F2.5. Lighting: Natural light.

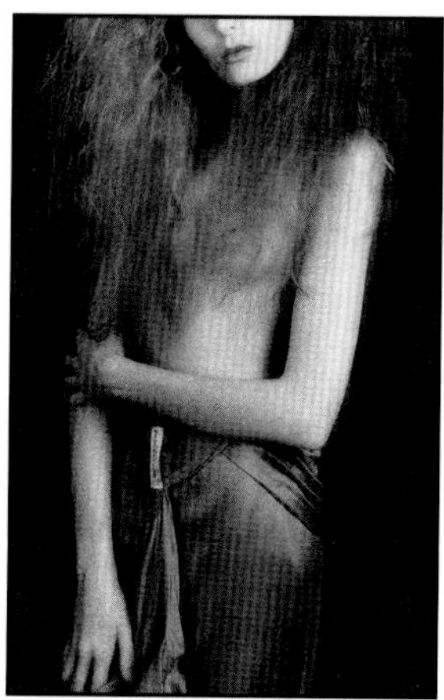

PLATE 68
Film: Kodak High Speed Infrared. Lens: 105mm F2.5 with red filter. Lighting: Softbox from right, and white reflector board on left.

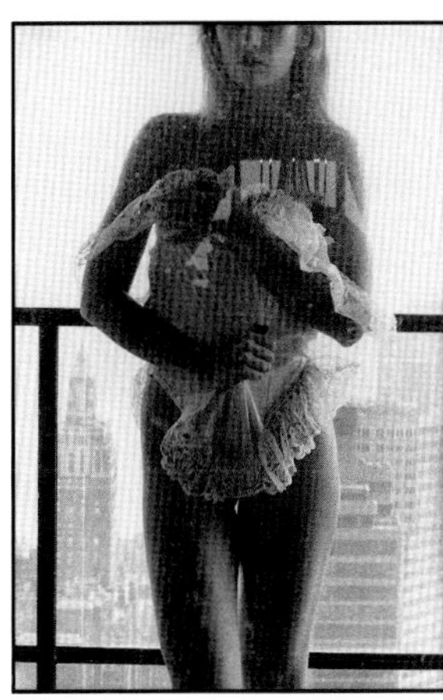

PLATE 69
Film: Kodak T-Max P3200 Professional. Lens: 35mm F2. Lighting: Natural light.

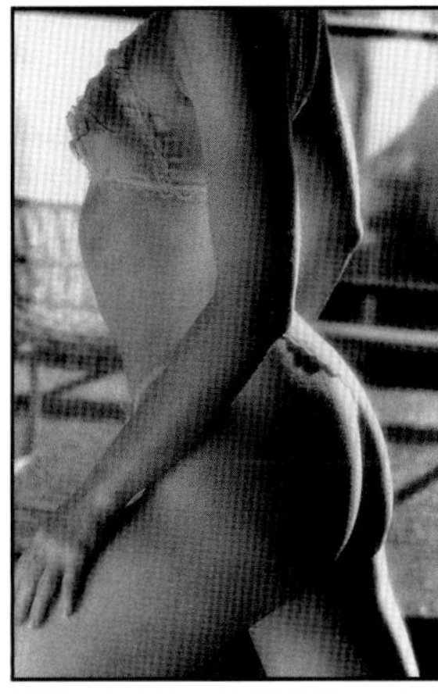

PLATE 70
Film: Kodak High Speed Infrared. Lens: 105mm F2.5 with red filter. Lighting: Natural light as main light, and strobe aimed into shoot-through umbrella as fill.

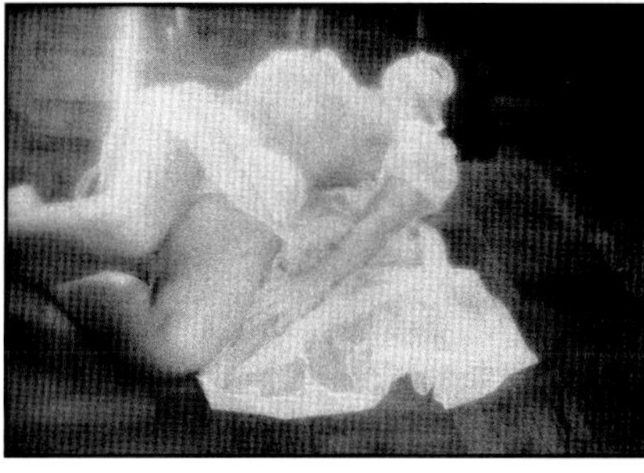

PLATE 71
Film: Kodak High Speed Infrared. Lens: 35mm F2 with red filter. Lighting: Direct strobe.

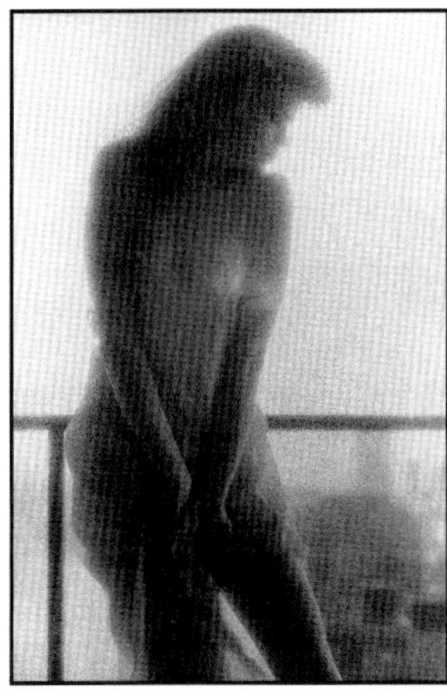

PLATE 72
Film: Kodak High Speed Infrared. Lens: 35mm F2 with red filter. Lighting: Strobe aimed into shoot-through umbrella as fill from above right. Photographed through glass.

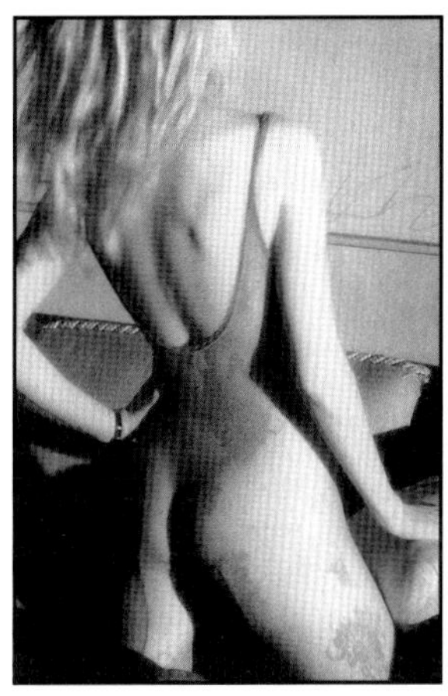

PLATE 73
Film: Kodak High Speed Infrared. Lens: 35mm F2 with red filter. Lighting: Ambient light.

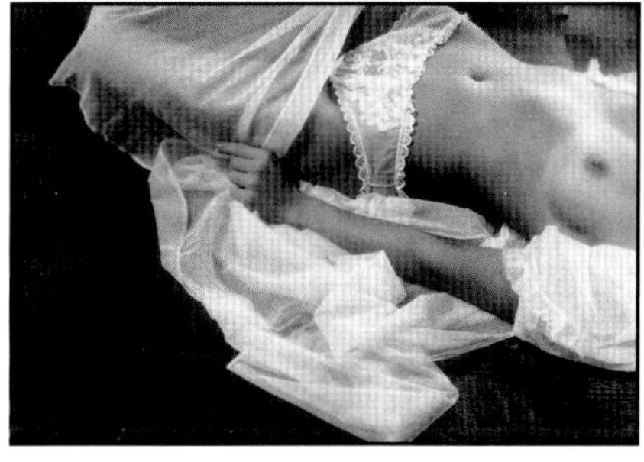

PLATE 74
Film: Kodak 5060. Lens: 35mm F2. Lighting: Direct strobe from above.

CREDITS

Cover
Model: Gregory

Plate 1
Statue in Italy

Plate 2
Model: Lynn

Plate 3
Model: Shawn Maratea

Plate 4
Model: Regina Hawkins; Hair: Timothy Downs; Makeup: Peter Brown

Plate 5
Anonymous

Plate 6
Model: Giorgio

Plate 7
Model: Andrea Van Raalte

Plate 8
Model: Shawn Maratea

Plate 9
Anonymous

Plate 10
Model: Regina Hawkins; Hair: Timothy Downs; Makeup: Peter Brown

Plate 11
Model: Regina Hawkins; Hair: Timothy Downs; Makeup: Peter Brown

Plate 12
Model: Peter Cruz

Plate 13
Model: Peter Cruz

Plate 14
Model: Carmela; Hair: Timothy Downs; Makeup: Peter Brown

Plate 15
Model: Carmela; Hair: Timothy Downs; Makeup: Peter Brown

Plate 16
Model: Carmela; Hair: Timothy Downs; Makeup: Peter Brown

Plate 17
Model: Carmela; Hair: Timothy Downs; Makeup: Peter Brown

Plate 18
Model: Kenn Wells; Body Makeup: André Pretorius

Plate 19
Model: Kenn Wells; Body Makeup: André Pretorius

Plate 20
Model: Kenn Wells; Body Makeup: André Pretorius

Plate 21
Model: Kenn Wells; Body Makeup: André Pretorius

Plate 22
Model: Kenn Wells; Body Makeup: André Pretorius

Plate 23
Model: Kenn Wells; Body Makeup: André Pretorius

Plate 24
Models: Karen Thorton and her son, Taharka Owens

Plate 25
Models: George and Kyle Alvarez

Plate 26
Models: George and Kyle Alvarez and Kasey

Plate 27
Models: Sam Paxhia and Barry Campbell

Plate 28
Models: Sam Paxhia and Barry Campbell

Plate 29
Models: Julie A. Walker and Donna K. Knasiak

Plate 30
Models: Donna K. Knasiak and Julie A. Walker

Plate 31
Models: Donna K. Knasiak and Julie A. Walker

Plate 32
Models: Donna K. Knasiak and Julie A. Walker

Plate 33
Models: Maria Elena Gonzalez and Jocelyn Taylor; Hair and Makeup: Peter Brown

Plate 34
Models: Maria Elena Gonzalez and Jocelyn Taylor; Hair and Makeup: Peter Brown

Plate 35
Models: Kim Hardy and Sari

Plate 36
Models: Kim Hardy and Sari

Plate 37
Models: Nadine and Dean Moretti

Plate 38
Models: Dave Jordan and Phil Schichtel

Plate 39
Models: Giorgio, Heather, and Lynn

Plate 40
Model: Giorgio

Plate 41
Model: Helen

Plate 42
Model: Seth Kornblau

Plate 43
Model: Boushelle Alvarez

Plate 44
Model: Chris Niemi

Plate 45
Model: Chris Niemi

Plate 46
Anonymous

Plate 47
Model: Carmela

Plate 48
Model: Carld Jonaissaint

Plate 49
Model: Carld Jonaissaint

Plate 50
Model: Carld Jonaissaint

Plate 51
Model: Carld Jonaissaint

Plate 52
Model: Tim Regal

Plate 53
Model: CC

Plate 54
Model: Garry Cohn

Plate 55
Model: Garry Cohn

Plate 56
Model: Garcia

Plate 57
Model: LaStrega

Plate 58
Model: LaStrega

Plate 59
Model: Sweet Adeline

Plate 60
Model: Lisa Zari

Plate 61
Model: Lisa Zari

Plate 62
Anonymous

Plate 63
Model: Kasey

Plate 64
Model: Peggy Palmer

Plate 65
Model: Holly Moyes

Plate 66
Model: Jules Warren; Hair and Makeup: Jules Warren

Plate 67
Model: Shannon Conley

Plate 68
Model: Stephanie

Plate 69
Model: April

Plate 70
Model: Kathleen Vigeland

Plate 71
Anonymous

Plate 72
Anonymous

Plate 73
Model: Wendy Benarz

Plate 74
Model: Lisa Zari

INDEX